DARK SPIRITS

ALSO BY A.J. RATHBUN
Wine Cocktails
Luscious Liqueurs
Party Snacks!
Good Spirits
Party Drinks!

DARK
SPIRITS

200 classy concoctions
starring Bourbon, Brandy, Scotch, Whiskey, Rum, and more

A.J. RATHBUN
Photography by Melissa Punch

The Harvard Common Press
Boston, Massachusetts

The
Harvard
Common
Press
5 3 5
Albany
Street
Boston
Massachusetts
0 2 1 1 8

www.harvardcommonpress.com

Printed in China | Printed on acid-free paper

Library of Congress Cataloging-in-Publication Data
Rathbun, A. J. (Arthur John), 1969-
Dark spirits : 200 classy concoctions starring
bourbon, brandy, scotch, whiskey, rum, and more /
A.J. Rathbun.
p. cm. Includes index.
Summary: "A collection of 200 cocktail recipes featuring bourbon, brandy, Scotch, whiskey, rum, and other dark spirits"—Provided by publisher.
ISBN 978-1-55832-427-5
1. Cocktails. I. Title. TX951.R166 2009
641.8'74—dc22 2009001422

Special bulk-order discounts are available on this and other Harvard Common Press books. Companies and organizations may purchase books for premiums or resale, or may arrange a custom edition, by contacting the Marketing Director at the address above.

Book design by Vivian Ghazarian
Photography by Melissa Punch
Drink styling by Brian Preston-Campbell
Production/prop styling by Lauren Niles

2   4   6   8   10   9   7   5   3   1

For those fellas who have continued
to buy me darkly spirited drinks over the years—
Ed, Jeremy, Markie B., Jon, Joel, and Shane—
here's to you.

Contents

Acknowledgments viii

Introduction x

How to Unleash the Dark Spirits 1

Dark Classics 25

Bartender's Choice 55

Bubbly Refreshers 93

Dim the Lights, Chill the Cocktails 137

Dark Drinks That Go Bump in the Night 183

Powerful Punches 237

Hot Stuff 273

Measurement Equivalents 293

Index of Drinks by Primary Liquor 295

General Index 297

Acknowledgments

The darkly spirited waters are delicious, but not the sort of thing one wants to traverse completely alone. Luckily, I was blessed with a whole host of trusty tipplers to assist me along my liquor travels. With that in mind, I'd like to shake up big thanks for those who helped as I was putting together this collection of drinks and bar talk, with a couple of extra-heavy pours (and thanks) for a few specific folks. The journey couldn't even have been started without the editing prowess of Valerie Cimino, whose keen ear and eye helped form the following pages from the first keystroke. I'd also like to pour out overflowing thanks to every one of the dandy and spirited Harvard Common Press crew, who were always there to answer questions, help pull the oars, and give incredible amounts of time and energy in making sure this book sailed smoothly. HCPers, you most definitely rule, and I'm really lucky to be able to work with each of you (and a little extra thanks to Bruce Shaw, for pulling together such a lovable bunch).

I wouldn't even leave the dock to take a trek into these dimly-lit-but-heavily-ice-cubed tales and tall glasses without my agent and pal Michael Bourret, which means he not only gets a heaping helping of "you rule" and "you rule" again, but also means that the next drink's on me, pally. Without the various life preservers you throw out to me on a regular basis (not to mention introducing me to the amazing WeatherUp—hey, thanks to Miguel for this, too, and for always coming out for drinks in rad NYC spots), I wouldn't be able to make it through the month. Thanks times ten.

Big boozy technicolor thanks and praise must be delivered to the best drink photographer in the world: Melissa Punch, not only do you have the best surname for shooting these concoctions I love sipping, but also the finest vision and sense of style. It's my lucky day, every day, because I'm able to have you give my books so much artistry. And thanks to Brian Preston-Campbell, for his food-styling genius, and Karen Wise, for catching mistakes and polishing prose with keen copyediting brilliance.

Of course, putting together a biggish tome of beverages has required even more help, especially when pulling together recipes from near and far. With that in mind, let me stir up a river's worth of praise for every professional and home bartender who aided me with a recipe, a technique, an idea, a story, or a classic-book tip—with a spotlight on those slingers in the Bartender's Choice chapter (page 55) and an extra garnish for a few: Andrew B., thanks for making Seattle a tastier place to drink; Kenny P. and Jeremy S., thanks for not forgetting your Midwestern brother of the bar from way back; Bradley Parsons, thanks for the support, the Lillet tips, and the books; Andrea S., thanks for the writing assistance, the workaday sanity checks, and the occasional lunches; and Robert Hess, Gary and Mardee Regan, and David Wondrich, thanks for being so darn inspiring.

It also helps to have friends on every shore to pick up a random tab, test out a fresh mix, give beneficial suggestions, and show up at tailgating parties that don't get past the driveway. I'm pretty well bursting with pride that I get to be a part of a posse of pals like this, and so thanks to each of you, with a serious shout-out to Brad Kosel, who goes above and beyond the call of pal-ship when videotaping and directing nutty drink videos (and thanks to his wife, Christi, and son, Cash, too); to the wonderfully encouraging and rad Lisa Ekus and the whole charming Lisa Ekus team; to Leslie P., Web genius (readers, y'all need to get your Schtickers now!); to pals Megan and baby Beatrix; Jill M.; dog-sitter extraordinaire Erika; Andy and Deena; Eric and Rebecca; Brett and Chelsea; Bob Wafflehouse; the mighty Mahlin household; the Hays Norris clan; KT, Ed, and Miles; Keith and Tasha; Baydra; Nicole S.; the Amazon Appliances team; Kristine M.; Christy S.; Londoners Ean and Reba; Argentineans Kyla and Mike; Matt and Amanda; and above all to the Fuller, Rathbun, James, Davis, and DeMaranville families (with a special thanks to my nephews Kaiser and Coen, who keep things jumping here in Seattle).

Without music in the bar, the dark spirits often get pretty darn grim, so I'm happy to be able to shake my rump and bang my head to the particular soundtrack this book was written to, which is composed of a healthy dose of Truck Stop Love, GFB and DGRE, Tales from the Birdbath, the Malinks and Withholders communal love fest, Artie and the Horsefeathers, Tom Waits, National Trust, Ghost Stories, The Table of Contents, Robots in Disguise, old tapes of the Moving Van Goghs and Sufferbus, and anything played or sent out by pop-master Yarges.

Barking thanks must go, in addition, to two of my nearest and dearest who can't even read but who entertain me and whom I love to no end: Sookie and Rory, y'all settle down, because this dark spirits ride is about to start—and stop sniffing the liquor bottles, 'cause dogs shouldn't drink so much. And quiet down, puppies, because before the final drop drops into the glass, I need to say loudly that the largest thanks go out to my wife, Natalie, who always makes sure that we're stocked up with Strega and snacks, refills the ice trays, and keeps me from ever forgetting that parties, and drinks, are an out-of-sight, fantastic, and fun journey. Here are a million darkly spirited toasts to you, Babycakes—and I promise to never again take the last sip of Prosecco.

Introduction

Gather round the campfire, my pretties, come close to where the flames are licking the shadowy corners that seem to creep in on us, get a little nearer so you can hear every word that I'm going to say, every nuance of the story I'm going to relate to you. It's a story that comes from the hazy edges of small out-of-the-way towns, from crossroads where the birds fly far overhead, from lonely distilleries, from babbling brooks where a few drinkers gather together, like we are now, to discuss the ways and means and meanings (and drinks) of a certain type of spirits. Welcome, fellow traveler, to the dark side. *Bwa-ha-ha-ha. . . .*

Okay, dropping cloaks and exaggerated stage whispers to the side for a moment, let me say that we're in the middle of one lucky time period, what I like to think of as a cocktail revolution (and, as I always say, "*Viva la revolución!*"). We're surrounded by a wide range of innovative cocktail creators, of both the professional and home variety, and we get to see and hear about—and, best of all, taste—new drink combinations at every turn. These combinations do not use solely traditional ingredients either, as more and more liquors and liqueurs are becoming available everywhere you can think of, thanks to better distribution, higher demand from consumers and better selection by retailers, and an overall renewed interest in imaginative mixes. The creativity doesn't just stop with the alcohol side, either, as drink slingers are also experimenting with a wider variety of fruits and herbs and other mixers. And as if that weren't pleasant enough, many older mixtures, from yesteryear and beyond, are being rediscovered, polished up, and polished off by eager consumers.

With this liquid explosion, the dark spirits, often resigned to being sipped solo by serious-minded sorts in the past, are finally coming into their own. But, even though they're becoming more regular components of cocktails and highballs where they're mingling with others, they remain a bit mysterious to many. It's their deep nature and renowned strength, combined with (I believe) the magic contained within their bottles. Delving into the dark spirits can seem a bit scary to even the most intrepid trekker of the liquor shelves. For some of you folks, it's just been easier to stick to those light liquors when pouring a drink for yourself, for you and a friend or partner, or for you and a passel of pals.

Don't let fear rule, friends. This book in your hands is waiting to guide you into the ins and outs of the dark spirits, either to serve as your tour guide as you start on your journey into the dark lands, or (if you're already a bit of a dark spirits aficionado) to walk and shake and stir with you as you discover new dark-spirited treasures. The world of the dark spirits is one to savor and not to miss. And, of course, it's also one that's most enjoyable when you're sharing it with another, when you have the dark spirits as a part of a conversation with one or with many.

At heart, this is what the dark spirits journey is about: not just introducing you to unknown dark spirits mixes, or reintroducing you to artistic classics, but setting the liquid stage for conversations and good-spirited times between you and friends, family, and loved ones. The dark spirits are especially proficient in this regard, as they tend to remind us (due to the loving care they're made with, and their fortitude) that life shouldn't always be lived at a feverish pace. That slowing down for a joke or a story at the bar or in the backyard while sipping a well-made drink is one of the important things. That having a few pals over for an agreeable darkly based cocktail means as much as—or more than—using every waking moment to rush, rush, rush around. Step back, the dark spirits chant, relax, have a drink with someone you care about, and make a few memories instead of passing by without a second glance.

Of course, being able, during these moments, to introduce your friends and paramours to a fresh and delicious drink (even if it's a rediscovered drink from last century) is a dandy way to accent the moment, too. Since so many drinks have tales to tell (or lead to legendary tales that you create), they help start the conversation. If the drinks are being introduced to a whole plethora of pals, and the conversations start flowing in many directions, and then you and yours and your dark spirits are having a spirited affair that lasts long into the night, well, that's the way cocktails drive memories. (And isn't it grand when you're the one *introducing* these mixes to friends? What a great day to be alive.) That's when this book becomes a member of the party, as it brings you closer to the dark side of the spirits world in an enjoyable and conversational way, with drinks for many occasions, from immortal mixes to innovative minglings, from hot combos to cool bubblers and everything shaken in between. It's time to let go of your fears and embrace the dark spirits side.

How to Unleash the Dark Spirits

Many worthy cocktail compendiums are broken out by base liquor (rum, whiskey, brandy, and so on); others by alphabetical order of drink names. *Dark Spirits* follows its own shadowy path and is, instead, divided into thematic chapters. For example, the Dark Classics chapter contains drinks that have attained historically sinister heights (because they've infiltrated so much of the communal cocktail consciousness), while Bartender's Choice is stocked with contemporary liquid numbers from some of today's top drink creators, both those who are currently being paid for their endeavors and those who are plying their trade for friends at home or online. Other chapters rally around certain party situations, such as Bubbly Refreshers, which sparkles with drinks designed to take the edge off a hot day; Powerful Punches, with recipes built for bigger parties; and the heated drinks in Hot Stuff, designed to help get winter off your back. Then there are those chapters gathering their dark children under more personality-driven themes, such as the spooky shenanigans populating Dark Drinks That Go Bump in the Night, and the smooth romancers in Dim the Lights, Chill the Cocktails. In the chapters themselves, the drinks join the party in alphabetical order, for easier uncovering and finding (and re-finding), with each recipe designed to make one drink, unless noted otherwise. In addition, for easy reference, there are two indexes at the back of the book, one that categorizes each drink according to its primary dark "base" liquor, and a general index. And here you thought you'd have to head to that part of the library that's usually cordoned off and shrouded in mist to find your dark spirits.

The reason for the thematic approach to our delicious treats? To make it easier for you, as party planner, to track down a drink that fits your particular occasion perfectly. If you want a classic, they aren't hard to find; by the same token, if you know that the mercury's edging up your thermometer and you want to cool it down a bit, you can flip to the proper place and start searching out the right chilly mix without breaking a sweat. This organizational setup of bottles and booze also makes it a snap for you to browse for a couple of well-matched signature drinks for an upcoming celebration of any sort. Having these "signature" drinks then makes your shindig stand out from all the other, more mundane, affairs people are having, which is never a bad thing. And, finally, having the chapters set up in this way is just a whole shakerful of fun, meant to reflect a good conversation between friends at the bar or the atmosphere of a really memorable party. Even though the spirits are dark in the drinks, they are also enjoyable and entertaining, and that's just how I hope you'll find this book.

THE SPELL OF A WELL-STOCKED DARK BAR

Merlin never said a spell by mumbling over the words, and he wouldn't have instructed Arthur to pull that sword out of the stone without preparing him a bit first—reminding Arthur that things could go south, but that being prepared and studying up a bit would allow him to control the situation. Houdini didn't wake up one day and say, "Fellas, lock me in a trunk, trundle it up with chains, and then submerge me in that big tank of water." He spent a bit of time (a lot of time, actually) getting to know the tools of the escape artist and the magician, like every first-rate practitioner of the prestidigitator's arts. Even in fiction, famous comic book magician Zatanna spent time learning how to speak backward so that her spells came out in heroic fashion. You, as a soon-to-be master of the dark spirits, should take note of the practices of these masters. To reach a high level, both of the dark spirits and of the home bar, you'll need the right tools and supplies to ensure that your guests are as enthralled by your parties and party-throwing acumen as the audiences were for the master mystics throughout history.

First, realize that preparation is the key to most successful affairs. There is much to be said for an impromptu shift to your home bar—say it's getting late at the local pub, but you don't want the exuberance and frolicking to fade away, so the idea to invite pals back to your pad pops up in your mind like flowers from a conjuror's sleeve. These spur-of-the-moment gatherings can be full of kicks. But even they, with a little basic preparation, can be even more fun, can be taken up another notch. For those parties where you're going the signature drink route, those merrymakings that you want to be remembered for more than a month, that you want everyone to refer to as "the party" for years—well, for those events, proper planning is a must. The nice part? You can do all the planning and preparation without a ton of stress or a large outlay of the coin of the realm. It's really not that hard to get the key basics, and a few extras, in place. And, let me assure you, this will also make it easier for you as host or hostess to enjoy your own party without worrying yourself into a frizz the whole evening—which is what you want, of course, because why shouldn't you experience a little magic at your own party? You should, indeed.

ESSENTIAL SPELL INGREDIENTS: DARK LIQUORS

To begin weaving a dark spirits spell, you must, naturally, start with *actual* dark spirits, or dark "base" liquors. For this book, the dark bases in the recipes (with only one or two notable exceptions) are dark rum, the members of the whiskey/Scotch/rye/bourbon family, and the members of the brandy/Cognac/Armagnac family (almost sounds like we're going to start a three-way round of *Family Feud*). With this in mind, if you're stocked up with at least one bottle in any two of those families, you're on your way to being able to make many of the drinks in this book, as well as being able to cover a variety of individual tastes. Having at least two of the dark spirits around also means that if you have someone over who doesn't like rum, you can instead make them a brandy drink without a hassle, and everyone's happy.

There have been many dandy books written about each of the base liquors above, books that delve deeply into the history, legends, and lore of the individual liquor, that trace out theories on the hows, whys, whens, and wherefores in often amusing and entertaining fashion (as well as imparting a whole bottleful, or caskful, of knowledge). While I don't want to get nearly as deep into them, because that'd keep us away from the recipes— and keep us a bit behind on making up these dark spirit-based spells—it is worthwhile to get at least acquainted with each. When calling up a dark spirit, you want to know a little more than its name, so that you can act appropriately (much in the same way an evil warlock would want to know a little more about a demon before conjuring one up).

Rum

Our first dark base, rum, is in some ways the most interesting "dark" spirit, because it has a corresponding "white" or clear sibling, and because it's often hard to pin down. What exactly constitutes "dark" rum? In this book, we're going with all those rums that have a richer color, running from amber to light brown, and a richer, deeper taste than their crisper, lighter brethren. When I make the majority of these recipes, I use something like Mount Gay Eclipse, Cockspur, Barbancourt 4-year, or Bacardi Dark, which are all readily available. There are also even darker rums, aged longer, which are most often sipped solo—although they can be mixed into cocktails if you use a very delicate hand. I shy away from using these so-called black or brown rums in drinks except for certain specific concoctions. All rum is originally distilled clear and made from sugarcane juice or molasses, and then fermented and aged in different manners to affect the taste and coloring and depth. Because of these varieties of processes, rums' flavors can range a bit, with some having a stronger molasses undertone (especially some of the more aged varieties) with thick notes of spices such as nutmeg or cinnamon coming through, while others will have a slightly crisper taste with fruity overtones, and still others might have more of a nutty consistency, with a caramelized sweetness showing its head, or hints of chocolate swirling around.

Is your rum crystal ball still a little cloudy on what rums to use in the cocktails contained within this book? Not surprising, but let me try to whisk away the clouds a bit. As rum's character can be wide-ranging, depending on source, you may end up with slight variations in taste if you try the same cocktail using two different dark rums. This, though, shouldn't keep you from experimenting, because as long as you stick to rum that's called "dark," or rum called "golden" that has a deep amber color, you're going to end with a pleasant mix. It just means that you can play around a little, and have some fun with it. As Wayne Curtis—whose book *And a Bottle of Rum: A History of the New World in Ten Cocktails* (Crown, 2006) is a must-read for all rum-o-philes—says, "Rum embodies America's laissez-faire attitude: It is whatever it wants to be. There have never been strict guidelines for making it." Following up on this is the explosion of a number of "flavored" rums on the market—those that have had something added, such as coconut, for example, or other fruit flavors. Stay away from these when making your dark rum mixes, unless specifically asked for, as they'll change the flavor of your cocktail too much.

Where does the word *rum* come from, though? It's a bit of a devilish task to track down, and no one is exactly sure. It could be from the Latin word for sugarcane, *saccarum*, or the Gypsy *rum*, standing in for "grand" or "potent," both theories that match up well with the spirit. Mr. Curtis suggests that it probably comes from *rumbullion* or *rumbustion*, which were British terms for "tumult" or "uproar" that started being used around the same time as rum started being consumed—both good matches with this sometimes wickedly perceived base liquor. Rum's worn other names, too, most following up on its once-thought-threatening nature, such as *hydra-monster*, *cursed liquor*, *kill-devil*, and *that demon rum*. While rum has shed much of its sinister skin, and found its way into reserved moments of contemplation as well as onto higher-priced shelves in stores, it still carries a lot a shadowy history in every sip.

Rum's ancestry goes back a long way in history, too, since it's essentially a sugar-based liquor, and sugar has been a popular item for, well, almost ever (while rum's progenitors haven't been around quite as long, drinks produced from fermented sugarcane juice trace their way back to ancient times in India or China). As European explorers started to reach the islands of the Atlantic, including the Canary and Azores first, and then the Caribbean, they planted sugarcane there (and later in Brazil, leading to rum's cousin cachaça). As the Caribbean proved to be such a great spot for growing sugarcane, production soared. It was then discovered that sugarcane's byproduct, molasses, would ferment without much trouble, and soon enough it was being distilled into a spirit—which became very popular worldwide.

And eventually it was distilled in more places, including the yet-to-be-united states, as the first rum distillery in Boston opened around 1700. Rum became a big, big hit in the colonies, as not only the most popular potion in colonial taverns, but also a booming business for traders—some of whom were also slave traders, or at least involved in the slave trade (rum hasn't always been the friendliest of spirits). During the Revolutionary War, with the British blocking ports and unsettling trade, rum's popularity began to decline, just at the time that whiskey was starting to grab hold of the hearts and minds—and taste buds—of drinkers.

As different kinds of sugar production were going on worldwide (thanks a lot, beets), Caribbean sugarcane production began to dip, leaving less molasses around. For a while, it looked like rum was going to stop being an international drink. But then people started traveling more, and this brought more people back to the islands, where they tried the local drinks, mostly made with rum, realized how great they were, and spread the word.

Whiskey

The next dark spirit to raise its dusky head (fittingly, since it took over from rum once already) is really a whole dark family, the whiskey family (spelled *whisky* for Scottish and Canadian varieties), full of relatives from various locales and carrying various calling cards. The word *whiskey*, no matter how you spell it, likely derives from *uisce beatha*, Gaelic for "water of life," which itself in all likelihood derives from the Latin *aqua vitae*. (It's dark histories like this that lead to late-night discussions, discussions helped along by drinks made with the very liquors being discussed.) In its most basic break-down, whiskey/whisky is an alcoholic beverage distilled from a grain mash and aged in wooden casks. Whiskey production is much more regulated than that of rum, though you'll find whiskey-style liquors in most places where some kind of grain is harvested, which leads to many of whiskey's traits being dependent on geography and farming.

American Whiskey Okay, let's start right here in the United States. American whiskey is made with a grain mash that contains at least 51 percent and no more than 79 percent of a single grain (corn for bourbon, rye for rye), and it must be aged in charred oak barrels. The one difference is corn whiskey, which is made from at least 80 percent corn. That's keeping it to the straight and narrow (which you might not expect from a dark spirit, but remember, many spells must be followed to the letter—too much eye of newt and we've got a problem). If an American whiskey is taking one of the above names (bourbon or rye, that is—we'll skip corn whiskey for a second), it is distilled to less than 80 percent and aged in oak casks. If it goes longer than two years in the cask, it's called straight rye, or straight bourbon, but if it has less than 51 percent of the signature grain, it's just straight whis-key. Corn whiskey doesn't have to be aged—however, if it is, it's done in new barrels and for only six months or even less.

A blended American whiskey usually consists of a couple of straight whiskies combined with a grain spirit, at different percentages, depending on how light or dark you want it and on the taste you're going for. Tennessee whiskey is somewhat like bourbon (in that it's 51 percent or more on the grain side), but it has to go through a special process of filtration where it passes, slowly and smoothly, through sugar maple charcoal before being returned to the cask.

Canadian Whisky Tending toward agreeability, lightness, and flexibility, Canadian whiskies go well in many kinds of cocktails and mixed drinks. But this doesn't mean that they're made all willy-nilly. These whiskies must be aged in oak barrels (almost always previously used oak barrels) in Canada for a minimum of three years, though often longer. They must be mashed and distilled in Canada, and are made of wheat, corn, or rye, sometimes with barley or barley malt, but usually some combination, as most Canadian whiskies are blended. You may see Canadian whiskies being called "rye whisky" or "Canadian rye whisky," but this doesn't mean that they're held to the same standards in relation to the amount of rye as in American rye whiskey.

Irish Whiskey To jump continents, Irish whiskies come in three forms: single malt (pure malted barley), pot still (malted and unmalted barley), and blended (malted and unmalted barley as well as corn or other grains), with every type aged for three years in oak casks and distilled three times. For the singular pot still whiskey, only 100 percent barley may be used, and the distillation takes place in a pot still made of copper; it's made using unpeated malt, dried away from fire and smoke. This process gives it a signature taste, spicy and yet with honey accents and a touch of sweetness. The pot still and the single malt varieties are usually sold as they are, but they could also be blended.

Scotch Whisky Scotch whiskies must be constructed in a distillery in Scotland and must contain water and barley, though other grains may be brought in as well; they must be aged in oak casks for at least three years and a day; and they must be double-distilled and have their malt dried over a fire of peat, which gives Scotch its singular smoky flavor. Scotch whiskies are either single-malt (which consist of 100 percent malted barley and tend to be sipped solo rather than mixed) or blended. In the case of the latter, if the label states a specific age, it's the age of the youngest part of the blend. In addition, blended whisky can come as blended malt (mixed single malts), blended grain (mixed grain whiskies, although you might see "single grain" Scotch, too), or blended Scotch (a combo of malts and grains).

The Scotch Whisky Association delineates five distinct whisky regions in Scotland: Campbeltown, the Highlands, Islay, the Lowlands, and Speyside. Each has a number of distilleries, and though not all whiskies from each region taste alike, there are similarities. Whiskies from Campbeltown are spicy and a bit salty and peaty, for example, while the Highlands (the largest area) provide whiskies that are fuller of lingering peat and smoke. Islay, an island, yields very smoky and strong whiskies, which challenge the drinker a bit with their tough nature and warming fortitude (my favorite single-malt, Lagavulin, is an Islay). The Lowland region has the fewest distilleries; Lowland whiskies are lighter and a little less aggressive on the tongue, with a less earthy touch. Finally, Speyside whiskies tend to be a touch sweet and to have a very intricate flavoring, both smoky and spicy. In addition, a number of whiskies fall under the "Island" rubric, made on smaller islands off the west coast. These are more diverse but share an oceanic quality—that is, a bit of brine and salt.

"Scotch-style" whiskies can be made outside of Scotland; for example, the Clear Creek Distillery in Portland, Oregon, makes a lovely "Scotch" using ingredients shipped in from Scotland, though the actual construction happens over here. Then, as any liquor store habitué knows, there are numerous blended varieties of whiskies, some of which have their own regulations based on country of origin and spell-caster. Once popular in cocktail-making, whiskey and Scotch (outside of a few timeless wonders) took a dip as a cocktail ingredient during the middle and end of the last century, becoming more of an "over ice" player. Which was a shame, because this family's members play well with others, and have layers of personality that emerge when combined with the right partners. But, like many things in our current cocktail culture, whiskey and Scotch are both showing up on a more regular basis in drinks far and wide. This resurgence has encompassed rye, too, which until recently was very difficult in many places to even find, but which is (thankfully) now available in most liquor stores and online.

Brandy

Our final dark spirit base is one that has, even more than whiskey, gone through periods of unemployment in cocktails and highballs. Which is a low-down dirty shame, because (as our cocktailing ancestors knew well) it mixes up like a dark champion in situations ranging from sparkling summer slurpers to elegant diamond-esque cocktails boasting class and character. *Brandy*, the word, comes from *bradwijn*, or *brandywine*, which trails back to the Dutch, meaning "burnt wine." As brandy is, basically, a distilled wine, varieties of it have been around since ancient times. But for the actual name, the story goes to the early sixteenth century, when a Dutch trader invented a way to ship more wine in limited cargo space by distilling it and packing it in wooden casks. The goal was to "reconstitute" it at its destination, but he found that what he ended up with—brandy—was actually darn tasty, and the rest is dark spirit history. There are three main types of brandy: grape brandy (our basic brandy, plus its dolled-up sibs Cognac and Armagnac), brandy made from other fruits, and pomace brandy (brandy made from grape skins, seeds, and pits, the best known of which is grappa, which is clear, and so saved for another book). The most noted brandy, Cognac, is made from white grapes in the Charente district of France. The label *Cognac, fine champagne* denotes the finest types, which come from a small area around the town of Cognac. Armagnac is another well-known and delicious brandy, produced in Gascony, France. The major difference between Cognac and Armagnac is the distillation method: Armagnac is distilled once in a continuous copper still, while Cognac is double distilled, and Armagnac is aged longer than Cognac, often for more than 10 years. Other brandies are manufactured commercially in other districts of France, and in Spain, Portugal, Australia, Italy, South Africa, and the United States. Most brandies are distilled in pot stills and then blended and flavored, and finally stored in casks (preferably oak), where they mellow and take on a yellow color; they acquire a deeper tint from storage or additives.

As with our other base liquors, you want to make sure you have a good-quality bottle when a recipe calls for brandy, but there's no need to get a second mortgage on the house to purchase a specific bottle, as you'll be mixing it with other items. Look for brandies labeled VS (for "very special"), which are aged at least three years. If you find reasonably priced brandies that are VSOP ("very superior old pale"), aged five years in wood, or XO ("extra old"), aged six years if Vieille Reserve or four years if Napoleon, don't shy away from them, either.

As noted above, there are also a number of scrumptious fruit brandies, which, as you might expect, are distilled from fruits other than grapes. The range is as wide as the world of fruit, with apple, blackberry, cherry, plum, peach, and many more available. A few have become more famous over time, including Calvados, which is an apple brandy specific to a region in Lower Normandy in France, and Kirschwasser, a cherry brandy. You'll often see these fruit brandies as components in recipes, but they are also very nice when imbibed solo, chilled or over ice.

SPIRITED SIDEKICKS

After you've become sociable with the dark spirits base liquors, it's time to start expanding. While it's enjoyable to slowly sip many of the dark spirits, you'll want to enlarge the shelf space before many minutes have passed, to start filling in your home bar with other bottles so that you can start making drinks. I think the best way to approach this "filling in" is to just page through the book, pick out a few recipes that catch your fancy, and make a list of needed items. Then head on out to the liquor store (or power up the computer and head to an online liquor store, if you have the time and don't mind the wait, or if you're searching for an ingredient your local place doesn't carry), and when back at home, begin mixing up the dark drinks. Follow these same steps a few times, and soon your home bar or liquor shelves will start to twinkle with an assortment of beautiful bottles that allow you to make a multitude of dreamy dark drinks.

If you want to be prepared for those moments when the liquor store might be closed, or when you don't feel like traveling, you can stock up on key ingredients in advance and never feel sorry about it, because they show up in drinks in this book on a regular basis. The first is often considered (at least by me, because I love having it around so much, and use it on such a regular basis) a base in its own right, though not a "dark" base, naturally, and that's Champagne or sparkling wine. I never think it's a bad idea to have at least one chilled bottle of bubbly around, and having a backup or two will come in handy as well, as a wide range of drinks combine the dark and sparkling with wickedly good results. Two other old friends that you should think about stocking up on from the beginning are sweet (red) and dry (white) vermouths—also known as Italian and French, respectively—because they raise their lovely heads in lots of drinks (you can catch up with them in more detail on page 42).

Regarding the physical makeup of your liquor and liqueur shelves or home bar, I don't think you need to build a fridge into the wall, or bar, to keep anything chilled 100 percent of the time (though the sparkling wine should be kept in your regular fridge—make room, y'all). The dark spirits should be stored at room temperature, unless your room temperature is hovering around the average for a Bermudan beach. Don't let them get under the direct sunlight for a long period of time. As their name suggests, dark spirits like to stay out of the light, and rarely need, or want, a tan.

WEAVING THE MIXER'S WEB

Sure, you want your dark drinks to be a bit deep and enigmatic and dusky as dusk, but you don't want to go overboard into the darkness. Balance, via letting in a swatch of sweetness and light and bubbles and fresh notes, makes for even better drinks in many situations. That's where mixers make their appearance. Here, I'm letting the mixer category become fairly broad, covering such items as ginger ale and club soda, as well as the wide assortment of natural mixers, fruits, and fruit juices. While this leaves us with a large mixer array, there is one rule that all mixers (with two small exceptions, detailed below) should live under to remain in peaceful harmony: Fresh is best. Sounds nice, doesn't it? Live with it, make better drinks, and be a happier drinker and drink server—the latter because your guests will be happier, which will make you happier, and, for that matter, the world happier. (Really, it works like that.) This means that you want your lemon juice squeezed from the lemon via your own hand (or your own juicer) not long before it's to be used, and that you shouldn't be sweetening a Lover's Moon (page 161) with cream that's been sidling up to a stack of sturgeon in the fridge for weeks before using if you really want to woo your lover. In the same way, when unleashing a two-liter bottle of ginger ale, you want it to announce its presence with a resounding *hssss* and not a wimpy *wssss* as the last gasp of carbonation slips away. Remember that fresh is best, and become a serving star.

Since you'll be using fresh items, you'll want to find good examples of the species. When you're looking for fruit for juicing (and, if you follow this advice, you'll be leaving bottled juice in the store and seeking fresh fruit often), try to scout out pieces that aren't badly bruised, as bruising may point to an inside that's gone rotten. Find fruit that has agreeable, unblemished skin, with solid and bright coloring, and (for citrus fruits) a touch of give when picked up and squeezed. Don't fret, by the way, about handling fruit before you buy it. Pick it up, give it a good once-over, talk to it if it helps, take a whiff, whatever. Being thought of as strange in the supermarket is a risk one must take. Anyway, if the results are better drinks at home, then it's worth it (and perhaps a nice story to tell when sipping, too). If you absolutely can't find fresh fruit (because you're in an odd fantasy land beyond the horizon's edge where an evil sorcerer has outlawed fresh fruit, for example), then you could use frozen concentrate for juice. But, if possible, sneak in a bit of fresh fruit in garnish form to add flavor (see page 14 for more on garnishing). When you've made it home with your fresh fruit and are ready to release the juice, keep in mind a couple of hints for maximum juiciness. First, make sure the fruit's at room temperature. If not, you can put citrus fruit in a damp towel and microwave it for a few seconds to warm it up a bit, or just run it under some warm water to get the juices flowing. Rolling a piece of fruit under your palm, with steady pressure, helps, too.

In addition to taking time to find and juice the finer fruits, be cautious when buying your bubbly mixers as well. I understand about budgets, and balancing them out, but be wary when buying the bottom-shelfers. Your mixers, like your liquors and liqueurs, add what's in their personality to a drink. If they have a flavor that lowers itself into a bargain range too deeply, then your drink is going to suffer, and perhaps taste like a mud puddle instead of the elixir you want. Be wary when wading through the mixer waters, and your wariness will serve you. While being wary, be sure to pick up club soda when called for (and not seltzer), and shy away from flavored varieties unless specifically called for. (If you have your own CO_2-style soda water dispenser, then more power to you, pal, because they can really deliver. Call me up and I'll come over for demonstrations, because you have pizzazz.)

As alluded to above (see, I gave a warning), two mixers skip around the fresh rule a bit (not that either

Simple Syrup

Makes about 4½ cups

2½ cups **water**

3 cups **sugar**

1. Combine the water and sugar in a medium-size saucepan. Stirring occasionally, bring the mixture to a boil over medium-high heat. Lower the heat a bit, keeping the mixture at a low boil for 5 minutes, stirring occasionally.

2. Turn off the heat and let the syrup cool completely in the pan. Store in a clean, airtight container in the refrigerator for up to 1 month.

⬆ *A Note: If you find you're not using your simple syrup at the pace I do (hey, I'm a sweet guy), you might want to add ½ ounce high-proof neutral grain spirit or high-proof vodka to the bottle for preservation purposes.*

of these should be hanging around through the generations). The first is bitters, a category that until recently always led to much moaning on my part (though I'm normally chipper and cheery, some things do bring even a bouncy boy such as myself down) because of the lack of bitters available and used in modern bar parlance. But we're now seeing a bitters resurgence, which is grand—and which you can read more about on page 224. Bitters are what they sound like: a bitter flavoring agent, one that's made from an assortment of herbs, spices, roots, barks, fruits, and other items proficient bar magicians might use to instill personality into drinks. You can find bitters in liquor stores, grocery stores, specialty gourmet shops, and online, with brands such as Angostura, Peychaud's, and Regan's Orange Bitters, plus more becoming readily available. Never, ever skip the bitters in a recipe, or your drink will fall flat and curses will descend upon your head from bartenders who have passed into the great lounge beyond. Your bitters don't have to be completely fresh, as they tend to retain their flavor for a while—but not for years (you should be using them more, anyway).

Our last mixer, simple syrup, fits into this no-need-for-fresh scheme as well. An easy combination of sugar and water, simple syrup is a key component of many drinks, not only adding the sweetness, but also taking away some of a drink's sharper edges, and helping the drink's other ingredients play nice. Keep some around, chilling in the fridge in a bottle that matches up with the syrup's status. It should be usable for one month, as long as your bottle has a sturdy lid and seal (I like a snap-top variety). Having it there, in the fridge, is a crucial step in preparedness. A few recipes in the book call for flavored simple syrup, or a syrup made in a different manner, adjusted for taste and mouth feel. In those cases, the syrup construction is detailed within the recipe.

A CHILL IN THE DARK AIR: ICE FACTS

Outside of the little devils in the Hot Stuff chapter, the drinks in this book use ice in a big way. Because of this prominent position, you should treat your ice with the same love and care that you do other mixers—if you don't, your drinks will suffer. Keep your ice nice, and don't use ice that might have been tainted by the bananas you've been keeping in the freezer for a year (I'll make that banana bread someday, I swear). If you have old ice, make new ice (this is much easier than when you had to buy ice from the ice man, so take advantage of modern technology, kids), or buy ice if you must.

Many of these recipes call for ice cubes, and standard 1-inch ice cubes work perfectly for the shaking and the straining. If cracked ice is called for, then buy the bagged cracked ice you find in grocery stores, unless you have a cracked ice dispenser. Cracked ice has irregular shapes, melts a little faster, and brings a little more water into some drinks (which you need on occasion—don't discount a touch of water as an ingredient, 'cause it's usually there). You can also sub in cracked ice if you run out of cubes, or have tainted cubed ice (darn those bananas). It's better to sub in this situation than to have no ice or unintentionally flavored ice. Other types of ice that show up are crushed ice (like you'll find in fountain sodas), which brings a slushy fun to certain mixes, and shaved ice, which isn't around as much (though there are ice shavers out there for dedicated drink detectives), but which also adds that slushy and chilly touch with its freshly shaven fluffiness. If you have an ice shaver or are interested in investing in one, use it to shave ice for frothy drinks during summertime, as shaved ice will make a drink chilly fast—but will also water it down more quickly. If you don't have an ice shaver, you can also use crushed ice to good effect.

You see, depending on irregularities in the ice, and how many planes of contact it has with other ingredients, it's going to melt at different rates. Cracked ice melts faster than cubes, and crushed or shaved ice melts even faster (which is why they can be fun in frothy drinks). If you want to use an ice pick and a block of ice, you can end up with some really large chunks, which work well in a single glass (filling an old-fashioned glass with one big cube or chunk instead of multiple little ones, for example), because it'll keep things chilly but not melt as quickly. For many of the drinks in the Powerful Punches chapter, you can use a single large block of ice to snazzy effect in punch bowls. It looks sharp, keeps the punch cold, and shows off your party-throwing chops. Ice blocks can be bought in stores, or you could make an ice ring—why not?—with a Bundt cake pan or Jell-O ring mold.

INCANTATION INDISPENSABLES: GARNISHES

You wouldn't head to the dark spirits wizard's ball without your special pointed hat, would you? Likewise, after you've poured the dark spirits and mixers (and perhaps shaken and strained them), you wouldn't want to automatically rush off to serve them into waiting hands without adding the garnish, an indispensable addition to many of the drinks contained within this volume. The right garnish adds a key visual touch to drinks (bringing the liquid ensemble together, so to speak), but also adds important flavor flourishes. If a drink is missing the garnish, it's missing an important part of its makeup and just isn't finished. It's like Frankenstein without the bolts at the neck, or Dracula without fangs. Don't leave your dark spirit hanging—remember your garnish.

Though citrus fruits are the most common garnishes, the list goes on much longer and continues to grow as drink-making people get more inventive. You'll find a decent range of garnishes called for in the following pages, including citrus fruits, fresh mint and sage leaves, grapes, raspberries, nutmeg, butter mint candy, pineapple chunks, and others. Don't let the list give you a fright, though. Remember the friendly "fresh is best" rule from earlier and you'll be in good shape.

A few garnishes—citrus twists, wheels, and wedges—deserve more investigation because of their frequency of use, and seasoned travelers have learned some lessons about them that you can benefit from on your own dark spirits journey. Twists are the most used and the trickiest in some ways. Too often they are used only as decoration, when the main reason they're around is to release those essential oils found in citrus rinds into a drink. (When you see them just draped over a drink, or scraped off a fruit with a tool nowhere near the drink, letting that flavor escape into the air, feel free to shed a tear.) It's not hard to make a usable and attractive twist. Start by cutting off the bottom end of your fruit in one clean straight line, not taking too much—just enough to make a flat surface. Next, place that flat part of the fruit on a cutting board and then, with a sharp paring knife or garnishing knife, remove ½-inch-wide strips of peel, cutting from top to bottom, working to get as little of the inner white pith as possible while still maintaining sturdy pieces of peel. These peel strips are your twists, and you want to be able to actually twist them over the top of a drink, without breaking them into pieces, before releasing them into the drink's dark depths. And don't forget: The fruit that you've made the twist from can then be juiced (yay, fresh juice!).

Wheels and half-wheels, or slices, are a snap to make, as are wedges. For the former two, you just slice the ends of your fruit with your trusty knife—⅛ inch off the top and bottom is good—and then cut the fruit into equally sized wheels; cut the wheels in half and you're in slice town. If you want them to balance on the glass, notch the wheels or slices. Wedges are almost as simple. You start in the same manner, with those ⅛-inch pieces cut off each end of a piece of fruit. Cut the fruit in half lengthwise and lay each half, cut side down, on your cutting board. Make three lengthwise cuts through each half, angled toward the center line. You should have three equally sized pieces, which you then cut in half, or thirds if it's a large piece of fruit. (A note: On occasion, folks making drinks call these smaller pieces quarters, and call the longer pieces "wedges." This is okay, because nomenclature changes from place to place and person to person. But for this book, let's stick with calling the smaller pieces wedges, so I don't get confused.)

THE TOOLS OF THE DARK SPIRITS TRADE

Wait, wait, before you go off looking for wands and brooms and cauldrons (unless you're making a hot whiskey punch of some sort), let me put a halt on diving so deeply into the "dark" spirits idea. The place you need to start when thinking about drink-making tools is in another section of the store (or another store entirely). You must first find the top dog of the drink-making tool assortment: the cocktail shaker. Not every drink in the book is made with a shaker (there's a whole chapter of punches that don't sniff a shaker), but so many are that your home bar will be sadly deficient if you don't pick one up. When starting tool talk, the shaker comes first.

There are two types of shakers, the cobbler shaker and the Boston shaker. You can find both of them in stores near and far, online and off, and

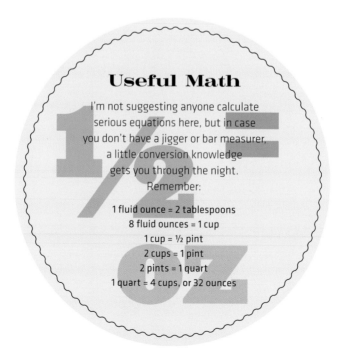

Useful Math

I'm not suggesting anyone calculate serious equations here, but in case you don't have a jigger or bar measurer, a little conversion knowledge gets you through the night.
Remember:

1 fluid ounce = 2 tablespoons
8 fluid ounces = 1 cup
1 cup = ½ pint
2 cups = 1 pint
2 pints = 1 quart
1 quart = 4 cups, or 32 ounces

both types are fairly easy to use and can have you, home bartending whiz, shaking up chilly mixes in no time. The cobbler shaker delivers cold results and is a snap to master. Most are all metal (though some have a glass component as well), and you should look for one that is made of 18/10 stainless steel, as it will stay in better shape and not stain. The cobbler consists of a larger bottom piece covered by a top that usually has a built-in strainer, and a small cap that can be used as a measuring device, a nice bonus. The process is remarkably simple, so dive right in: Add your ingredients to that larger bottom piece, secure the top (double-checking the "secure" part; spilling everywhere during the shaking process delays drinking, which isn't a plus), and get to shaking. Once done, strain, garnish, and serve.

The Boston shaker may take a tiny bit of practice to master, but it also delivers lovely and chilly results. The Boston shaker consists of two parts (plus you'll need a stand-alone strainer to help at straining time): a bottom cup made of glass and a top cup made of metal. As with the cobbler, you should look for one whose metal part is made of 18/10 stainless steel. Here's how it works: You add the ingredients to the glass bottom cup and then invert the metal top cup and place it over the bottom cup, like a cover. Using the palm of your hand (and thinking safety first) give the bottom of the upside-down metal cup a bit of a thump. You want to create a seal between the two cups, to keep them together securely. Now, turn the whole thing upside down and, holding both pieces firmly (you certainly don't want to spill now), start shaking. Once the shaking is done, set the shaker on a steady surface, metal side still down. Strike it carefully with your hand to break the seal, and then strain the drink into the appropriate glass or drinking vessel.

Whichever of these standout shakers you end up getting, I suggest shaking (unless a recipe specifically suggests otherwise) for 10 seconds, or up to 15. You want chilly results, sure, but you're also working on ingredient combination, and shaking long enough ensures it.

Now that you've invested in your tried-and-true boon companion on the road to dark spirits success, your shaker, there are some other tools to get, to help kit out that home bar. First, even if your shaker does have a built-in measuring device, you'll want to have a jigger for accurate measuring. There may be a time when you want to alter a drink recipe's proportions, but to serve better drinks from the get-go and reduce the chances of serving drinks that carry a taste of old sorcerer's socks, you'll want to get the right ingredient measurements. Get a jigger that's made of 18/10 stainless steel; I suggest one that measures 1 ounce on one side and 1½ or 2 ounces on the other, as these sizes should cover most mixings.

Finally, we get to your wands. Okay, not exactly a wand, but the next tool you'll want to get, a muddler, is somewhat like a wand, with its resemblance to a small baseball bat (usually with both a wider end and a slightly tapered end). Also like a wand, it's used to "muddle" ingredients together, so that the result is even tastier than the original components. You basically beat around (macerating, but not getting *too* wacky about it) fruit or herbs in the bottom of your shaker before shaking, or in a glass before pouring other things into it, to release their essential oils, as well as juices—all of which taste so devilishly divine. There are lots of muddlers currently available in stores, both wooden models and modern-y metal ones. Search out a muddler that fits your hand, and that you feel comfortable hefting (there's no need to get a giant muddler to show off—you'll end up blistered). Try to get one that isn't painted up, or varnished heavily, or the finish will come off in your drink; if you have to, sub in a sturdy wooden spoon until you find the right muddler for you.

For the fresh juices mentioned in "Weaving the Mixer's Web" on page 11, I suggest ponying up for a solid, reliable juicer. Because fresh juice is such an imperative addition to many drinks, it'll save you time—and up your drink-making reputation (never a bad thing)—if you have a juicer at the ready. There are nice handheld juice squeezers out there in a variety of shapes and sizes—Want a juicer that looks like a bird? No problem!—but if you throw parties for large groups, I suggest a lever-model juicer, as they juice faster and keep hands from getting into an overly sticky situation. Motorized juice extractors can be great, too, though with the smaller citrus fruits (limes and lemons), I find they impart too much pith taste.

To get fruits ready for juicing, and to make those great garnishes in the "Incantation Indispensables" section on page 14, you'll want to invest in a sharp, serious, thin-bladed paring knife (accompanied by a solid, non-shaky cutting board, if you want to keep your counters shipshape). When bandying that knife around, remember that care is of the essence with knives. Even a nick on a finger's tip when cutting fruit is going to dampen your ability to be a party champ. It's not a bad idea, talking cutlery, to have a larger knife handy for any out-of-the-ordinary garnishes that need chopping.

Two final tools come under the heading of "essentials" in my book (and then there's a small host of others below that you should consider getting cozy with): a blender and a pitcher. Saying this may have me maligned in some areas, but hold steady and I'll plead my case. First, the blender. Sure, there are only a few drinks in this particular book that call for a blender, and some blender drinks are overly saccharine and give an ice headache more readily than a pleasant drinking experience. But when made right, with a bit of balance and a bunch of love, a good blended drink is a summertime soirée soldier's greatest friend, as you can usually make them in bunches and know that they're going to bring a smile to sweltering guests (and making guests smile is a central theme to any gathering). And you can always use a good blender to make crushed ice, if you'd like to make any drink slushier. Plug in one whose jar holds at least 27 ounces, though I suggest a 40-ounce model or larger (depending on how many drinks you wanna make at once), and one that has multiple speed settings plus a pulse function and stainless-steel blades. Double-check that the blender has a tight seal and a pouring lip (and that the seal seals the lip when in use), and you're set. Now the pitcher may be an even harder "tool" sell to some, but I find a pitcher, really two pitchers, to be indispensable when making drinks for a group. Not just for serving either, but for constructing the drinks. Because of this, I think having two reliable pitchers is best, one with a bit of brawn for outside entertaining and one that's glass and sparkles a bit under candlelight, or faux candlelight, for indoor associations. Make sure that they have a pouring lip (so handy), and that they hold 50 ounces or more. A small pitcher holds 50 ounces; larger ones run 75 to 100 ounces, and that's a lot of lovely dark spirits in one spot, indeed.

Filling In: More Tools

While the crucial tools just discussed take center stage, it's not a shabby idea to increase your bar tool portfolio, both to ease the drink-making event and because, well, it's a lot of fun. Remember, drinking and drink-making are a kick, and more tools can raise the level of that kick even higher. Places to start include getting an ice bucket and ice scoop for easy ice access (this is going to sound like a chorus, but again, go for 18/10 stainless steel in this situation), a spice grater for nutmeg and hard spices, a foil cutter and a steadfast corkscrew for wine, a bottle opener, a long and slender stirring spoon that's always within arm's reach for those stirred drinks, and a clean and cute (it can be darkly cute, if you want) towel for whisking away any overflow (it's going to happen, so be ready). You can also dive in deep on bottle stoppers and pourers if you desire, colorful or plain toothpicks for balancing garnishes on glasses, shiny or artistic trays for taking cocktails from one corner of the house to another, and more. I tend to believe that every bar needs a little splash and style, so I suggest getting some colorful or quirky coasters and bar napkins (these aid in any overflowing at the drinking source as well), some swizzle and stir sticks, and some straws. You want your bar to be, at heart, a reflection of you, and I know you've got style.

GET YOUR GLITTERING GLASSWARE HERE

It's rare, I've found, that drinking a delish dark spirit-based drink out of one's cupped hand is a hoot (although this has a certain communal ring to it, too much of the mix ends up on the ground). And, while consuming out of oddly spectral containers sounds intriguing, it doesn't work nearly as well as matching up the right glassware with the right drink. That, dark spiriters, is a beauty to behold, and to sip on, a happy marriage that no one who doesn't drop their glass can tear asunder. You can switch up glasses on drinks here and there and not worry too much about a malevolent curse dropping on you out of thin air (though some old salts might give you the evil eye for it), but with a little glassware investment in a few key categories, you'll have most situations covered, and the only curses you'll be hearing will be joyful ones from fellow revelers.

The first, and most important, glassware to set yourself up with is the classic cocktail glass, often called the Martini glass. It's one that you'll recognize, as would most folks from Topeka to Timbuktu, by its graceful stem and bowl. The sizes have become much larger than when our fathers' fathers' fathers drank, as you can now find cocktail glasses from 3 to 12 ounces without straining eyes much. Many of the drinks in this book stay in that lower range, which is a more classically minded amount (so you can, as the legendary Harry Craddock said, consume the cocktail "while it's laughing at you"). I tend to believe this size of mix gets consumed while it's still nice and cold—a desired effect. This isn't to say that a larger cocktail, or cocktail glass, is bad, by the way. It's only when one ends up drinking a not-so-chilly cocktail that the dark spirits start to rumble. The number of cocktail glass choices, and glassware choices in general, is very wide today, especially if you like to add antique markets to your shopping sprees. Want a cocktail glass with painted cherries on the outside for your Quickie (page 165)? Not a problem.

Two other key glassware categories are highball and old-fashioned glasses, both of which are used a lot, and which are sort of opposites. Highballs tend to be tallish and slender, in the 10- to 12-ounce size range. Old-fashioned glasses are short and more squat in shape, with thick bottoms and the ability to hold 6 to 10 ounces. You can track down double old-fashioned glasses if you want, that reach up to a 15-ounce arena, and they can be handy to have on your glassware shelf. There are also some drinks in this book that call for a Collins glass, which is tall and in the 12- to 16-ounce range, somewhat like the highball's bigger sibling. The more generous size makes the Collins a nice receptacle for the larger bubbly drinks.

The wine glass family comes in handy, too, for a number of drinks. I'm bringing along the Champagne flute with this category, because it gets along well with the other wine glasses, as long as you let it step to the front of the line (ah, Champagne, so good, but a tad snooty). It does look lovely, though, with its thin and funneled shape. If you can find old-school bowl-style Champagne glasses (originally designed, as the legend goes, from a mold of Marie Antoinette's breasts), then you should try those out for both sparkling wine drinks and drinks usually served in cocktail glasses. I think a set of both red wine (goblet-style) glasses and the smaller-bowled white wine glasses are a bet you'll want to make, because they aren't shy either, and they show up regularly.

For the Hot Stuff category (and for a few other choice warm drinks here and there), you'll want a good set of mugs, ones that can take the heat without burning the hand, ones with a good handle that won't cramp anyone's drinking style. Both ceramic and glass mugs can step up to the heated dark spirit's plate, but if you have glass ones, it's not a bad idea to warm them under a warm water tap and dry them quickly before filling them up with a hot drink.

A punch bowl, as mentioned above, is necessary for many of the larger drinks in the book, and it's definitely something you'll want to lay your hands on. (Both hands is probably the best idea, because you'll want to be careful with it once you've brought it home.) Go for a thick-walled-but-still-sparkly crystal number, one that glitters a bit and that has a set of crystal punch cups trailing behind it like baby ducks following their mother (if the ducks were as shiny as a punch bowl, that is).

I sure like having a lot of cordial glasses around, but then again, between us, I'm a bit of a glassware addict. They tend to be a touch decorative, sometimes with long, long stems, sometimes with colored bowls, sometimes with each glass in a set having its own curve, its own personality, its own *je ne sais quoi* (see what a glassware obsession can lead to?). These glasses, friends, can provide oodles of amusement when serving smaller drinks, or giving solo tastes of liqueurs and liquors, and can make your bar shine above the rest. There are lots of glasses out there that can slake your glassware thirst once it gets going, from snifters for brandy (and drinks like the Drowsy Chaperone, page 66) to specific pousse café glasses to shot glasses of all sorts (be careful using them for measuring, though, as they are in no way regulated). But don't let glassware be a source of frustration. If you're lacking in white wine glasses and an intriguing recipe that's singing to you calls for them, instead use red wine glasses this time, or even punch glasses in a pinch. Glassware, like everything circling your home bar, should be a good time.

THE FINAL ENCHANTMENT: HERE'S TO YOU

Your bar is looking fine, with shaker, tools, and glasses, you've picked up some choice bottles, and your dark spirits adventure is about to begin. Though I've mentioned it before, let me underline in this spellbook one final ingredient you should never leave out of your drinks and drinking: fun. Whether it's good-natured tomfoolery for ten with punch perfectly positioned, or the more restrained glee of cocktails for two, this communal sharing of cocktails, highballs, and other drinks should at heart be enjoyable, a moment to savor in the midst of a world that's rushing by, sometimes at speeds that seem unstoppable. Which is why these moments of unharnessed joy, moments that are often few and far apart, are worth taking some time out for. And, in many of these situations, a perfect cocktail makes the moment even better, bringing out the best in everyone who's around. What a lovely day, with friends and good drinks and good spirits. This book, with dark drollery set aside for a minute, sets itself right in the middle of these moments with you, with about 200 darkly delicious recipes spread over its seven chapters, recipes combining tastiness, history, useful tidbits, silliness, and cheer, enough to help get the party started and, I hope, take it on into the evening—or early morning—hours. Don't stop here, though; turn the pages and let your own dark spirits begin to flow.

Dark Classics

This is where the seminar starts, as I'm going to lay out a multilayered, painstakingly researched, bloody-nailed, chicken-scratched, scientifically determined hierarchy of Dark Classics, backed by my first, second, and third rules of Dark Classics, ending up in an inarguable canon of ultra-exclusive cocktails, highballs, and etceteras—a canon that's laid out over a flow chart that flows as flawlessly as the Volga River and ends up being worthy of a poster posted in every bar school, to be chanted every morning by students who'll know, by gosh, what's good for them, once they've chanted said chart at least 365 times.

Nah, let's skip that exercise (as super-duper-scintillating as it sounds). Because often a "classic" is defined ten ways by ten people who have ten valid opinions. If I cut off their opinions, then why shouldn't they cut off mine? Then we're spending all our time cutting up each other's classicism instead of drinking together and singing bawdy songs. Which isn't to say opinions are bad—drinking opinions are swell, as long as they don't get in the way of drinking. But "classic" is a wibbly-wobbly word these days, and waffling over it for too long takes away from the very powerful drinks in the following pages.

They are powerful potions, by the way, that have stood a bit of time, and have been consumed by a pretty large pack of people during a significant dollop of the mixing-stuff-to-make-a-beverage time. Honestly, that's a mouthful that doesn't begin to describe the effect these drinks have had on those who've consumed them, as they've been a big part of people's lives, of celebrations and the drowning of sorrows, of marriage proposals and marriages, of toasts to new jobs and early retirements, of seductions and Sunday afternoons, of songs, stories, and plain old good times.

That makes them "classics" for me, the fact that they've been a part of so many lives while always retaining their good taste. They've been a part of histories big and small, been ordered by many folks near and far, and been made at home, too, with maybe some strange alterations along their historical way, but always making those who were drinking them pleased, if not outright joyous.

Perhaps when we end up alongside each other in a bar booth, or in lawn chairs, or while watching the stars slip into the sky while looking out an open garage door on a fall evening, you'll argue coherently, bravely, and honestly for a different set of Dark Classics. I'd sure be happy to listen, while I sip my Manhattan, smiling at how I'll remember the night, and the drink, forever.

Dark and Stormy It's

amusing that this drink from the highball family has such an intimidating name, one that conjures up a long night's deadly boat ride on an upset ocean, or at least a long night of the soul, when, in actuality, the Dark and Stormy pairs best with hot and lazy summer evenings, when there's a slow twang in the sweaty air and not much movement outside of the slight swaying of palm frond fans. The reason for this matching—and I think the reason the Dark and Stormy has been discovered and rediscovered by many, becoming an obsession with a number of discerning drinkers—is the drink's refreshing nature, and how the rum and ginger beer bring out the best in each other while taking the edge off a heated situation. Speaking of the rum, the aficionados (and historical preference) point to Gosling's Black Seal as the ideal choice—if you can't find it, at least use another Bermudan brand.

Ice cubes

2 ounces **dark rum**

Chilled ginger beer

Lime wedge for garnish

1. Fill a highball glass three-quarters full with ice cubes. Add the rum.

2. Fill the glass with ginger beer, but don't be wacky about it (no drink becomes a favorite if it bubbles over and stickies up the counter).

3. Squeeze the lime wedge over the drink, and then let it slide on in. Stir, but briefly.

Fish House Punch

"Now, this is the story all about how, my bar got stirred, stirred upside down, and I'd like to take a minute—just drink and don't carouse—I'll tell you how I became hooked on a punch called Fish House. In west Philadelphia, Fish House was born and raised, at the Schuylkill Fishing Company, where it spent most of its days, rumming out, Cognac-ing, relaxing all cool. . . ."

The Fish House Punch could be called a forgotten classic, a drink once in every book and bar and club and known throughout the drinking kingdom. Except, thankfully, more and more folks are unearthing it, introducing it to friends in their garages, printing it up in their books or on websites, and generally making the ghosts of those gentlemen who hung out in 1732 or thereabouts at the original Schuylkill Fishing Company in Philly (also known as the State in Schuylkill or the Fish House Club) very proud.

Serves 10

Block of ice (or **cracked ice**, if necessary)

One 750-milliliter bottle **dark rum**

15 ounces **Cognac**

7½ ounces **peach brandy**

7½ ounces **freshly squeezed lemon juice**

7½ ounces **Simple Syrup** (page 12)

1. Add the ice to a punch bowl (fill about three-quarters full if using cracked ice). Add the rum, Cognac, brandy, lemon juice, and simple syrup. Stir 10 times, while humming fishy songs or hymns to Pennsylvania.

2. Stir 10 more times. Serve in punch cups or wine glasses.

Horsefeather

Let me take a moment while we're going pitter-patter for classic dark spirit mixes (if you're one of those who nitpicks about definitions of words like *classic* while the rest of us are in the corner consuming said mixes, then you need to take a moment of your own and realign those priorities) and give a serious and lengthy toast to those mighty Midwestern barmen and barwomen. I mean those folks who poured me many beautiful drinks year-round, insulating me from snow and rain, helping me reroute dreary days and instilling a spring in my step, and (perhaps most of all) serving me Horsefeathers when the dusty afternoons parched me punchy. If you've spent a desiccated summer anywhere where a throat gets extra-arid, you'll know the kind of days I mean. And if you don't know what I mean, but end up stuck in Kansas in this situation, head to the Taproom in Lawrence or Auntie Mae's in Manhattan, Kansas, and let either Jeremy Sidener or Jeff Denny rustle up a Horsefeather for you—you'll soon be giving them toasts, too.

Ice cubes

3 ounces **Kentucky bourbon**

Chilled ginger ale

2 dashes **Angostura bitters**

1. Fill a highball glass three-quarters full with ice cubes. Add the bourbon (or watch happily as it's being added).

2. Fill the glass leisurely with ginger ale. Add the Angostura bitters. Stir well.

⌃ *A Note: Take the horses out with friends via the Horse's Neck, page 253.*

A is for Applejack

I never thought much of the saying "When you're really good, they call you crackerjack." Not that I dislike the popcorn mix called Cracker Jack (though when did the surprises in the packages become so lame?). It's only that if the saying were "When you're really good, they call you applejack," I'd feel much more desire to be really good. And it would have a little more historical relevance, as applejack, the apple brandy that is so, so good, dates back to the American Colonial era, and was a big part of the lives of those folks who founded the United States—even being used as currency (as the story goes) to pay construction crews mapping out some of the nation's first roads. Applejack has been made in two different ways, with regular distillation and with freeze distillation (which is how they did it way back when). The latter used to be known as "jacking," and hence led to applejack getting its signature snappy name. Laird & Company, which was the first commercial distillery in the United States, is perhaps the most well-known maker of applejack. It began with William Laird, who, after moving to the Colonies in 1698 from Scotland, where he had a hand in making Scotch, put his energy and skills into making a tasty beverage from what he saw all around him: apples. But the Laird applejack really made a splash in the public eye in 1760, when Robert Laird, a Revolutionary War soldier who was soldiering under George Washington, started to provide the troops with applejack—this after General Washington himself had tried it, and contacted the family for the recipe so he could produce his own version. You can see why I think it's better to be called an "applejack," after this historic mix, than any old crackerjack. And if you don't want to be called either, you can always call yourself "Jersey Lightning," which was an old name for applejack and which sounds pretty darn cool.

Hot Toddy

The toddy family traces its heritage back as far as the heated pools of the river Okeanos (which, in ancient Greek mythos, was the river that circled the earth), where drink-loving ancestors reclined to unwind and gaze at sun, stars, and moon (which rose and set out of the river's waters), sipping heated H2O swirled into mugs made of wood and mixed with our old pal brandy's progenitors and a smidge of sweetness (perhaps some honey, perhaps a little sugarcane, perhaps a sweet dried fig), taking a few moments to bandy, philosophically, about whether a lemon twist should be added to the mug's contents.

Since those far-gone days of yore, the Hot Toddy has grown up, raised a large family, become legendary, added and subtracted a few medicinal powers, been modernized, tripped into back alleys and byways, been revitalized, been stylized, been posturized, and today has once again become a favorite of many—and for good reason: The warming drink's simplicity is quintessential.

2½ ounces **water**

1½ ounces **brandy**

½ ounce **Simple Syrup** (page 12)

Lemon twist for garnish (optional)

1. Using a small saucepan or the microwave, heat the water until almost boiling.

2. Add the brandy to a prewarmed old-fashioned glass or a suitably historic mug. Add the simple syrup and stir briefly.

3. Pour the water carefully into the vessel. Stir once more. Garnish with the lemon if you desire.

VARIATIONS: The toddy can be made with multiple liquors. A hot whiskey toddy helps with the pain experienced when using the TV remote too rapidly (although no doctor has verified this), and a hot apple toddy made with apple brandy or Calvados is good for tennis elbow (again, not doctor approved).

Mai Tai

Mai Tai The decline of tiki time at the end of the past century brought frowns to many giant wooden masks that hung on humid bars and lounges during the movement's heyday, from the late 1940s until the '60s or thereabouts. (Movements, especially booze-related, have shaky borders.) I hope those who are reviving and celebrating tiki time are making the king of tiki concoctions, the Mai Tai, in a manner that wouldn't anger King Kamehameha. At its height of stardom, the Mai Tai was made any number of ways, many of which completely ignored the fact that the drink should be a balance of rums, fruit juice, and sweetness, and included crazy ingredients like so many decorative stir sticks.

Which **you can't completely blame anyone** for, as even the Mai Tai's origin is a little under debate. Most think it was created by Victor Bergeron, known popularly as Trader Vic, whose restaurant, Trader Vic's, was a tiki triumph and who said about the Mai Tai, "Anyone who says I didn't create this drink is a stinker." The story goes that he composed the original in 1944 for some friends from Tahiti who said after sampling: "*mai tai–ro ae*," which means "out of this world–the best."

The other possible progenitor was the other tiki giant striding the waves, Donn Beach, better known as Don the Beachcomber, who was really the kick-start for the whole tiki craze—well, that and society's desire to rebel against the staid 1940s and '50s. Donn may just have applied the name Mai Tai to a drink in the early 1930s that featured rums, lime and grapefruit juices, Pernod, Falernum, and Cointreau. While this is tasty and worth trying in its own tiki right, I prefer Vic's version myself.

Ice cubes

2½ ounces **dark rum**

1 ounce **white rum**

1 ounce **orange curaçao**

1 ounce **freshly squeezed lime juice**

½ ounce **Simple Syrup** (page 12)

¼ ounce **orgeat syrup**

Fresh mint sprig for garnish

1 to 2 **lime wedges** for garnish

1. Fill a cocktail shaker halfway full with ice cubes. Add the rums, curaçao, lime juice, simple syrup, and orgeat. Shake well.

2. Fill a highball glass three-quarters full with ice cubes. Strain the mix over the ice. Garnish with a fresh mint sprig and a lime wedge or two.

⤴ *A Note: It may be more authentic if you strain this over crushed ice or shaved ice, which makes it slushier. (Maybe a bit too slushy? You decide.)*

⤴ *A Second Note: Orgeat is an almond-flavored syrup available in gourmet stores, some happening grocery stores, and online.*

Manhattan

Whatever deity or otherworldly being or little green men you chat with when wanting to give thanks in some general way (even if it's solely the random hand of universal randomness), please pass along to them my thanks for the Manhattan. Or, if you somehow know exactly who first made this—the apex, in many ways, of the dark spirits pantheon—thank his ghost (since it was probably some first-rate forward-thinking bartender from the Manhattan Club in the late-to-middle 1800s or perhaps, as has been recently reported, a New Orleans colonel).

Why the panoply of thankfulness for this one drink, named after the sparkling city and ordered by many right now as I type? Because, silly, the Manhattan is the boss. Not in the political sense (it could, between us, use a little more in the lobbying department, though it's **been swilled by many back-room bargainers**) and, you could argue, not even in the purely popular sense, because it gets trumped today in orders by the Martini (spotlight-hogger that the Martini is) and probably by a host of ugly amalgamations having less to do with taste and more to do with rocket fuel (could you talk to the above powers about this ratio, by the way?). The Manhattan is the boss where it matters most. It's sophisticated, strong, simple (in the "perfect simplicity" sense), a cocktail that's like a solid wooden bar: reliable, comfortable, and always something to admire and savor.

Ice cubes

2½ ounces **whiskey** or **rye**

½ ounce **sweet vermouth**

2 dashes **Angostura bitters**

Maraschino cherry for garnish

1. Fill a cocktail shaker halfway full with ice cubes. Add the whiskey, vermouth, and bitters. Shake well, with another little "thanks" for the bounty you're about to receive.

2. Strain into a cocktail glass. Garnish with the cherry.

⬆ *A Note: I like a Tillen Farms (www.tillenfarms. com) all-natural Merry Maraschino Cherry with my Manhattan. You should try one.*

Mike Collins

I've had a number of friends named Mike, and while they were fine fellas up and down the list (no female "Mike" friends yet, sadly), I'm not sure that I like any of them quite as well as the Mike Collins (sorry, other Mikes). Well, curse me as disloyal if you want, but the Mike Collins is a lesser-known member of the enshrined Collins family, and I figure if I start touting how friendly Mike Collins is, my friends named Mike won't feel so bad. And if the Mike Collins becomes more famous, more Mikes will have drinks bought for them, which will make them happy. I mean, a free Mike Collins *is* worth a lot, especially when your name is actually Mike.

The Mike Collins follows the fairly lovely and uncomplicated formula of the family's now sort-of starry-eyed and most-written-about-by-paparazzi member, the Tom Collins, with a touch of sweet (of course, Tom's sweetness used to come from a sweetened gin, whereas Mike's sweetness has always emanated from outside the main base liquor, Irish whiskey), a touch of tang, and a touch of refreshing. I think the slightly less-sweet nature of Mike makes it ideal for those days when you want to cool down—but also keep your stiff upper lip stiff.

Ice cubes

2 ounces **Irish whiskey**

½ ounce **freshly squeezed lemon juice**

¼ ounce **Simple Syrup** (page 12)

Chilled club soda

Lemon slice for garnish

1. Fill a cocktail shaker halfway full with ice cubes. Add the whiskey, lemon juice, and simple syrup. Shake well, in celebration of all Mikes.

2. Fill a Collins glass three-quarters full with ice cubes. Strain the mix over the ice. Fill almost to the top with chilly club soda. Garnish with the lemon slice (stirring briefly if you want Mike mixed more).

"Drinkers, such as Horace, were regularly mentioned in the New Years Honours. Indeed, Horace's great ode on the defeat of Cleopatra begins, symbolically, with the words **'Nunc est bibendum': 'Now for a drink.'** It is as if some patriotic American poet, the late Robert Frost perhaps, were to have celebrated the annihilation of an infinitely seductive female Mao tse Tung by demanding a Manhattan."

PETER DICKINSON, "Love, Liquor, And Classical Learning," *The Compleat Imbiber 6*, 1963

Mint Julep

At one point (as many folks have mentioned for many years) there were many juleps. It was a whole class of fruity drinks, with offshoots, cousins, and icy branches. The word itself descends from the Arabic *julab*, which means rosewater, and has come to refer to seasoned water, fruity water, or boozy-fruity water. There is serious history with a julep, and maybe that weight is one of the problems keeping this, one of the world's ideal liquid compositions, mostly relegated to a particular very popular horse race held the first Saturday in May. Now, I love a Mint Julep on Derby Day as much as at least half of my close friends. (The other half? Insane for it. Dangerous for it. Raising their children to be Mint Julep madwomen and madmen on Derby Day.) However, I do feel a pinch pecked that the Mint Julep is not given its broader due. The Mint Julep is a prince or princess among drinks. Its harmony of spring water (who doesn't love the spring?), sublime sugar, fresh mint (which carries the heart of spring in every leaf, like a hope for sunshine and a blooming and better world), and then, finally, and most importantly, America's own bourbon, brings stability to the glass, to springtime, and to any occasion where it's served. All of these elements socialize, mingle, and combine to become an essential part not only of history, but of every gala where a drop passes lips. This, then, is a julep: a part of history and a part of making history. Remember that next time you're mixing one up. You're having a drink, but now you're also part of something larger than yourself.

I've quoted this before, but it bears repeating: "A Mint Julep is not the process of a formula. It is a ceremony and must be performed by a gentleman possessing **a true sense of the artistic**, a deep reverence for the ingredients, and a proper appreciation of the occasion."

S.B. BUCKNER, JR., *in a letter to General Connor*, 1937

4 to 5 **fresh mint leaves**

1 ounce **Simple Syrup** (page 12)

Crushed ice

3 ounces **Kentucky bourbon**

Fresh mint sprig for garnish

~~~~~~~~~~~~~~~~~~~~~~~~~~~

⬆ *A Note: Once upon a time, you picked your ice up in a block, then crushed it in a special ice-crushing bag. If you need to start with crushed ice, don't be too sad—or too happy—about it.*

1. Take one mint leaf and rub it over the inside of a metal julep cup (if you have one) or a highball glass. Be sure the mint comes into close acquaintance with all of the inside of the glass, then let the leaf come to rest in the glass.

2. Add the remaining mint leaves and the simple syrup to the glass. Using a muddler or wooden spoon, muddle the leaves and syrup well. Remember, only by being strong can you live up to the juleps that came before yours.

3. Fill the glass halfway full with crushed ice. Add the bourbon. Stir well—the glass should get icy.

4. Fill the glass almost to the top with crushed ice. Stir just once and garnish with the mint sprig and a bit of reverence.

Six Obscure Dark Spirit Facts to Bring Up at the Bar

Feeling that itch to impress the folks around the bar with your arcane drinking knowledge and ability to bring facts out of almost thin air to get a conversation started? Let me help you out with the six historical tidbits below.

1. Bourbon is the official spirit of the United States, by act of Congress.

2. The explorer Magellan, when getting ready to sail around the world in 1519, spent more of his sailing budget to stock up on sherry than to buy weapons.

3. The word *brandy* comes from *brandywine*, which is a derivation of the Dutch word *brandewijn*, which means "burnt wine."

4. During William III's rule over Great Britain in the seventeenth century, he once had a party where a fountain in his garden doubled as a punch bowl, being filled with a recipe that boasted 560 gallons of brandy, 1,200 pounds of sugar, 25,000 lemons, 20 gallons of lime juice, and 5 pounds of nutmeg, as well as a bartender rowing around in a boat, filling up the glasses of guests around the fountain.

5. By 1717, the British colony in Boston was producing more than 200,000 gallons of rum annually.

6. In Cleveland, it was long illegal for two men to drink out of the same whiskey bottle and get drunk at the same time.

Old Fashioned

Ah, the Old Fashioned. It's a testy mix. Well, the drink itself isn't so testy—when made right, that is. That's where the testiness starts, because it's a classic that's made cattywampus more often than not. Sometimes you see more fruit than on a Carmen Miranda hat. Sometimes there's enough soda water to float a battleship. Sometimes (and I bow for my mistake here) you think that the original club where this drink was poured, the Pendennis Club, was in New Orleans (as certain books say), instead of in Louisville (which is right). There's one way around this fuddling and fussing: Combine the classic drink from antiquity with a modern marvel, the website of Mr. Robert Hess—a.k.a. DrinkBoy—the world's leading voice on the Old Fashioned. DrinkBoy (whom you can find at www.drinkboy.com and read more about on page page 58) fills us in on the ins and outs of the Old Fashioned, tells us some spots to get a good Old Fashioned, and **entertains in a way that could never be called old-fashioned**. And if you like your Old Fashioned without an orange slice muddled in (like I tend to), he won't even laugh. Much.

1 **sugar cube** (or 1 teaspoon **granulated sugar**)

2 dashes **Angostura bitters**

Orange slice (optional)

Ice cubes

2½ ounces **bourbon** or **rye**

Lemon twist for garnish

Maraschino cherry for garnish (very optional)

1. Put the sugar in an old-fashioned glass, of course. Add the bitters and the orange slice, if you wish.

2. Using a muddler or very solid wooden spoon, muddle up the sugar and bitters, along with the orange slice if you are using it.

3. Place a couple of ice cubes in the glass. Add the bourbon, slowly and with reverence.

4. Twist the lemon twist over the glass, then let it take its part in history (by dropping it in the glass). If you must have a cherry (because you're cherry deficient), drop it in now. But be quiet about it.

Planter's Punch

Because it once was (and still is, if you take into account the copious permutations served in six or seven different beach-bound spots within a few coconuts of each other) a more general term referring to common rum-based punches, Planter's Punch **should never cause any arguments** about definitive recipes. Arguing about this, unless one recipe contains gasoline, is cutting into what you should be doing like a machete cuts into a pineapple. What you should be doing, of course, is having a Planter's Punch–Off, with a number of punch-loving pals over to make up the judging panel. While the punchy judges taste and taste and taste some more (if they judge like me), I suggest you recite this poem (first printed in an August 1908 edition of the *New York Times*) for luck: "This recipe I give to thee / dear brother in the heat. / Take two of sour (lime let it be) / to one and a half of sweet, / of Old Jamaica pour three strong, / and add four parts of weak." If you recite it in a rousing manner, that may sway any waffling judges over to your side.

Serves 6

Ice cubes

12 ounces **dark rum**

12 ounces **freshly squeezed orange juice**

12 ounces **fresh pineapple juice**

3 ounces **freshly squeezed lime juice**

1½ ounces **freshly squeezed lemon juice**

3 ounces **Simple Syrup** (page 12)

6 dashes **Angostura bitters**

6 to 12 **pineapple chunks** for garnish

6 **orange slices** for garnish

1. Fill a large pitcher halfway full with ice cubes. Add the rum, orange, pineapple, lime, and lemon juices, simple syrup, and bitters to the affair. Stir well with a spoon, in an iambic manner.

2. Fill six goblets or sturdy wine glasses three-quarters full with ice cubes. Pour the punch into the glasses, being sure no one feels shorted (that's a sure way to irritate a judge).

3. Garnish each goblet with a pineapple chunk or two and an orange slice, securing them with toothpicks if you need neatness.

VARIATIONS: There are many, as you well know. If you want to alter the above with a splash or two of grapefruit juice, or remove the bitters, or play around with other kinds of bitters, go right ahead—I'll still be happy to sit on the judging panel. Just give me a call.

Rob Roy

If it seems outlandish, don't dress like a legendary Scottish outlaw when you drink a Rob Roy. Don't don a kilt, and don't march around with your bosom cohorts crooning and gently carousing and saying words like "whilst" and "thou" and "prithee," and don't shoulder a few faux animal skins, and don't perch an exceptionally outlaw-esque hat on your head. Don't do any of those, while drinking a Rob Roy, if you aren't feeling it (and if you're a stick-in-the-mud kind of person). But at least don't pout, and don't whine, and **don't bother those folks having a hoot** while drinking their Rob Roys (which is the proper way to consume them). Remember what Fandral said in *Marvel Spotlight on Warriors Three* (Marvel Spotlight Issue 30, 1976) to the guy who bugged him when he was drinking a Rob Roy (at least I think he was): "Churl! Hast thou no manners? Never interrupt a man whilst he is drinking!"

Ice cubes

2½ ounces **Scotch**

½ ounce **sweet vermouth**

2 dashes **Angostura bitters**

Lemon twist for garnish

1. Fill a cocktail shaker halfway full with ice cubes. Add the Scotch, vermouth, and bitters. Shake thee well.

2. Strain into a cocktail glass. Garnish with the lemon twist. Methinks you'll be happier for it.

⏶ A Note: You could go lighter on the Scotch, and heavier on the vermouth, for a sweeter Roy, and still not be called a varlet.

A VARIATION: Wanna take a wee trek away from the Rob Roy? Swap Angostura for orange bitters, and skip to a Highland Cocktail.

Introducing Vermouths

Vermouth has long been a key component in a wide assortment of drinks. It's often called an "aromatized" wine because it has been infused or closely cuddled with some items to modify the flavor—items such as herbs, spices, roots, flowers, sugars, and more. The herbal qualities of most vermouths for many years led to their being thought of as medicinal products (and they may still be thought of that way today by true vermouth lovers).

The varieties of vermouth used on a regular basis in this day and age, dry and sweet, or French and Italian, might lead you to think that the name, and the drink, originated in one of these countries. But in actuality, the word derives from the German *vermut*, which means "wormwood," which was a favorite additive in fortified wines from that country back in the day.

The dry, or French, variety of vermouth was most likely developed in the early 1900s by Joseph Noilly. It's a clear—though here and there called white—wine and, while popular in cocktails, is also happily consumed by many as an apéritif. The other vermouth in regular rotation is the red, or Italian, variety, which takes its Italian legacy from Antonio Benedetto Carpano, who created what may have been the first of this style of vermouth in the late 1700s in Italy. It's also a cocktail favorite, while also being consumed (especially in its mother country) as an apéritif.

There is a third variety of vermouth, bianco, which isn't seen as often. A touch sweeter than the red, it should be used sparingly at first, until you become better acquainted with it. Also, when in other countries, you may see rosé vermouth, as well as orange and lemon varietals. In the spirit of a true cocktail explorer, I suggest trying as many as you can get your hands on. You may end up with a new drink that changes the cocktail landscape (or, at least, *your* cocktail landscape).

There are many brands of vermouth, including well-known names such as Martini & Rossi and Cinzano (both made in Turin, Italy) and Noilly Prat (made in France), and some newer players, such as Vya, which is made in California. There are also vermouth brands that have such individual flavors that you'll find them called out by name, such as Punt e Mes or Carpano Antica. Always track these down when they are recommended, to get the full flavor of a drink.

Rusty Nail

Some might quibble with the venerable-ness of the Rusty Nail. *Pshaw*, is what I say to them. In the Midwest, there are bevies of Rusty Nail dousers dotting the landscape (as well as many old fences, ba-dump-bump). They keep reappearing, and transferring their love of Rusty Nails to their progeny, because of the Scotch's potency combined with the Drambuie's touch of melodiousness (which is birthed by combining Scotch, honey, and secret ingredients that have been passed down from generation to generation in whispers and ciphers).

Remember this venerable-ness if you're in a watering hole of an evening, and saunter up to the bar to order a Rusty Nail, only to have other patrons question your choice. If, after you bring up the tastefulness of the drink, the hassling continues, ask them if they know what Drambuie means in Gaelic. And when they don't, tell them it's "the drink that satisfies." That should make them realize who the chief drink-orderer is, and they'll sit silently.

Ice cubes

2 ounces **Scotch**

1 ounce **Drambuie**

Lemon twist for garnish (optional)

1. Place ice cubes in an old-fashioned glass until they reach the halfway point. Let the Scotch and then the Drambuie cascade into the glass.

2. Stir, but not tackily. Add the lemon twist, if that's the way you play.

Sazerac

I love the Sazerac so intensely it's nearly hard for me to talk about it. But while I'm working up to it, remember that talking and typing is thirsty work. Please head over to the bar and fetch me one of these elegant and amazing cocktails, which harmonizes resurgent rye with a slip of sweet, a bite of bitters, and an altering and awesome addition of now-legal-again absinthe, and then lets itself be tantalized by a touch of lemon oil, sparkling across the top of the drink like stars sparkle across the Milky Way. Yes, get me a Sazerac, the official cocktail of New Orleans, to help keep my spirits elevated and my mind working at a pitch only **properly described as powerfully pleasant**, letting me reach the mountainous tops of speechmaking. So find your way to the bar thinking of Horace, who two thousand years ago wrote about the Sazerac—or so I like to imagine—"With thee, 'tis happiness to live, / And life, without thee, can no pleasure give." With those immortal lines ringing, and with the Sazerac you were so kind to procure for me in hand, I feel fortified enough to begin to sing its praises. Right after I finish it, naturally.

¼ ounce **absinthe**

Ice cubes

2 ounces **rye** or **bourbon**

½ ounce **Simple Syrup** (page 12)

2 dashes **Peychaud's bitters**

Lemon twist for garnish

1. Carefully pour the absinthe into an old-fashioned or rocks glass, then swirl it around respectfully so that it coats the glass's inside walls, then fill the glass with ice cubes.

2. Next fill a reliable cocktail shaker halfway full with ice cubes. Add the rye (or bourbon, if it comes to that), the simple syrup, and the bitters. Shake well.

3. Strain the shaken ingredients into the glass, then garnish with the lemon twist, and a few short words.

A Note: If you have a chilled glass, you can skip the ice cubes in step 1. Also, if you're worried about bruising that precious rye or bourbon during the shaking step, try stirring with a long spoon instead. Just be sure to get a good chill on.

"The two Sazeracs had loosened her up a little and it looked as if we might become buddies."

JAMES L. RUBEL, *No Business for a Lady*, 1950

Sidecar

Does anyone ever drink Sidecars in sidecars anymore? Not that I'm suggesting doing it while the motorcycle to which said sidecar is attached is moving, but **imagine how tough you'd look** in a sidecar with one of those *Wild One* Marlon Brando hats cocked on your noggin and a Sidecar gripped in your hand. Perhaps you're slowly sipping it, and also talking in a mumble-y and guttural fashion. Tough, I tell you, and tougher-looking than having your Sidecar with a heavily sugared rim, which is how it's served in brightly lit joints and even some local hooch parlors.

You can show up at my table bringing me a Sidecar that's sugared up and I'll drink it ('cause my momma didn't raise no fool), but I'll shake my head a little and mumble at you, too. If you do decide that having me mumble doesn't outweigh your sugar addiction, then see the note below. Me, I watch the sugar on my Sidecars (even perhaps having a heavier Cognac-to-Cointreau ratio than some). It helps me keep my girlish figure.

Ice cubes

2 ounces **Cognac** or **brandy**

½ ounce **Cointreau**

½ ounce **freshly squeezed lemon juice**

1. Fill a cocktail shaker halfway full with ice cubes. Add the Cognac, then the Cointreau, then the lemon juice. Then shake it like you mean it.

2. Strain it, also like you mean it, into a cocktail glass.

⤴ *A Note: As promised, if you want a sugared rim, you need to (before anything else) take a lemon wedge and rub it around your cocktail glass's outer rim. Add a bit of sugar to a saucer or small plate, then warily rotate that rim through the sugar, focusing on getting sugar only on the outside of the glass (there's no need to taint the contents).*

⤴ *A Second Note: In his book* Straight Up or On the Rocks *(North Point Press, 2002)—a must-read for anyone who wants to learn about the history of the cocktail—cocktail historian William Grimes says, "Do not pour serious Cognac into your Sidecars." It's a good point to remember. You're mixing it up with other pals here, so there's no need to break the bank on an ultra-expensive Cognac. Not even if you want to impress someone, 'cause foolish spending isn't impressive.*

Six Current Cocktailian Reads

Not only is it a refreshing time to be drinking cocktails and highballs and their ilk (thanks to the many folks unleashing unburied drinks, new drinks, and new spins on old drinks), it's also a great time to be reading about the subject. There are many bubbly reads out there to delve into, but these five are a good way to start. (Plus my other books, naturally. I mean, we gotta look out for each other as well as ourselves, right?)

1. *Imbibe! From Absinthe Cocktail to Whiskey Smash, a Salute in Stories and Drinks to "Professor" Jerry Thomas, Pioneer of the American Bar*, by David Wondrich (Perigee, 2007). Learn about the first real celeb bartender and have a hoot (and some good drinks) doing it.

2. *The Joy of Mixology: The Consummate Guide to the Bartender's Craft*, by Gary Regan (Clarkson Potter, 2003). Learn how to classify cocktails according to families, not just base ingredients, while sipping on stories and history and having a rollicking time.

3. *And a Bottle of Rum: A History of the New World in Ten Cocktails*, by Wayne Curtis (Crown, 2006). Learn the colorful history of rum while tracing the history of drinking in America, and pick up some recipes and lore while taking the trip.

4. *The Craft of the Cocktail*, by Dale DeGroff (Clarkson Potter, 2002). Learn the ins and outs of becoming a bar-master from the King of Cocktails himself, with recipes, tips, and tales, as well as a huge helping of good humor and fine spirits.

5. *Mixologist: The Journal of the American Cocktail,* Volumes 1 and 2 (Mixellany, 2005 and 2006). Learn about the many corners of the cocktail universe with these bound booze-y volumes edited by Anastatia Miller and published by Jared Brown, which collect essays by today's top sippers on everything under the bottled sun.

6. *The Essential Bartender's Guide: How to Make Truly Great Cocktails*, by Robert Hess (Mud Puddle Books, 2008). Learn how to bartend, from the basics to more advanced skills, from one of the friendliest and most knowledgeable shakers in modern cocktailing.

Stinger

When I was young (but of consuming age—I don't want any retroactive problems with the sheriff) and rolling the dice on some of the middle-of-Kansas mean streets (which were, in actuality, dirt roads, often nicknamed things like "the beach" because they were so sandy), I took a lot of flak for my love of Stingers. "That's a granny drink," behatted bronc-busters would bellyache, while tight-jeaned fillies would laugh, joking, "You're a fogey for drinking brandy," and everyone would cackle at my black-and-yellow bee suit (worn in honor of the Stinger). I persevered, though, because I believe a scintillating liquid socialization like this needs to be remembered, consumed, and loved. Try one, and I think you'll agree the minute its sting hits your tongue. And remember those kids who made fun of me? They're now drinking Stingers by the barrelful, wondering why they waited so long to catch up.

Ice cubes

2½ ounces **brandy** (or **Cognac**, if you're feeling it)

½ ounce **white crème de menthe**

1. Fill a cocktail shaker halfway full with ice cubes. Add the brandy and crème de menthe (be sure it's the white kind, 'cause green gets icky). Shake, while proclaiming your Stinger affection loudly.

2. Strain the mix into a cocktail glass, being sure not to spill any on your bee costume.

A VARIATION: On occasion, Stinger aficionados have placed a bantam bit of lime juice into the shaker in step 1. I don't always do so myself, but adding the lime juice certainly won't keep you from being transported from a dead-end dirt road into Stinger heaven.

Vieux Carré Cocktail

What an exquisite name this French Quarter favorite has, and if it's not a favorite with everyone visiting the French Quarter currently—like those knuckleheads who tend toward drinks poured into gallon buckets—it should be, as it's named for the French term for the area, the "old square." The taste is exquisite, too, multifaceted and adult and lovely, a creation of Walter Bergeron, who in the 1930s strode the bar boards as the head shaker at the Monteleone Hotel (one report even narrows down his creation of the Vieux Carré to the year 1938). The Monteleone now features the Carousel Lounge, in which the customers revolve around a center bar. The revolving is steady, giving you changing views as you sip your cocktails, but **not so speedy as to cause consternation**. After a few rounds, and a few Vieux Carrés, you may find your equilibrium a little off, but in a way that's purely pleasant.

Ice cubes
1 ounce **rye**
1 ounce **Cognac**
1 ounce **sweet vermouth**
½ ounce **Benedictine**
Dash of **Peychaud's bitters**
Dash of **Angostura bitters**
Lemon twist for garnish

1. Fill an old-fashioned glass halfway full with ice cubes. Add the rye, Cognac, and vermouth.

2. Add the Benedictine and both bitters, and stir slightly.

3. Twist the lemon twist over the drink, and drop it in before anything revolves out of view.

"As Johnny placed the champagne goblet and my refill in front of us, the blond boy **said in a tentative voice**, 'And one Whiskey Sour, please.'"

EDWIN ROLFE AND LESTER FULLER, *The Glass Room*, 1948

Whiskey Sour David A. Embury

may here and there seem a wee bit cranky, like an older uncle who knows a lot about dominoes, but who doesn't necessarily seem like someone you'd want to sit down and play dominoes with for a long period of time. In his truly dandy cocktail guide, *The Fine Art of Mixing Drinks* (Doubleday, 1948), he says, plainly enough, "a Sour is simply a combination of citrus juice (lime or lemon or both), sugar or other sweetening, and liquor." Simple, and it's the basic formula for the whole Sour family, which includes more drinks than one can count on fingers and painted toes, and which used to encompass a range of items now living high on the hog all on their own (think about a Rum Sour, made with lime juice—sounds a lot like a Daiquiri, another point Mr. Embury makes).

But in this modern imbibing world (and here I'm speaking about diminutive barrelhouses in Birmingham and holes in the wall in Helena, places where the jukebox plays songs with refrains like, "When I'm not drinking, I'm thinking about drinking," as well as the gilded cocktail palaces dotting the landscape), the Sour you hear called for most is the Whiskey Sour. It's a drink many milk during their formative years, which is good, if it's made right, because it can initiate these budding tipplers and prepare their tantalized taste buds for exploring more and more classic cocktails.

Ice cubes

2 ounces **bourbon**

½ ounce **freshly squeezed lemon juice**

½ ounce **Simple Syrup** (page 12)

Lemon twist for garnish

1. Fill a cocktail shaker halfway full with ice cubes. While thinking of the many Sours served to souses before (don't try to say that out loud, though, while doing this), add the bourbon, lemon juice, and simple syrup. Shake well.

2. Strain into a cocktail glass. Garnish with that twist.

⬆ *A Note: I like my Sour solely with that single lemon twist 'cause I'm a loner—no, I'm kidding, I like you, really, and people in general. I serve the sole twist out of Sour respect; it's like a salute. But some—a lot, really—serve it with a cherry, maybe an orange, or a stick of rhubarb. If you need to go there, go there.*

A VARIATION: To shout out to Mr. Embury once more (hey, he's listening somewhere, I hope), let it be said that he asserts, "A Whisky Sour without the sugar is sometimes called a Palmer."

⬆ *A Second Note: I believe in the bourbon here, but I wouldn't riot if it were changed to rye. Heck no.*

Zombie

Must have drink with many rums and then stumble around in reanimated fashion. Or, at least, that's my theory on Zombies. According to the legend (not the legend detailed in books about zombie wars, or in movies about zombies running around the U.K. or U.S. countryside), venerable tiki troubadour and progenitor Donn Beach (or Don the Beachcomber) did first serve this knockout to a particularly weary customer (and, by weary, I mean hung-over to the green gills), who then said he felt like "the living dead." Sneaky monkey, that Donn, curing a sickly imbiber in such a manner.

If only we knew exactly how he did it. Donn didn't write the recipe down, and since he passed away (to hang out with other zombie bartenders at that great zombie bar, one hopes), there have been too many Zombie recipes to easily count. (Besides, zombies don't count counting as one of their signature talents. Thoroughness, sure. Persistence? You better believe it—especially if they're chasing you.) I believe this recipe gets the basics in and tastes good to boot (and is close, from what I've heard, to the original). It does have the 151 rum floating on it, but if that seems silly even for a silly-ish drink, feel free to omit. Even if you omit it, and even if you are well stocked in Cornetto (the treat of choice in the movie *Shaun of the Dead*, a must-watch for any serious zombie fan), this can still knock you into stultification pretty rapidly. Be warned, then, of the Zombie, and kill (or rekill) only a few at a time.

Ice cubes

1 ounce **dark rum**

1 ounce **white rum**

1 ounce **gold** or **amber rum**

¾ ounce **freshly squeezed lime juice**

¾ ounce **fresh pineapple juice**

½ ounce **apricot liqueur**

½ ounce **papaya juice** (if you can't get it, sub in **passionfruit juice**)

½ ounce **Simple Syrup** (page 12)

½ ounce **151-proof rum** (optional)

Lime wheel for garnish

Lemon wheel for garnish

Maraschino cherry for garnish

2 **fresh mint sprigs** for garnish

Confectioners' sugar for garnish

A Note: *If you must use bottled pineapple juice that is presweetened, then nix the syrup and double the pineapple juice. Also, if you're feeling flighty (for a zombie, that is), sub in some fresh pineapple on the garnish train, or even a star fruit slice.*

1. Fill a cocktail shaker halfway full with ice cubes. Shuffle in the dark, white, and gold rums, lime juice, pineapple juice, apricot liqueur, papaya juice, and simple syrup. Shake unlike a zombie (meaning, shake well).

2. Pour everything into a Zombie glass, large Collins glass, or other 14-ounce glass.

3. If you wish, float the 151 rum on top of the drink. Garnish with the lime wheel, lemon wheel, cherry, and mint sprigs.

4. Lightly sprinkle confectioners' sugar over the whole mess. Serve with a straw and a little groan.

VARIATIONS: As alluded to, there are many variations you could live through. For example, it has been suggested that Pernod was an original ingredient, or a little absinthe—this might be an enjoyable addition. Often, orgeat (an almond syrup) shows up, replacing the maligned apricot liqueur. I'm not as fond of this but can wake up to the point.

5 Scary Movie Sippers

Wait, why won't the light switch work? And what's that *tap-tap-tapping* noise behind you as you walk down the hallway? And, for that matter, why is one knife removed from the knife block? If you're having a fright-fest of monster movies or slasher cinema hits, I suggest serving one of these.

1 Leprechaun (page 210)

2 Thumper (page 228)

3 Derby Widow (page 63)

4 Warlock (page 230)

5 Crimson Slippers (page 195)

Bartender's Choice

I believe it was Samuel Johnson who first said, speaking for the multitude of skilled professional and home bartenders, "For we that live to please, must please to live." Admittedly, he had already partaken of a number of his favorite drink creator's freshest liquid concoctions (a recipe sadly lost to history). But the point comes across in this chapter, which is filled with new combinations created by an assortment of bartenders—creations made to entice, entrance, and enthrall a drinker, to please that recipient of a freshly made mixture, that friend, friendly customer, or reader who's hanging loose at the bar, in the backyard, or on the spinning stool or cuddly couch.

The act of drink creation has been around for as many years as drink itself (ah, those Greeks and their flower'd wines). If mixed drinks weren't around the very day the first alcoholic beverage sprang into happy existence, they likely came into being the day after, when that first hairy bartender began to realize that with experimentation, he could make his cave the most fabulous on the block, and soon have every cave-crew in the hollow hanging out there, banging stone drums and wiggling in dance. Sounds pretty fun, doesn't it?

And it's still fun today, maybe even more fun, as we revel in our very own cocktail explosion, with a wide assortment of intriguing ingredients showing up in mixes such as the mysterious Ognam, the Left Hand, the Polynesian Donkey, and the Human Factor, and combining now-known-to-be-agreeable essentials in hits like the Lion Tamer, the Haitian Witch, and the Occidental. This chapter is a modern-day drinker's Library of Alexandria, with inventive imbibables coming from top hot spots and top hot reads, as well as from those bars out on the front lines. *Mes amis* of the bar, we are blessed by all this bounty. Be glad.

ASAP

Alacrity is of the essence, excitable ones, as the throng descends like a winter's evening (I'm not saying it *is* winter, by the way), and you've promised to have a fantastic fusion of liquors, liqueurs, juices, and frisky hours when the peeps fall into place at your pad—but, on the flipside, you don't want to fret about the frolicky nature of many fizzy and non-fizzy coalescences. No worries. **This drink's first-rate and ready** as soon as you want it to be.

Ice cubes

1½ ounces **dark rum**

½ ounce **Falernum**

½ ounce **Tuaca**

½ ounce **fresh pineapple juice**

Chilled ginger ale

Lime slice for garnish

1. Fill a highball glass three-quarters full with ice cubes. Add the rum, Falernum, Tuaca, and pineapple juice. Stir, but only twice.

2. Top the glass off with ginger ale. Stir once more. Garnish with the lime slice.

⊙ *A Note: Falernum is a flavored syrup (think lime, with a bit of ginger and other accents) that sometimes has an alcohol content and sometimes doesn't. Either version works here—check online if you're having trouble tracking it down in your local liquor or specialty food stores.*

⊙ *A Second Note: Tuaca is an Italian liqueur that has hints of citrus and vanilla. The legend goes that it was created by Florentine Renaissance mover-and-shaker Lorenzo de' Medici. Tuaca became popular in the United States in the 1950s, after World War II servicemen who had been stationed in Italy started asking for it at American bars.*

Black Feather

This titles echoes ominously, as if it were an artifact that would be presented by a dark woolen-jacketed messenger when you were in trouble with a mountainous mob, or to let you know that war was approaching your borders. A slight shiver snakes up the arm thinking about it. Which is the height of goofiness, because this drink is in reality **the house cocktail of one of the friendliest cocktailians on the planet**, Robert Hess, the Drink-Boy, whose online site, www.drinkboy.com, holds a wealth of information; and whose MSN group, groups.msn.com/DrinkBoy, with its online message boards, is the spot where many of the fine imbibing folks on the forefront of our current cocktail uprising got together for the first time; and whose book, *The Essential Bartender's Guide* (Mud Puddle Books, 2008), is a great boon to any bartender. So, believe in the Black Feather not only as a splendid mix, but also as a congenial signal, and leave that doom-and-gloom behind.

Ice cubes
2 ounces **brandy**
1 ounce **dry vermouth**
½ ounce **Cointreau**
Dash of **Angostura bitters**
Lemon twist for garnish

1. Fill a mixing glass or cocktail shaker halfway full with ice cubes. Add the brandy, vermouth, Cointreau, and bitters. Using a long spoon (an actual feather does not work here), stir well.

2. Strain the mix into a cocktail glass, then garnish with the lemon twist.

⌃ *A Note: On the DrinkBoy site, no type of bitters is specified, providing a little wiggle room. I've suggested Angostura here, but play around (and if you can get a bottle, or eyedropper, even, of Mr. Hess's house bitters, then use them).*

⌃ *A Second Note: A word from the wise DrinkBoy himself: "When in doubt, add a little extra brandy." Sage advice, indeed.*

Buck Owens

Pioneering and prolific country singing meets up with essences of the Far East in a Ballard, Washington, alleyway via this amiable companion created by raconteur, bash master, and generally entertaining lad Keith Kyle (whose amigos and admirers—one of whom you'll be five seconds after meeting him—call him "Cookie"). After much slaving away testing proportions, he (with some aid, I'll bet, from his wife, Tasha) discovered the perfect balance in this meeting of distant cultures. Worth a song, I think.

Ice cubes

1 ounce **Maker's Mark bourbon**

1 ounce **Yazi ginger vodka**

½ ounce **lemongrass-flavored simple syrup** (see A Note)

1½ ounces **chilled club soda**

1. Fill a cocktail shaker halfway full with ice cubes. Add the bourbon, vodka, and lemongrass simple syrup. Shake well.

2. Fill a rocks glass or old-fashioned glass three-quarters full with ice cubes. Pour the club soda over the ice.

3. Strain the shaken mix into the glass. Stir briefly with a straw.

A Note: To make lemongrass simple syrup, follow the recipe on page 12, adding ½ cup chopped fresh lemongrass in step 1. Let the syrup cool completely, and strain the lemongrass out before bottling.

Coronado Heights Flip

Coronado Heights is a castle on top of a hill outside of Lindsborg, Kansas (which happens to be where I spent my formative years, growing up surrounded by Swedes and rolling hills). The castle isn't as ancient as you might believe—it's only from 1932, like the stone picnic tables and fire pits surrounding it—but supposedly Coronado did traverse the hill it sits on, and no one doubts that the lovely panoramic views have been in place longer than any structure in the whole state. Neither does anyone doubt that Jeremy Sidener is one of the best drink slingers in that central state (and in the whole central United States). He also happens to be **one of the true gentlemen of modern bartending**, and he first gave me this recipe. Check him out when in Lawrence, Kansas, at the Eighth Street Taproom (and learn more online at www.eighthstreet-taproom.com).

Ice cubes

2 ounces **Harveys Bristol Cream sherry**

1 ounce **Kahlúa**

2 heaping tablespoons **freshly whipped cream**

1 **egg**

1 teaspoon **granulated sugar**

½ teaspoon **grated Mexican chocolate** for garnish

Thin orange twist for garnish

1. Fill a cocktail shaker halfway full with ice cubes. Add the sherry, Kahlúa, cream, egg, and sugar. Shake well.

2. Strain, slowly, into a Champagne flute. Garnish with a sprinkling of the chocolate and the orange twist.

❌ *A Warning: As this drink contains a raw egg, it shouldn't be served to the elderly or those with compromised immune systems.*

The Curtis Hotel

The last time I checked, this wasn't being served at the Curtis Hotel in downtown Denver, but I'm hoping they'll put it on their next menu, because this is **the ideal combination of punch and panache** for those about to head over the mountain passes (not directly after consuming a few of these, of course) or those who have made it through those passes. This is especially true if there is snow involved, and if you are driving an RV with four friends. I'm not saying that these factors will necessarily lead to a desire for this drink, but they probably will.

Ice cubes

1 ounce **Bushmills Irish whiskey**

1 ounce **Johnnie Walker Red Label Scotch**

½ ounce **dry vermouth**

½ ounce **sweet vermouth**

Dash of **Peychaud's bitters**

Orange twist for garnish

1. Fill a cocktail shaker halfway full with ice cubes. Add the Bushmills, Johnnie Walker, the vermouth cousins, and the bitters. Shake well, in a mountainous style.

2. Strain the Curtis into a cocktail glass, and garnish with the orange twist.

*⬆ **A Note:** You could sub in another Irish whiskey, and a different Scotch, but this is the way Jeremy (Husky Boy) Holt taught me how to make this, and I sure wouldn't want to travel a different route.*

Derby Widow

It's fortuitous how many delectable drinking spots are popping up from Portland, Maine, to Portland, Oregon, and everywhere in between—spots that make enticing libations, serve scrumptious bites, and set up smiles on pleased patrons. Spots such as the Tigertail, right in my own backyard here in Seattle (not literally—if Johnny Law happens to be reading this—but nice and close), where you can sip a Derby Widow, listen to rocking music, and snack on Asian-influenced eats like rainbow chard pot stickers.

4 **lemon wedges**

Ice cubes

2½ ounces **Maker's Mark bourbon** or **Crown Royal whisky**

1½ ounces **St-Germain elderflower liqueur**

1. Add the lemon wedges to a cocktail shaker. Using a muddler or long wooden spoon (but definitely not a feline tail), muddle the lemons well.

2. Fill the cocktail shaker halfway full with ice cubes. Add the Maker's and St-Germain. Shake well.

3. Strain into a cocktail glass.

↑ A Note: Even amongst the finest bar staffs, there are some disagreements—and isn't this a proper occurrence, keeping the boredom at bay? At the Tigertail, genial owner Carl thinks the Widow is best with Maker's, while smiley bartender Heather goes the Crown route (as she believes the Maker's is a bit too sweet). When whipping this up at home, you'll have to make the choice for yourself. To find out more about the Tigertail, be sure to check out www.tigertailbar.com.

↑ A Second Note: St-Germain is made from fresh, hand-selected, handpicked French elderflowers, and has taken the drinking universe by flowery storm in the past few years.

Dr. Blinker

Drinks take intriguing twists and turns, popping up here and there and then everywhere. You often find you've managed to see, or even taste, a drink a couple of times—a good drink, a worthy drink—but it hasn't made your regular rotation, and then you see it (or drink it) again, and maybe it has a slight variation, and there's that crystalline moment (which I believe Blake referenced first) when every sip makes sense. This is how Dr. Blinker is for me, as I saw this particular recipe once in Ted (Dr. Cocktail) Haigh's bouncy book of lore, recipes, and stories, *Vintage Spirits and Forgotten Cocktails* (Quarry Books, 2009), but then saw it again in *The Museum of the American Cocktail's Pocket Recipe Guide* by Robert Hess (Ready Writers Publishing, 2007), and the second sighting got me hooked.

Ice cubes

2 ounces **rye**

1 ounce **freshly squeezed grapefruit juice**

¼ ounce **raspberry syrup**

Lemon twist for garnish

1. Fill a cocktail shaker halfway full with ice cubes. Add the rye, grapefruit juice, and syrup. Shake well, fast as a blink.

2. Strain into a cocktail glass. Garnish with the lemon twist.

Drowsy Chaperone

Hey, chaperones, don't start believing that you should consume this while watching over the young'uns at the ninth-grade sock hop (those ninth graders can be tricky—keep your peepers peeled). Rather, save this relaxing brandy repast for post-chaperoning. Savor it at the moment when you're propping your feet up on the couch's armrest, a book of poems (perhaps *Mister Skylight*, the latest by Ed Skoog, as he's the poetic bee's knees, one of the finest bar companions known, a happening home entertainer, and the pappy of this very potion) in one hand and this slow warmer in the other, once the chattering children have slipped into dreamland—but before you do.

1 **buttermint candy**

1½ ounces **brandy**

½ ounce **crème de pêche**

¾ ounce **Cointreau**

***

⬆ *A Note: Buttermints (they're also called pillow mints) are those soft, individually wrapped mints that restaurants sometimes give you along with the check.*

1. Add the buttermint to a snifter or large cordial glass, then add the brandy and crème de pêche to the glass.

2. In a sturdy mug, briefly heat the Cointreau in the microwave for about 15 seconds. You don't want it boiling at all, just well-warmed—it should steam in the glass a bit.

3. Carefully pour the Cointreau into the glass. Ah, swilling, relaxing, and reading—the ideal end to a chaotic day.

Fu Manchu

Unearthing an oasis when meandering through a city you don't know like the back of your cocktail shaker is as important as finding **a cooling beverage on a hot day** —and by "oasis" I mean a good bar, and by "cooling beverage" I mean this tall tiki tippler. But you probably already guessed that (if you've read this far in the book). If in your oasis you meet a bartender like Gary at the Tiki Lounge in Pittsburgh, Pennsylvania (where I found the original Fu Manchu, adapted below)—a bartender who laughs at your out-of-town-isms, makes you over-flowing rum treats, and lets you play pinball for free—the moment's moved from finding an oasis to thinking you may have reached nirvana.

Ice cubes

1 ounce **dark rum**

1 ounce **citrus-flavored rum**

1 ounce **ginger brandy**

½ ounce **freshly squeezed lemon juice**

½ ounce **freshly squeezed lime juice**

Chilled ginger ale

Lemon slice for garnish

Lime slice for garnish

1. Fill a large mug that looks like a deadly mus-tachioed villain, or a Collins glass or other large-ish glass, three-quarters full with ice cubes. Add the rums, brandy, lemon juice, and lime juice. Stir briefly.

2. Fill the glass almost to the top with ginger ale. Garnish with the lemon and lime slices and give it another slight stirring.

Five Snug Bars and Lounges to Stop At

They may not have room for your whole co-ed touch football team (or at least not for both you and your opponents), but these comfy spots are always pleasant to sneak into with a certain someone or two, for good times and close companionship.

1. Hazelwood, Seattle, Washington

2. The Matchbox, Chicago, Illinois

3. PDT, New York, New York

4. Franklin Café, Boston, Massachusetts

5. Ernie K-Doe Mother-in-Law Lounge, New Orleans, Louisiana

Cherry Heering

Heering cherry liqueur, sometimes referred to as Peter Heering, or the world's most famous cherry liqueur, or cherry Heering (which is how you see it listed in many bar books), traces its history through the spirited byways to a creation back in 1818. It became a popular worldwide brand, though, with traveling Brits in the early days of the nineteenth century, as they (the story goes) took it with them on their adventures around the world so that they could make tasty cocktails after a day of hunting, polo playing, or colonizing. Since that time, this Danish-made liqueur has become a feature in many cocktails, including (perhaps most famously) the Singapore Sling and the Blood and Sand (page 239). While it's a cherry brandy, with a brandy base, its lush liqueur nature gives it more in common with other fruit liqueurs, and less with the more bracing fruit brandies—though don't take that to mean that cherry Heering is overly saccharine, because it balances out its delicate sweetness with a strong black cherry flavor that is truly one of a kind, emanating from specific Stevns cherries, which are known for their rich, dark coloring and taste. These cherries are crushed (with stones and pulp and all) and then placed into oak casks for at least three years with the base spirit and the requisite secret spice list that many liqueurs have (usually hidden away in a secret chest in the ancestral home). As ever, the result is something to cheer about.

Haitian Witch

Summoned to life by incantation, the burning of unnamed incenses, and boogie-licious dance—the regular mystic machinations of Joel Meister, longtime bartender at Chicago art spot Rodan, the Haitian Witch conveys you and your partisans to planes of party pleasantness. A witch this rich in taste and able to cast enchantments powerful and felicitous must emanate from a number of influences, which according to our conjuror include classic Northwest band the Sonics, which had a song called "The Witch"; Big Dipper, a power-pop Boston band from the 1980s that had a song called "Meet the Witch"; and Sonic, the fast-food/drive-in chain that has, as Joel says, "made cherry limeade a romantic concept for Midwesterners." I believe the songs and snacks accompanying the Haitian Witch during this charmed soirée are now set.

Ice cubes

2 ounces **Barbancourt dark rum**

1 ounce **modified sour mix** (see A Note)

½ ounce **Heering cherry liqueur**

1. Fill a cocktail shaker halfway full with ice cubes. Add the rum, sour mix, and cherry liqueur. Shake witchingly well.

2. Strain into a cocktail glass, bottoms up, and have a spell put on your evening.

⌃ *A Note: To make the modified sour mix, combine 2 parts freshly squeezed lime juice, 1 part granulated sugar, and 3 parts water in a small saucepan, and place over medium heat. Cook, stirring occasionally, until the sugar has dissolved completely. Remove from the heat and let cool. Bottle and refrigerate; it will keep for at least 1 month.*

Hot Shot

I get a shiver in my step even considering the winter months in the Midwest (or, for that matter, in the Northeast, and even some days in other, more temperate spots), with the prettily deadly ice, the dumped dunes of snow, and that mercury in the thermometer skidding so low. **Give yourself a break** next time you find yourself stuck in the doldrums from these dreary days by getting out the old liquid prescription pad and giving yourself a Hot Shot. Created in Minneapolis's Town Talk Diner, the Hot Shot takes the edge off. If you happen to be in that city, though, you might as well stop in and learn the ins and outs of warm drinks from the source: bar manager Nick Kosevich or friendly bartender Tim Baker.

6 ounces **apple cider**

1 ounce **brandy**

½ ounce **Apfelkorn**

½ ounce **Heering cherry liqueur**

2 **sour cherries**

⬆ *A Note: This warmer-upper was originally printed in* Food Network Magazine, *in order to keep readers warm, too.*

⬆ *A Second Note: Apfelkorn is a German apple liqueur, slightly sweet but with a full apple taste.*

1. Add the apple cider, brandy, and Apfelkorn to a large, hearty mug. Stir briefly. Heat until almost boiling (30 to 40 seconds in the microwave).

2. Add the Heering and the sour cherries to a white wine glass or large cordial glass that's been preheated by running it under warm water and then drying it rapidly.

3. Pour the hot cider-brandy-Apfelkorn mix slowly and carefully into the warmed glass over the Heering and the cherries.

The Human Factor

The amplified announcements are blaring from city to city: The Human Factor is not a mutant strain of virus released by accident into the water supply of a major metropolitan area that only one professor could figure out a formula to counteract, if only he weren't in the corner bar slurping up a mingling of **heft layered with light lavender** and a teeny hint of herbs and oranges, accented by two frozen green grapes. This drink is, in fact, the real Human Factor.

Ice cubes

2 ounces **brandy**

1 ounce **Loft lavender liqueur**

½ ounce **Lillet Blanc**

Dash of **Peychaud's bitters**

Dash of **orange bitters**

2 **frozen green grapes**

1. Fill a cocktail shaker halfway full with ice cubes. Add the brandy, lavender liqueur, Lillet, and both bitters. Shake well, and quickly, for gawd's sake.

2. Add the 2 grapes to a cocktail glass. Strain the Human Factor into the glass over the grapes.

⊙ *A Note: Loft lavender liqueur (like other Loft liqueurs) is made with all organic ingredients, including agave nectar for sweetening.*

Irreverent Reverend

We're blessed, *mes amis*, by the plentiful number of inspired **cocktails being fashioned by wizards** of the bottle at hotspots and homes today. There are so many to choose from that it can be a smidge daunting. Even the number of worthy new bars is overwhelming, and perhaps more so in Manhattan than anywhere else. Far be it from me, a simple slurping scribe, to single out one spot. But, I suppose I could say that if you get the chance, slip past the nondescript door and thick curtains and into Death + Company and find a seat in its cozy confines to have an Irreverent Reverend. I mean, I am a preacher's son.

Ice cubes

2 ounces **Elijah Craig bourbon**

¾ ounce **freshly squeezed lemon juice**

½ ounce **yellow Chartreuse**

1. Fill a cocktail shaker halfway full with ice cubes. Add the bourbon, lemon juice, and Chartreuse. Shake as if Prohibition were on its way.

2. Strain into a cocktail glass. Enjoy.

Six Party Packages

Say you want to throw a memorable, signature, stand-out-from-the-pack kind of a party, and you're not sure what to theme it around, what drinks and snacks to serve, and what to spin on the turntable. Let me take the pressure off with the following party packages, ready-built for fun.

1. Circus Fantastic. Date: Anytime you feel it's okay to wear a big hat, a red clown nose, or acrobatic attire. **Drinks:** Lion Tamer (page 79) and Golden Panther (page 250). **Snacks:** Circus peanuts, popcorn, and cotton candy. **Music:** The Great American Main Street Band, *Under the Big Top: 100 Years of Circus Music*.

2. Speakeasy Evening. **Date:** Sometime after the sun has set, and whenever you can find a tough-cut suit. **Drinks:** The Manhattan (page 33) and Dutch Charlie's (page 199). **Snacks:** Sautéed chicken livers, salmon and mushroom toasts, and savory cheese balls. **Music:** Various Artists, *Nipper's Greatest Hits: The 20's*.

3. Summer Solstice Soiree. Date: June 21, near June 21, or any day you wish were June 21. **Drinks:** Summer Dream (page 168) and Fair Skies (page 104). **Snacks:** Fruit salad, half cobs of grilled corn, brandied cherries. **Music:** The Beach Boys, *Sounds of Summer: The Very Best of the Beach Boys*.

4. Hayrack Roundup. Date: Sometime in fall (if you're not in the mood to actually take a hay ride, just dot the yard with hay bales). **Drinks:** Horsefeather (page 29) and WOW (page 292). **Snacks:** Caramel apples, pumpkin pie, and pumpkin seeds. **Music:** Bill Evens, *Bill Evens Plays Banjo*.

5. Summer Camp Revisited. Date: Anytime in summertime when you can get whistles, nametags, and arts-and-crafts projects. **Drinks:** Pony Punch (page 261), Vick's Zither (page 132), and Drowsy Chaperone (page 66). **Snacks:** Mac and cheese on crackers, sloppy joes. **Music:** Twin Sisters, *102 Camp Songs*.

6. Painters on Parade. Date: Late spring or early fall (when it's comfortable to set up easels outside and wear smocks). **Drinks:** Artist's Special (page 185), Bobby Burns (page 189), and Brainstorm (page 190). **Snacks:** Cheese, olives, grapes, and lots of French bread. **Music:** The Minutemen, *Buzz or Howl Under the Influence of Heat*, or The Soft Boys, *Underwater Moonlight* (depending on what kind of inspiration your artists need).

Karlita

Try out this grapefruit-ed glass of liquid genius either on the next August afternoon when the sweat's starting to stain the inside brim of your cap, or on the next December Saturday night when you're **rocking it out at a loud-but-cozy club** (listening to The Table of Contents, perhaps—a dandily named band you can see more of at www.myspace.com/thetableofcontents), or on the next April morning when you're about to hit the golf course (mini-golf counts, people) and need a picker-upper. It rolls out the remedy in each of these situations.

Ice cubes

1½ ounces **gin**

4 ounces **freshly squeezed grapefruit juice**

1½ ounces **bourbon**

1. Fill an old-fashioned glass three-quarters full with ice cubes. Add the gin, then the grapefruit juice. Stir briefly.

2. Pour the bourbon carefully over the gin and grapefruit. Now, you can start your drinking motors here, or you can again stir briefly. Pal Karl, who is the ideal garnish for any of the situations described above, and who taught me the ways of the Karlita, is okay with either.

Who Let the Drinks Out: 5 Animal Drinks

Unleash your tiger, go running with the wolves, or purr yourself into a little ball on the table. I won't laugh, because I know there's an animal side to all of us. Embrace it by serving one of these.

1 The Eagle (page 282)

2 Polynesian Donkey (page 84)

3 Gaslight Tiger (page 202)

4 Honey Bee (page 154)

5 Lion Tamer (page 79)

KP Cocktail

Wait, wait, don't think you have to survive some sort of kitchen patrol duty to **be engulfed in this effervescent invigorator's realm**. The KP here stands for Kicking Parties into high gear, as well as for Keel-hauling Potable and Keen Potion. However, the number-one definition for the KP is Ken Pingleton, longtime bartender and manager at Manhattan, Kansas, restaurant and booze parlor the Hibachi Hut (where he gave me much of my own early schooling in the alcohol arts, before moving on to sling drinks and wisdom at Lawrence and Kansas City celebrity spots). Currently he's a bartender, bar manager, drummer, and rock star about town in Lawrence. If you're there, ask anyone to point you in the direction of the bar he's currently slinging drinks at, and then head there immediately.

1 teaspoon **thinly sliced fresh ginger**

3 **fresh mint sprigs**

1 teaspoon **confectioners' sugar**

Juice of ½ **lime**

Ice cubes

2½ ounces **Gosling's Black Seal rum**

Chilled ginger beer (see A Note)

1. Place the ginger, 2 of the mint sprigs, sugar, and lime juice into a highball glass. Using a muddler or large wooden spoon, muddle them well.

2. Fill the glass almost to the top with ice cubes. Add the rum, and stir well.

3. Top the glass off with ginger beer, and garnish with the remaining mint sprig and a large straw. Don't forget that straw, now.

⊕ **A Note:** Not feeling the love for the ginger beer? Sub in ginger ale and don't fret—KP won't be upset.

Left Hand

It's phenomenal that so many new, newly discovered, and newly exported liquors and liqueurs are now available in many more peachy places. It's darn fine. But it's also phenomenal that so many more varieties of bitters are available (for more on bitters, see page 224), providing those accents and notes that take certain cocktails **from mundane to mighty, from pretty tasty to tastylicious**. Some top bitters being born at this writing are concocted by the friendly folks at Bittermens bitters (Janet and Avery Glasser, to be precise)—I hope that by the time you read this they'll be available everywhere (be sure to find out at www.bittermens.com). This cocktail was first concocted by Sam Ross of the amazingly excellent New York bars Milk and Honey and Little Branch, and I've been told it was one of the original drinks to feature Bittermens Sweet Chocolate Bitters on a menu.

Ice cubes

1½ ounces **bourbon** (Elijah Craig is the suggested pick)

¾ ounce **Carpano Antica vermouth**

¾ ounce **Campari**

2 dashes **Bittermens Sweet Chocolate Bitters**

Brandied cherry for garnish

1. Fill a mixing glass or cocktail shaker three-quarters full with ice cubes. Add the bourbon, Carpano, Campari, and bitters. Stir well with a long spoon.

2. Strain the mix into a cocktail glass. Garnish with the cherry.

⬆ *A Note: Carpano Antica is red vermouth made from a secret formula (so secret the drink hasn't even been available in the United States for long). It can be had solo as an apéritif, but it also plays well with others in drinks such as this.*

⬆ *A Second Note: Can't get a brandied cherry? Use an unbrandied one, but don't tell the other hand about it.*

Grand Marnier

As a classier version of triple sec (or at least a kissing cousin), Grand Marnier is well known as an ingredient in a number of famous or infamous drinks, such as the B-52, higher-end Margaritas, and some Sidecars (though not the one on page 46), and it is becoming well known in more mysterious concoctions such as the Black Hood (page 187). The liqueur traces its history back further than these mixes, though, with a story that began to germinate in 1827, when one Jean-Baptiste Lapostolle decided to start a fruit liqueur distillery in Neauphle-le-Château, France.

The big blooming happened, however, in 1876, when Jean-Baptiste's granddaughter got hitched to one Louis-Alexandre Marnier, starting the Marnier-Lapostolle family. It was Louis-Alexandre who decided that it would be a good idea to blend his beloved Cognac with Citrus Bigaradia—a bitter orange from the Caribbean that is now commonly known as a Seville orange—into a liqueur that manages to hold on to the luxurious taste of both the Cognac and the oranges.

Since then, that original secret recipe for Grand Marnier has entertained and delighted the taste buds of heads of state and high-class entertainers; the liqueur was stocked on the *Titanic*, was used by master chef Escoffier in a soufflé, and has continued to garner many awards. Though run by the same family, the Grand Marnier liqueur line has expanded, and now includes Louis-Alexandre, named after the creator, which boasts a bit more Cognac and a drier taste; Cuvée du Cent Cinquantenaire, launched in 1977 to celebrate the company's 150-year anniversary and featuring aged Cognacs; Cuvée du Centenaire, made first in 1927 to celebrate the company's 100th anniversary and using rare petite and grand Cognacs; and, of course, the original Cordon Rouge (or "red ribbon").

Lion Tamer

The circus, like the workplace, can be fraught with danger, excitement, breathtaking wonder, clowns, and ferocious jungle beasts. To navigate the big top (and the big building), you need to balance like an acrobat and be able to handle the big cats. This drink **walks that high wire in its poised fashion**. Writer, editor, and carney compadre Andrea Swangard (who's a bit of a lion herself, as well as the creator of the Lion Tamer) says it best: "There are times when you can settle the score by killing someone with kindness. Other times you've got to fight fire with fire. The best lion tamers know how to get their way using an even dose of both. This drink involves tasty layers that start out with a punch of rum, then soothe with sweetness."

Ice cubes

4 ounces **cream soda**

1 ounce **GranGala**

1½ ounces **dark rum**

Orange twist for garnish

1. Fill an old-fashioned glass or ringmaster's hat halfway full with ice cubes. Add the cream soda.

2. Pour the orange liqueur on top of the soda, then top that with the rum. Stir gently—you want the layers to blend just a bit.

3. Top with the orange twist (or other whip-like garnish).

⚡ *A Note: Andrea says that, much as there are different lions that one must tame, it's fun to try your taming skills with other orange liqueurs besides GranGala, such as Grand Marnier or Cointreau.*

⚡ *A Second Note: GranGala is an award-winning Italian orange liqueur. It's made by infusing VSOP brandy with an array of delectable oranges from around the world. If you, sadly, can't find it, you could slip in another orange liqueur here. But I'd watch for rain in that case.*

Millennium Cocktail

The big bad millennium (Y2K and all that) seems far in the rear view already—a time I have to imagine certain parties will be calling "retro" before long (if it hasn't already happened). One part of the millennium that won't ever be outdated, though, is this turn-of-the-century mix, crafted by none other than Gary and Mardee Regan, cocktailians extraordinaire, who hang out at www.ardentspirits.com and whom I was lucky enough to work with via an Amazon.com connection way back when (they were writing recipes for the site, and I was putting the recipes on the site). It was amazing for me, because I was able to learn bucketfuls about cocktails and making cocktails and having fun with cocktails during the workday. For example, I learned about this one, which was later reprinted in Gary's out-of-sight book *The Joy of Mixology* (Clarkson Potter, 2003).

Ice cubes

2½ ounces **bourbon**

½ ounce **peach schnapps**

3 dashes **Angostura bitters**

Lemon twist for garnish

1. Fill a mixing glass or cocktail shaker halfway full with ice cubes. Add the bourbon, schnapps, and bitters. Stir well (with a leftover New Year's Eve 1999 party favor if you must).

2. Strain into a cocktail glass and let that lemon twist do its thing.

The Occidental

Travelers are continually uncovering exotic and novel drinks and (if we are, as Lover-boy said, one of the "lucky ones") introducing them to friends, family, and whoever happens by. Such is the case with the Occidental, introduced to me by pal and pro party-thrower Mark Butler (with help from his wife, Leslie). The fact that he uncovered it at home makes not a whit of difference. But what is the Occidental about? As Mark says best, "No esoteric ingredients, no exotic undertones, but a tasty combination nonetheless. I picture it being like what might have been considered **a tropical cocktail in 1965 Duluth or Eau Claire**. . . . The drink actually looks like a sunset, with the cherry juice putting a little fire into the dark rum, and the cherries glowing like flaming orbs. The origin of the term *occident* is from the Latin *occidentem*, meaning 'western sky,' the part of the sky in which the sun sets."

Crushed ice

2½ ounces **apple juice**

2½ ounces **chilled ginger ale**

1½ ounces **dark rum**

Dash of **cherry juice**

2 **maraschino cherries** for garnish

1. Fill an old-fashioned glass halfway full with crushed ice. Add the apple juice, ginger ale, rum, and cherry juice. Stir briefly.

2. Garnish with the maraschino cherries—and be cheery about it!

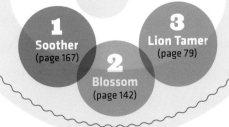

3
Potions to Pacify

Coming home with a bit of the ol' bad news? Want to diffuse a silly argument that's about to get out of hand? Need to calm the anger waters after a night where you stayed out too late without a phone call? Don't think that because the beverages below are *dark* spirit–based that they can't pitch in perfectly to help the pacification process along.

1 Soother (page 167)

2 Blossom (page 142)

3 Lion Tamer (page 79)

Ognam

A rumbling drum whose echoes float over the snow-tufted mountaintops and **mingle in the jungle vines**, Ognam is approaching, over land and sea and sea turtle when necessary (not hurting the turtles any, I assure you), heralded by smoke signal, carrier pigeon, Morse code, this very book, and Internet video. Ognam is approaching, approaching, trumpeted by its high priestess, Natalie Fuller, approaching your backyard, which is in need of Ognam this day, as Ognam knows how to turn your warm-weather wingding from wipeout into sunshine-y daydream.

Ice cubes

2½ ounces **mango juice**

1½ ounces **brandy**

½ ounce **Aperol**

Chilled club soda

Lemon slice for garnish

1. Fill a highball glass with ice cubes. Add the mango juice, brandy, and Aperol. Stir well.

2. Fill the glass almost to the tippy top with club soda. (Ognam insists on words like tippy top. Don't infuriate Ognam.) Stir again, well. Squeeze the lemon slice over the glass and drop it in.

Polynesian Donkey

International bon vivant, renowned in locales known and unknown, Jeremy Holt (the Husky Boy, of the much loved and somewhat lamented—as there hasn't been an issue in a while—*Husky Boy* magazine, and of the Husky Boy blog, thehuskyboy.blogspot.com) is also, I'm tickled to say, a close pal of mine. In addition, he is the creator of this multi-faceted amalgamation that could get you out of, or into, a fix, depending on how many are consumed, with whom, and where. It is, as you'd expect if you know the HB, very charming, and also holds a hearty wallop. And though some may dispute the fact, it is, definitively, where the phrase "drunk as a Polynesian donkey" comes from.

Ice cubes

1 ounce **Mount Gay gold rum**

1 ounce **POM Wonderful pomegranate juice**

½ ounce **brandy**

½ ounce **cachaça**

½ ounce **Hpnotiq**

½ ounce **fresh pineapple juice**

½ ounce **Simple Syrup** (page 12)

Chilled ginger ale

Pineapple chunk for garnish

1. Fill a cocktail shaker halfway full with ice cubes. Add the rum, pomegranate juice, brandy, cachaça, Hpnotiq, pineapple juice, and simple syrup. Shake while kicking.

2. Strain into a cocktail glass. Add a splash of ginger ale. Garnish with that pineapple chunk (either on a toothpick or dropped into the drink, depending on the company kept)

⬆ *A Note: Jeremy says that as long as you follow the ratios, you can scale this one up for more folks, even making a punch bowl of it. Believe him and stay glad.*

The Search for Delicious

Concocting inventive beverages is often **an expedition through the wilderness of liquors**, liqueurs, juices, and other ingredients, starting perhaps on a wisp of a trail or quickly using a shaker like a machete to strike your own path. That's why bartender Kirk Estopinal (drink slinger at Chicago's cocktail haven the Violet Hour, at this moment at least) is now among the great explorers (take that, Ponce de León), after going off roads and off trails into the deepest depths of the drink jungle, not stopping or allowing himself to be dead-ended, determined to make the Search for Delicious.

2 ounces **Cynar**

1 ounce **Punt e Mes vermouth**

6 dashes **Regan's Orange Bitters No. 6**

2 pinches **salt**

¾ teaspoon **freshly squeezed lemon juice**

3 pieces **lemon rind**

Ice chunk or **chunks**

1. Add the Cynar, vermouth, bitters, salt, and lemon juice to a mixing glass or cocktail shaker. Using a long spoon, stir well.

2. Twist all 3 lemon rind pieces over the glass, and drop the third one into the glass.

3. Add one large chunk of ice, or a few fairly large chunks, to an old-fashioned glass. Pour the mix over the ice. Serve deliciously.

⬆ *A Note: Cynar is a sepia-toned Italian liqueur made from a number of herbs and spices (13, to be exact), with artichoke being the headliner. It doubles as an apéritif and a digestive, as well as being a hit in cocktails.*

⬆ *A Second Note: Punt e Mes is a red vermouth, one with a slightly more bitter outlook than other vermouth relations.*

Short Timer

Celebratory drinks are what it's all about—"it" here being life, if I can be so bold. (Not that I mean it's the only thing life is about, but a fresh drink celebrating an occasion is certainly one part of it.) A celebratory drink created by one of the foremost cocktail bloggers—in this case Paul Clarke, from the if-you-miss-it-you're-nuts blog the Cocktail Chronicles, at www.cocktailchronicles.com—is maybe even better. And if said cocktail is created to celebrate Mr. Clarke leaving his day job to concentrate fully on blogging, editing up the bubbly mag *Imbibe*, and writing for places such as the *San Francisco Chronicle* and the website Serious Eats (www.seriouseats.com), then the whole drinkers' universe should stop and join the celebration. This appetizing liquid socialization is in fact an adaptation of a drink called the Coin Toss, created by Phil Ward at Death + Company (for more from Death + Company, see page 72).

Ice cubes

2 ounces **Pampero Aniversario rum**

¾ ounce **Carpano Antica vermouth**

¼ ounce **Giffard Ginger of the Indies liqueur**

¼ ounce **Rhum Clément Créole Shrubb**

2 dashes **The Bitter Truth's Jerry Thomas' Own Decanter Bitters**

1. Fill a mixing glass or cocktail shaker halfway full with ice cubes. Add the rum, vermouth, liqueurs, and bitters. Stir well.

2. Strain into a chilled cocktail glass. Here's to celebrations.

⬆ *A Note: Giffard Ginger of the Indies liqueur has notes of ginger, obviously, but also vanilla, cardamom, and orange. If you can't find it, try Paul's substitution suggestion, Domaine de Canton Ginger Liqueur.*

⬆ *A Second Note: Rhum Clément Créole Shrubb is made in Martinique, with a base of multiple rums, orange peels, and sugarcane syrup. Search for it online, at www.thedrinkshop.com, for example.*

⬆ *A Third Note: The Bitter Truth (the-bitter-truth. com) makes artisanal bitters and other cocktail ingredients, including aromatic bitters, orange bitters, and lemon bitters.*

Cynar

When folks fear the Cynar (pronounced *CHEE-nar*), it's
not the dark brown coloring that's intimidating; usually
it's the artichoke—the ingredient that takes top billing in
this liqueur. But, even if you dislike artichokes, don't let
that stop you from trying the Cynar, because I'm guessing that once you get past your initial reluctance you'll fall
for it, especially if you enjoy a bit of bitter taste in your
apéritifs and digestives. Thanks to its balance of bitter
and sweet, this liqueur can really fall into both categories
without stepping on any culinary toes. The taste isn't just
artichoke, either; 13 all-natural herbs and spices come
together to bring about an adventure for both the mouth
and the nose (as Cynar boasts an array of floral and herbal
aromas).

Good on its own, Cynar also mixes well, whether it's
simply with soda water over ice, perhaps topped with an
orange slice or twist, or as a component in more complex
creations, such as the Search for Delicious (page 85). In
France, it's even used as an addition to beer.

Cynar was first introduced in 1952 and developed a
core following that enjoyed its unique flavor—and wasn't
opposed to the many health benefits that the herbs are
thought to impart. It was in the 1960s that Cynar began to
take off for a larger audience, thanks to some television
commercials featuring Italian movie and TV star Ernesto
Calindri. In the spots, he (a perfect Italian gentleman)
would often end up sitting at a small table in the middle of
a busy street, sipping Cynar, or Cynar and soda, reading the
paper without a care in the world. Those health benefits,
and Cynar's ability to relax that stress away, aren't to be
taken lightly.

Sweet Louise

If someone is named "Wolfgang," you have to believe that he'll be either an illustrious composer, a spectacular villain (even a wrestling villain), or one seriously sublime bartender (and I hope not a woman). We're (and I use the inclusive *we* here to mean every one of us drinking types) golden, 'cause Andrew Wolfgang Bohrer decided on the last path. As one of Seattle's top itinerant bartenders, writer of the Cask Strength blog (caskstrength.wordpress.com), magician of drinks like the Sweet Louise, and host of events such as bring-your-own-homemade-bitters afternoons, Andrew is continually thinking about how to serve better cocktails, make better cocktails, and teach people better cocktail-making. As I said, we're golden.

1 **plum**, pitted

Ice cubes

2 ounces **brandy**

1 ounce **green Chartreuse**

1 ounce **freshly squeezed lemon juice**

Orange twist for garnish

1. Add the plum to a cocktail shaker or mixing glass. Using a muddler or wooden spoon, muddle well.

2. Fill the cocktail shaker halfway full with ice cubes. Add the brandy, Chartreuse, and lemon juice. Shake well.

3. Strain into a cocktail glass. Garnish with the orange twist.

⬆ *A Note: Andrew says that you need to make sure your strainer is a fine-mesh one, to ensure no plum bits get stuck in your teeth.*

⬆ *A Second Note: Chartreuse is an herbal liqueur that's been made from a hush-hush recipe by monks for many years. There are two readily available varieties, green and yellow.*

Tombstone

In the old-timey saloon set-up, there was a cowpoke who slung the Tombstone for the first time, **leaving others scratching for their shakers** (help came in the form of shaker holsters tied tight to the thigh for easy access, with an ice bucket holster on the parallel hip). He strode a wide swath and, pardners, still does, with books that shine like stars on the open range, such as *Imbibe!* (Perigee, 2007), where this very nugget of liquid gold is panned from (note: no actual gold in recipe). I'm jawing on about this cocktail buster, without even a name, so let me correct myself: This bearded scribe of the bar's brand is David Wondrich.

Cracked ice

2 ounces **rye**

1 teaspoon **rich simple syrup** (see A Second Note)

2 dashes **Angostura bitters**

1 **thin lemon twist**

1. Fill a cocktail shaker halfway full with cracked ice. Add the rye, rich simple syrup, and bitters. Shake well.

2. Strain into a cocktail glass (chilled if you can wrassle it down), and twist the lemon twist over the drink like a lasso over a runaway calf, and then drop it in.

⌃ *A Note: Mr. Wondrich suggests 100- or 101-proof rye here. Don't anger him.*

⌃ *A Second Note: To make rich simple syrup, add 4 cups Demerara sugar and 2 cups water to a saucepan, and place over low to medium-low heat. Cook, stirring occasionally, until the sugar completely dissolves. Let cool. Bottle with ½ ounce grain alcohol if you would like this to keep longer than a month.*

Touchless Automatic

Don't let this **strong-but-savory coupling** fade away like a shipboard romance or, more exactly, like the song that shares its name, a touchingly indie love-song-of-sorts by onetime Midwestern powerhouse Sufferbus (with this particular song penned by bassist and pop master Brian Harris, aided by drummer Ken Pingleton and guitarist and singer Mitchell Leggs) that is currently forgotten by far too many. Too many are sitting outside wishing they had a song to sing right this instant, mirroring those who are wishing they had this drink right now. You, tuneful one, can ensure this drink doesn't fade away, by making one for those needy folks.

8 **fresh pineapple sage leaves**

Ice cubes

2 ounces **Scotch**

1 ounce **St. Elizabeth Allspice Dram**

Lemon twist for garnish

1. Add all but one of the sage leaves to a cocktail shaker. Using a muddler or wooden spoon, muddle well.

2. Fill the cocktail shaker halfway full with ice cubes. Add the Scotch and the St. Elizabeth. Shake while humming a song you once forgot.

3. Strain into a cocktail glass. Garnish with the lemon twist and the last sage leaf.

A Note: I think a nice blended Scotch works well here, such as The Famous Grouse (which is one sweet Scotch name, as well). If you're into experimenting, though, play around with a single malt or two. Then report back.

A Second Note: St. Elizabeth Allspice Dram combines Jamaican rum and allspice berries into a lovely herbal liqueur. Sometimes you'll see an ingredient in older recipes called "Pimento Dram"— use St. Elizabeth in those situations. You can get it online, if you can't find it at your local liquor store.

A Third Note: No pineapple sage in a big barrel in the backyard? Sub in regular sage and take no guff.

WeatherUp

There's something special about a good neighborhood bar, one that's intimate and a bit cozy, one that has its own style and is a reflection of the surroundings and the people who inhabit it. These local parlors tend to be good spots to hang out in, much like the WeatherUp in Brooklyn, which is a bit **more secretive than some locales**, but so enjoyable to sit and drink in, because of the relaxed-but-cool atmosphere, the friendly staff, and the right-on drinks made by tiptop bartender Gabe Harrelson. The following drink, which shares the bar's name and is the baby of Sasha Petraske and Kathryn Weatherups, also mirrors the bar itself: perfectly balanced, lovely in its simplicity, and tasty.

Ice cubes

2 ounces **Lazzaroni Amaretto**

1½ ounces **Landy Cognac**

1 ounce **freshly squeezed lemon juice**

One **3-inch piece orange rind** for garnish

1. Fill a cocktail shaker halfway full with ice cubes. Add the amaretto, Cognac, and lemon juice. Shake well.

2. Strain the mix into a chilled wine glass. Twist the orange rind over the drink so the oil sprays nicely, and then drop it over the glass's rim.

Four Ingredients to Experiment With

There are a ton of new brands and slants on liqueurs and liquors weighing down the shelves of stores, but when you're coming up with an inventive drink all your own, why not see if you can slip in one of the following ingredients? You might end up with amazing results and be the talk of the town—or at least the talk of three of your friends.

1. Mango nectar or juice: Available in international food stores and some grocery stores, this viscous juice goes well with rum.

2. Fresh ginger: Be sure it's peeled and finely chopped, and perhaps even muddled up, when using this to add extra flavor and zing to punches and more.

3. Raspberry syrup: Go for a thick variety (not raspberry jelly, but something that oozes a bit), and use it to raise the sweetness quotient of a drink while also upping the flavor.

4. Dried hibiscus flowers: Tracked down at local apothecaries, health food stores, botanical companies, or spice shops (or online at spots like Dandelion Botanical, www.dandelionbotanical.com), this exotic treat brings a floral touch and island accents to creative combinations.

Bubbly Refreshers

Sing it loud, y'all: School and work and any sort of situation that might drag you down and keep you from kicking it—these are out for summer. Or for a summer-like afternoon. Or for a cloudy day that old Mr. Steamy Stuff, Mr. Sunshine, shakes a ray into. Or even a winter evening where you've cranked that heater up to summertime levels. Or a couple of hours when you're sauna-ing, or hot-tubbing, or taking a warm, warm bath. Or, between us, anytime you feel like inserting a bit of bursting summer into your life. Because you've made it to the chapter that's here to cancel out any overheating, to get the sunshine superstar party swinging. Ladies and gentleman of the sun, let me present . . . Bubbly Refreshers.

It's a shame, in my opinion, that we reserve the dark spirits (with maybe the exception of bathing beauty dark rum, but even that a little bit) more often for the dreary months, for the cold days and colder nights. Those nights do at times demand a more serious prescription, a darker component to handle their long sunless hours. But don't strand the dark spirits the rest of the year, leaving them to languish alone in the back of cupboards, shaded from the bright ball in the sky, shrouded in mystery like an insane twin chained to a corner of the attic in an old horror movie. Don't treat our beloved companions the dark spirits in such second-class fashion for six months or more every year, like a sort of anti-Persephone. Let them live, I beg you, year-round! Let them live.

Or else I promise even more melodrama, and you're going to be the one suffering for it, because you'll be missing out on a serious assortment of bubbling beverages using our dark spirits—beverages that are bound to become faves at hot houses and hot backyards if you unleash them. Whether it's brandy bringing the bursts in the Snow Ball or Washington's Wish, or bourbon bouncing through your day with a Lazy

Hazy or becoming the Class of the Race, these spirits are ready to bring their playful sides to the light of day.

So invite rye out to the club next time via the Golf Links Highball, or have it give you a Spring in Your Step. Take Scotch out under the next late August moonlit night by stocking up on Mamie Taylors, or invite a lovable Roffignac—with its Cognac, club soda, and raspberry hints—to the lake house. And don't forget about dark rum when bustling around the dark spirits' effervescent possibilities and its favorable sandy position as a key part of the Beach Bubble, the Rum Rascal, and others. I'm feeling warmer, then cooled down, already. What about you?

Beach Bubble

Living beach style, you might think even bubble-blowing is too much effort—won't it take away from all that persistent relaxing you should be doing, there on that sand-strewn Hawaiian stretch (or other tropical locale)? Well, when you construct a Beach Bubble, you won't be overwhelmed by the effort, just the results. It probably won't stick to your face like bubble gum, either. Unless you have a tendency toward really high levels of messiness.

Ice cubes

2 ounces **dark rum**

2 ounces **fresh pineapple juice**

1 ounce **mango juice**

Chilled ginger ale

2 **pineapple chunks** for garnish

1. Fill a Collins glass or large goblet three-quarters full with ice cubes. Add the rum, pineapple juice, and mango juice. Stir, but with respect for the beach's mellow demeanor.

2. Fill the glass up with ginger ale. Stir, but again, mellowly.

3. Spear the pineapple chunks on a toothpick, and float them in the glass (watch out for that toothpick when drinking).

A VIRGIN VARIATION: You'll want to title this the Beach Ball, as it doesn't have the same bubble (or maybe call it the Beach Bubble, Popped), and you'll also want to omit the rum and add 1 more ounce each of the pineapple juice and the mango juice. It'll still taste tropicalicious.

Blue Train

Everybody, sing along: "You must sip the Blue Train, to go relaxing with some fruit and brandy. If you find you missed the Blue Train, you'll find you missed the quickest way to fruit and brandy. Hurry now, get on, it's shaking. Watch those bubbles a-sparkling. All aboard, sip up the Blue Train. Soon you will be drinking fruit and brandy."

Ice cubes

1½ ounces **brandy**

1 ounce **fresh pineapple juice**

Chilled brut Champagne or **sparkling wine**

Pineapple chunk for garnish (optional)

1. Fill a cocktail shaker three-quarters full with ice cubes. Add the brandy and pineapple juice. Shake well, humming all the time.

2. Strain the train into a Champagne flute. Top with chilled bubbly, almost to the top. Garnish with a pineapple chunk if you like, on a toothpick or just dropped carefully into the glass.

⟳ *A Note: Mr. Ellington, please, wherever you are, forgive me, remembering that imitation is the sincerest form of flattery.*

Bring the Noise

Folks acting a little dull at the spring spree, when you were hoping for a rump-shaking, or a head-banging, or at least a bopping and shoulder-shrugging affair? Serve up one of the following five drinks paired with one of the five songs listed (mix-and-match as desire and volume demands). Your neighbors will be complaining (or coming up, down, or over to join the fun) before you can say "pish-posh."

Bring the House Down
(page 242)

Southstreet
(page 266)

Spring in Your Step
(page 130)

ASAP
(page 56)

Golden Lady
(page 108)

"You Dropped a Bomb on Me"
The Gap Band

"Live Wire"
Mötley Crüe

"Sister Havana"
Urge Overkill

"Corona"
Minutemen

"We're in the Music Biz"
Robots in Disguise

Chicago

Whether it's catching a cab to roll from a chic spot downtown to a hip hideaway in Wicker Park (the bar Rodan, perhaps, on a Tuesday for live music and wasabi fries), spending a few hours transporting yourself through time while viewing the Thorne Miniature Rooms collection at the Art Institute, walking along the river under the twinkling lights on a cold night while cozying up with that special someone, or teaching the friendly folks at the delicious restaurant Crofton on Wells how to make this very drink—there are few ways to better enjoy a couple of days than hanging out in the Windy City.

Ice cubes

1½ ounces **Cognac**

½ ounce **orange curaçao**

Dash of **Angostura bitters**

Chilled brut Champagne or **sparkling wine**

1. Fill a cocktail shaker halfway full with ice cubes. Add the Cognac, curaçao, and bitters. Shake well.

2. Strain into a Champagne flute, and top with Champagne.

A Note: As alluded to in the intro, this drink has sadly fallen off most bar menus, in the city of big shoulders as well as in most other cities. But when in Chicago, you shouldn't shy away from ordering this; just ease the kind bartender into it, and don't forget to tip well.

Class of the Race

When consuming the Class of the Race, please, please resist the urge to get all Pheidippides-esque and consume the whole stretch at once, racing to get it down without stopping for breath. To be the class of the race, you must pace yourself. Because that way you get to have more of these slightly herbal, slightly stylish, slightly assertive refreshers, which in the long run is going to make you the winner.

Ice cubes

2 ounces **bourbon**

1 ounce **Benedictine**

½ ounce **Simple Syrup** (page 12)

2 dashes **Peychaud's bitters**

Chilled brut Champagne or **sparkling wine**

1. Fill a cocktail shaker halfway full with ice cubes. Add the bourbon, Benedictine, simple syrup, and bitters. Shake well (but not so well that you expire from the effort).

2. Strain the mix into a Champagne flute. Top with the bubbly.

⬆ *A Note: Pheidippides was the original marathoner, running from Marathon to Athens after a battle in 490 B.C. without stopping once, announcing, "We have won," and then reportedly dying.*

⬆ *A Second Note: It seems, in honor of old Pheidippides, that real Champagne should be used here. But I know the road is long, and if that means you go with a good sparkling wine, I sure won't say anything against it.*

Corn Popper

This drink (which traces back at least to Harry Craddock's 1930 *Savoy Cocktail Book*) uses no fresh corn, but it does traditionally contain corn whiskey, along with other assorted ingredients (and I do mean assorted). In later tomes, you sometimes see bourbon substituted in, and while the results are tasty, I think if you can get the corn whiskey, use it. One warning, though: While this drink sounds like a kitchen appliance (one you'd use to make corn fritters, perhaps, or a better version of the Corn Baller from the sadly canceled show *Arrested Development*), **don't use any appliances** after a few of these. That's just asking for trouble.

Ice cubes

1½ ounces **corn whiskey**

½ ounce **heavy cream**

½ ounce **grenadine**

1 **egg white**

Chilled club soda (preferably the traditional White Rock, if you can find it)

Freshly grated nutmeg for garnish (optional)

1. Fill a cocktail shaker halfway full with ice cubes. Add the whiskey, cream, grenadine, and egg white. Shake well (as if you were a corn kernel popping).

2. Fill a highball glass halfway full with ice cubes. Strain the mixture into the glass. Top with club soda, and stir.

3. Sprinkle the drink with a little grated nutmeg if you're feeling poppy.

❌ *A Warning: As this contains raw egg, it's best not to serve it to the elderly or those with compromised immune systems. And go for fresh organic eggs—you'll be glad you did.*

Côte d'Azur Cooler

I sense a lot of bronzed bodies at the beach party (perhaps on the Riviera?) where this brandy-based sunbather's daydream is served up chilly. I first slipped this drink out of the book *International Cocktail Specialties from Madison Avenue to Malaya* by James Mayabb (Castle Books, 1962), and I suspect you'll want to lather on the sunblock—a drink that sounds as smoothly Mediterranean as this will probably have you in a skimpy swimsuit in no time.

Ice cubes

1 ounce **brandy**

½ ounce **fresh pineapple juice**

½ ounce **freshly squeezed lemon juice**

¼ ounce **maraschino liqueur**

Chilled club soda

1. Fill a cocktail shaker halfway full with ice cubes. Add the brandy, pineapple juice, lemon juice, and maraschino liqueur. Shake well.

2. Fill an old-fashioned glass halfway full with ice cubes. Strain the mix into the glass (sort of like sliding yourself into a swimming pool). Fill the glass with club soda. Stir briefly.

⬆ *A Note: Feeling this is too naked even for a hot beach? Add a pineapple chunk to the glass for modesty's sake.*

5 Accented Drink Ideas

Feeling a yearning to appear a swatch continental at your next—as the Italians say—*grande festa eccellente*? I suggest, then, you pick one or two of the drinks listed below for your menu, as they'll allow you to slip into an accent like you'd slip into a seasoned dinner jacket.

1 Côte d'Azur Cooler (above)

2 Lalla Rookh (page 115)

3 Crimean Cup à la Marmora (page 247)

4 Ti Penso Sempre (page 174)

5 Nuit de Noces (page 163)

Dark Water

Dark Water can run deep—deep enough that you may be wary when dipping in that first toe (or when tipping back the glass for that first swallow). **Have no fear** of these waters, though—save that fear to decide whether it's a good idea to go swimming in the ocean at midnight after watching one of the *Jaws* movies—because this combination of rum, vodka, soda, and lime is nothing to be scared of, unless you dabble in more than three of them. By the way, it's never a good idea to go swimming in dark waters after drinking three Dark Waters. At that point, just rewatch the movie with the shark and you'll feel much better in the morning.

Ice cubes

2 ounces **dark rum**

½ ounce **vanilla vodka**

Chilled club soda

Lime wedge for garnish

1. Fill a cocktail shaker halfway full with ice cubes. Add the rum and vodka, and shake well.

2. Fill a highball glass or 8-ounce hollow plastic shark three-quarters full with ice cubes. Strain the rum-vodka mix into the glass (or shark). Top with club soda.

3. Squeeze the lime wedge over the glass and drop it in.

A VARIATION: This might sound odd at first, but try subbing in chilled ginger ale for the club soda. Call it Dark Water in Georgia (or DW in GA for short).

Don't Have a Naked Bar

I'm not saying that you shouldn't make drinks in the buff here and there—that's your own decision. But even so, your actual bar needs the following five items, both for whipping up preplanned drinks and for those last-minute mash-ups.

1. Liquor.

2. Glassware. You can fake some types of glassware, but not with plastic (unless you've been transported to the plastic planet).

3. Cocktail shaker of some sort (one you're comfortable with is best).

4. Measuring device (sub in a jolly attitude if your shaker is already equipped with this).

5. This book. Or, a good pitcher for larger party populating. Or, a good mixing device—which could also be this book.

Derby Fizz

The Derby Fizz is **a good rip-snorter** for the morning *after* the Kentucky Derby, but don't get confused and have this the day of, as that privilege is reserved for the Mint Julep (page 36), and you surely don't want to get a Mint Julep upset with you. And, really, the whole egg inside the Derby Fizz both makes it a dandy morning drink and provides you with a bit of breakfast (not to mention taking the edge off if you were too friendly with the Mint Juleps the day before).

Ice cubes

1½ ounces **bourbon**

½ ounce **Simple Syrup** (page 12)

½ ounce **freshly squeezed lemon juice**

¼ ounce **orange curaçao**

1 **egg**

Chilled club soda

1. Fill a cocktail shaker halfway full with ice cubes. Add the bourbon, simple syrup, lemon juice, curaçao, and egg. Shake exceptionally well (even while also shaking the cobwebs out of your eyes).

2. Fill a highball glass halfway full with ice cubes. Strain the mix into the glass.

3. Slowly fill the glass with club soda, stirring at the same time if possible.

✖ *A Warning: As this contains raw egg, do not serve to the elderly or those with compromised immune systems.*

Fair Skies

Ah, look above you on a late after-noon in late April (after the thaw has hit and winter's beginning to be a cold, fading blip in your memory), or on a day you've skipped out a bit early from the job (or, if on a weekend, skipped out from the yard work), or you're with four or five friends who **understand how lovely life can be**. Look above you between drinks of this bubbly-but-a-bit-bracing beauty, and take in that big blue canvas stretching out. Fair skies, indeed.

Ice cubes

1 ounce **Armagnac**

½ ounce **GranGala**

½ ounce **Simple Syrup**
(page 12)

Chilled brut Champagne or **sparkling wine**

Orange twist for garnish

1. Fill a cocktail shaker halfway full with ice cubes. Add the Armagnac, GranGala, and simple syrup. Shake, while looking at those skies.

2. Strain the mix into a Champagne flute. Top with chilled Champagne and garnish with the orange twist.

A VARIATION: Armagnac, Cognac's older cousin from up the French road a bit, works especially well here, with its slight and tender fruit aspects. If you have only Cognac around, experiment with it, but you have to call the final product Fair Skies with One Little Cloud.

"I'll tell you what. We'll drink a little bottle of Champagne. **I feel happy**. And I like talking to you."

PETER CHEYNEY, *Another Little Drink*, 1940

GranGala

GranGala is a rich orange liqueur that's showing up more and more in an assortment of drinks (the Fair Skies, opposite, and the Lion Tamer, page 79, for example). It's made in lovely Trieste, Italy, from Mediterranean oranges and Italian VSOP brandy. While it uses sweet oranges to bring out a bright orange taste, the liqueur itself is not overly sugary (luckily), thanks to the brandy that gives it that solid base to build on (and that also lets it mix well into such a wide assortment of drinks, both shaken cocktails and bubbly highballs). This combination of oranges and brandy helped it win a gold medal at the 2008 San Francisco World Spirits competition and rate highly in a number of other competitions. (And though the Margarita isn't a dark spirit–based drink, I'd be a bit remiss if I didn't suggest you try GranGala in one instead of triple sec, because it's pretty dreamy.)

Created as an Italian answer to the top orange liqueurs made in other countries, especially Grand Marnier (don't put a bottle of GranGala next to a bottle of Grand Marnier on a shelf in your liqueur cabinet—I don't know that you wouldn't end up with a premium orange liqueur showdown that could get downright sticky), GranGala was first blended by Lionello Stock in 1884, and the secret recipe (though it's admitted that the oranges come from Sicily, and the VSOP brandy from Italy itself) is still made by the House of Stock in Trieste. The recipe is said to be instilled with Italy's history of art, culture, and craftsmanship, all of which is reflected in the liqueur's sensuous yet serious taste.

Foppa

From the Italian book *Cocktail: Classici & Esotici* (Demetra, 2002), the Foppa is an international blend, mingling Scotch whisky, amaretto, dry vermouth (sometimes known as French vermouth), and ginger ale. Think about taking a trip to where all those ingredients originate, and you're all of a sudden a world traveler. Or, if you can't manage to coordinate the multitude of flights, serve these up when putting together a puzzle of a map of the world with friends, or sip one when finally reading that copy of Hendrik van Loon's *The Story of Mankind*, a book that trots the globe (and that may, between us, demand a refreshing Foppa to go along with reading it).

The original version of this recipe suggests single-malt Scotch, but I like using a nice blended version, which I think works well with the other ingredients (something like Dewar's is a dandy choice). It also suggests using Disaronno amaretto, which traces its secret recipe back to 1525. This is a suggestion you should follow. (Who wants to argue with all that history? And the almond taste is just right.)

Ice cubes

1½ ounces **Scotch**

½ ounce **amaretto**

½ ounce **dry vermouth**

Chilled ginger ale

1. Fill a highball glass three-quarters full with ice cubes. Add the Scotch, amaretto, and vermouth. Stir with a long spoon.

2. Top the glass off with ginger ale. Stir again.

Golden Lady

A sweetheart with a few hints of orange, a hint-and-a-half of Cognac, and a whole hatful of hints of sparkling wine, the Golden Lady plays well both on fifth dates (by which time you're probably close enough where you can start calling that special someone "golden" and not feel too ooky about it) and fiftieth anniversaries, especially if either of these occasions are occurring under a starlit spring or summer sky. I believe that a sweeter sparkling wine or Champagne (of the demi-sec variety, even), or the Italian sparkling wine Prosecco, rises to the special occasion in a manner most fitting. Be extra-safe when popping that cork, though, as nothing ruins one of these singular evenings more than a runaway cork.

Ice cubes

1 ounce **Cognac**

¾ ounce **Cointreau**

¾ ounce **freshly squeezed orange juice**

Chilled demi-sec Champagne, sparkling wine, or **Prosecco**

Orange twist for garnish

1. Fill a cocktail shaker halfway full with ice cubes. Add the Cognac, Cointreau, and orange juice. Shake well.

2. Strain the almost-golden lady into a large cocktail glass. Fill the glass carefully with the Champagne. Twist the orange twist over the glass and drop it in.

⊕ *A Note: This is often made in a flute. I like the way it looks and disperses in a cocktail glass, but if I were served this on my fiftieth anniversary in a flute, I wouldn't turn it away.*

⊕ *A Second Note: I'd be remiss if I didn't say that Golden Lady is also a wonderful brand of Italian tights. If you want to give some of those as a present with your Golden Lady beverage, I'll bet you get a gold star.*

Golf Links Highball

At the Bruntsfield Links in Edinburgh, Scotland, in 1456, the site of an awfully old golf game (the one that boasts the oldest surviving records of it having happened), they did not, sadly and against all my ideas (retroactive ideas, to be sure) and against all logic and sports-person-ship, serve any Golf Links Highballs. Since that sad day, golfers have become not only more civilized but also more hydration-conscious, and have never played a round of golf without **this invigorating and revitalizing amalgamation.** If a golfer has, well, give him or her some pity. But don't follow that lead the next time you're on the links.

Cracked ice

1½ ounces **rye**

¾ ounce **sweet vermouth**

½ ounce **freshly squeezed lemon juice**

½ ounce **fresh pineapple juice**

¼ ounce **dark rum**

Chilled club soda

1. Fill a highball glass three-quarters full with cracked ice. Add the rye, vermouth, lemon juice, pineapple juice, and rum. Stir slightly (you don't want to strain your putting arm).

2. Fill the glass with club soda, almost to the top. Stir well (but again, no straining).

Four College Town Bars Worth Returning to School For

There are college bars, and then there are bars in college towns. The latter tend to be the driving forces behind going to back to visit the ol' alma mater. And they tend to be fantastic places to find those friends who never left school.

1. Auntie Mae's Parlor; Manhattan, Kansas; Kansas State University
2. Chubs Pub; Fargo, North Dakota; North Dakota State University
3. Zanzibar; Ann Arbor, Michigan; Michigan University
4. El Rancho; Durango, Colorado; Fort Lewis College

Hour Glass

Don't dwell on looking at these as you drink them up, dreading that last sip as you get closer to the bottom of the glass and thus (as you'd dread that last grain of sand passing through an actual hourglass, because it always seems so ominous) not enjoying the fun you had getting there. This Hour Glass isn't hard to make, so you can always **whip up another one** for you and your friends. Also, don't be confused into thinking the fun should last only an hour (like the comic book hero Hourman's powers after he took the miracle drug Miraclo). It's just the opposite: After an hour spent in the company of friends and a few Hour Glasses, the fun is just beginning.

Ice cubes

1 ounce **Cognac**

¾ ounce **Cointreau**

½ ounce **absinthe**

Chilled club soda

Lemon twist for garnish

1. Fill a cocktail shaker halfway full with ice cubes. Add the Cognac, Cointreau, and absinthe. Shake well (and don't even glance at the clock).

2. Fill a highball glass three-quarters full with ice cubes. Strain the timely mix over the ice, and fill the glass almost to the top with club soda.

3. Squeeze the lemon twist over the glass and drop it in.

⊕ *A Note: Finally, after long last, certain types of absinthe are again available in the United States. If your local liquor store isn't stocking them yet, try online sources like www.internetwines. com. If you can't track any down, replace the absinthe in this recipe with Pernod or Herbsaint.*

"They entered a small café and took an absinthe together, then resumed their walk along the pavement. Morissot stopped suddenly. 'Shall we have another absinthe?' he said. 'If you like,' agreed Monsieur Sauvage. And they entered another wine shop. **They were quite unsteady when they came out**, owing to the effect of the alcohol on their empty stomachs. It was a fine, mild day, and a gentle breeze fanned their faces."

GUY DE MAUPASSANT, *Two Friends*

Irish Rickey

Like many old drink families (even the breath-of-fresh-air ones like this, ones that you'd think would top the invite list at any spring or summer soiree), the Rickey has had many of its branches pruned off, to the point where you see only the Gin Rickey, if you see a Rickey, period. It's a sorry state of affairs, because the other Rickeys are also pleasant, and also **have that little smooch** of savoir-faire when you introduce them. I think the Irish Rickey is delightful from St. Paddy's Day until the setting sun on August 31. You don't even have to wear green every time you have it (though green looks so nice on you—why not wear it?).

Ice cubes

2½ ounces **Irish whiskey**

1 ounce **freshly squeezed lime juice**

½ ounce **Simple Syrup** (page 12)

Chilled club soda

Lime wedge for garnish

1. Fill a highball glass halfway full with ice cubes. Add the whiskey, lime juice, and simple syrup. Stir once.

2. Fill the glass with club soda, squeeze the lime wedge over it, and drop it in. Stir well.

VARIATIONS: As mentioned, there are many, many Rickeys—really, you can substitute in any base liquor for the Irish whiskey and you'll have a rum Rickey, brandy Rickey, and so on. You can also sub in liqueurs for the Irish whiskey and drop the simple syrup (as the liqueurs are already sweet). Two to try that make especially nice warm-weather play dates are apricot liqueur and maraschino liqueur (add maybe a splash of simple syrup with the latter). The one constant to remember is that you must use lime juice. Sometimes you see it made with lemon juice, and, well, that's not a Rickey at all.

King's Peg

It's good to be the king or queen. You get to sport a jeweled crown, drink King's Pegs from dusk till dawn, and wear one of those expansive, super-soft robes that are always dyed a deep red with a few gold sparkles and have that rim of fur around the top—a feature that's both warm and flattering. You also get the first choice of drumsticks, and get to sleep in a four-poster bed with whomever you want, and get to make proclamations and **have songs written about you** and played by the top lute-playing bards. In addition, you get to lay down taxes to pick up new robes, put down rebellions, execute popular anti-royalty politicians, watch as the people rise up, and perhaps spend a sour moment at the headman's block. You know, thinking about it, maybe drinking a bunch of King's Pegs while sitting in a lawn chair wearing a red T-shirt and a paper crown is the better route to take.

Ice cubes

2 ounces **Cognac**

Chilled brut Champagne or **sparkling wine**

1. Put one or two ice cubes in a Champagne flute. Add the Cognac.

2. Fill the flute with Champagne. Stir with a tiny scepter.

VARIATIONS: Supplant the Cognac with gin and you have a Queen's Peg. Bring in brandy instead, and you've only made it to a King's Pet. Add ½ ounce Simple Syrup (page 12) to the Cognac and Champagne, and you have an Ambrosia II. (For the original Ambrosia, see page 275.)

The Basics of Bubbly

Ah, there's nothing quite like the sound of a cork popping out of a bottle of Champagne or sparkling wine. The immense potential for a classy kind of fun, the gloss of shiny black shoes and shimmery pearls sliding around a dance floor, the chandelier sparkling off the smiles and the bubbles sliding up the sides of every glass—that cork removal is like the beginning of a really good dream brought to life. At least that's the way I think of it, which is why I enjoy not only the bubbly by itself, but also mixed with other items into drinks such as the Blue Train (page 96), Fair Skies (page 104), the Golden Lady (page 108), and many more. I enjoy it so much that I sometimes think of Champagne and sparkling wine in the same category as the main base liquors—though of course it's actually wine. A different kind of wine (which is somewhat stating the obvious but is good to remember), thanks to the second fermentation that it has within the bottle, which causes the bubbles. Though the fables may make it seem that the bubbling process and Champagne were invented by a French monk, Dom Perignon, this isn't really true. However, he did help modernize the production of Champagne, and he also helped to spread it and the love of it around. As far as I know, sparkling wine was first sold in the Limoux area of the Languedoc region within France around 1535. Since then, Champagne and sparkling wines have become more and more popular (with a nice bump in the 1700s), not to mention developing a long association with wedding toasts and other celebratory functions.

There are five types to watch for, going from driest to sweetest: brut, extra-dry, sec, demi-sec, and doux. To be called "Champagne," a sparkling wine has to be made in the region of France that shares its name (thanks to the Treaty of Madrid signed in 1891), but there is a host of other worthy sparkling wines, from France and throughout the world, that are also tasty and carry the same bubbly nature as the standard bearer, and it's fine to slip these in when making drinks that call for Champagne. It's a good idea to stick to a mid-range sparkler (but still one you know and trust) when mixing it, because other ingredients are going to alter the taste—and, as a bonus, the mid-range will help you save a few dollars without sacrificing taste, leaving more money to spend on more drinks.

"This relic of the Gay Nineties is a syrupy-sweet and **wholly deceptive** concoction."

DAVID A. EMBURY writing about the Lalla Rookh in
The Fine Art of Mixing Drinks, 1948

Lalla Rookh

A historic drink mostly lost in the annals of history, the Lalla Rookh traces its name back to a poem by Thomas Moore, first published in 1817. The poem is about the daughter of a Mughal emperor (her name is Lalla Rookh) who's engaged to some prince, but who meets a poet who sweeps her off her feet with poems and poetic-ness (those poets are so tricky, especially this one, as he turns out to be—*spoiler alert*—the prince). As you might expect from such a lovely tale, this one's a sweet sipper, best on those romantic summer evenings when the coo-coo between you and yours needs a trace of bubbly-ness for balance.

Ice cubes

1 ounce **Cognac**

1 ounce **dark rum**

1 ounce **vanilla liqueur**

½ ounce **Simple Syrup** (page 12)

½ ounce **heavy cream**

Chilled club soda

1. Fill a cocktail shaker halfway full with ice cubes. Add the Cognac, rum, vanilla liqueur, simple syrup, and cream. Shake poetically (which here means shake a lot, rhythmically).

2. Fill a highball glass halfway full with ice cubes. Strain the mix into the glass. Top with club soda and stir well (again, poetically).

Lazy Hazy

Golly, those lazy, hazy days of summer are swell (and if I sound too much like a kid in the 1950s, back off a little there—summer lets everyone **slip into a reverie** of their own choosing). Wait, let me make an addendum. Golly, those lazy, hazy days of summer are swell, provided you have the right assortment of liquor, liqueur, juice, and bubbles chilling in a glass in your hand, and the right assortment of pals, power-pop musical hits, and summer duds (think "less is more," 'cause it's hot out). Now, with that laid out like a Slip 'n Slide, *swell* doesn't sound so far off, does it?

Ice cubes

1½ ounces **bourbon**

1½ ounces **freshly squeezed orange juice**

½ ounce **Rhum Clément Créole Shrubb**

Chilled club soda

Orange slice for garnish

1. Fill a highball glass three-quarters full with ice cubes. Add the bourbon, orange juice, and Créole Shrubb. Stir briefly.

2. Fill the glass with club soda, stir well, and garnish with the orange slice.

Mamie Taylor

Gather round the kiddie pool, kiddies, and let old Uncle A.J. regale you with the tall tale of Mamie Taylor. Able to take the edge off a sweltering desert day, while still retaining her effervescence and keeping on her 10-gallon hat (or lemon slice—this tall tale's admittedly a little dusty in spots), Mamie Taylor was at home from the highlands to the high seas to the high plains—whenever and wherever revelers wanted to whip together an easy-but-tasty favorite. But then, sadly, she drifted into the sands of time, seemingly lost forever. But, kiddies, **you can bring her back**. Do it, and you'll soon have your own tales to tell.

Ice cubes

2 ounces **Scotch**

Chilled ginger ale

Lemon slice for garnish

1. Fill a highball glass three-quarters full with ice cubes. Add the Scotch.

2. Carefully fill the glass with ginger ale, and garnish with the lemon slice.

A VARIATION: No Scotch? Deputize dark rum in its place, and then switch the garnish from a lemon slice to a lime slice. You'll be drinking a Susie Taylor, and you'll want to talk about it.

Rhum Clément Créole Shrubb

A freshly popular orange liqueur that's only recently become available (and by "recently," I mean practically as I'm writing this—by the time you're reading this, I hope this liqueur will be available everywhere at all times), Rhum Clément Créole Shrubb comes from, like many of its brother and sister liqueurs, a legendary family recipe, passed from generation to generation, and contains an ingredient list that is kept mostly in secret. But there are a few key points known. First is the fact that it's made from a combination of white and aged rums. The aged rum traces its history back to the 1800s, when Homère Clément (a physician) decided to take a new route in making rum after researching Cognac and Armagnac distillers, using sugarcane (instead of the traditional molasses), which he crushed and fermented into a sugar wine, which was then distilled. This individualistic base of the Créole Shrubb is then mixed with white bitter curaçao orange peels and the alluded-to series of secret Créole spices. From this history and ingredient list was born a liqueur that's moderate in its sweetness, not quite as sweet as other orange varieties, one with a bright clean taste that boasts echoes of oranges as well as grapefruit and vanilla, cloves, cinnamon, nutmeg, and a hint of pepper on the back end. This creative flavor combination has made Créole Shrubb not only a blooming favorite with cocktail creators and slow sippers (as it's also superb solo over ice), but with cooks and chefs as well, as it makes a welcome addition to many savory dishes and desserts.

Morning Glory Fizz

Fizzes have been a bar staple since carbonation (or thereabouts), though at one point they were called "Fiz" with just one "z," as that extra "z" would have been thought of as ostentatious in the late 1800s, even in the A.M., which always was and ever should be the time of day a Fizz is consumed (see Derby Fizz, page 103, for another example), as they make mighty morning mixes, especially when you've had a few too many potent potables the night before. Of all the Fizz family, the Morning Glory, as might be expected from its name, is perhaps the one to break out in the most critical morning situations, as its bracing powers and ability to cut through the haze are mighty indeed. Admittedly, it may put you back into a haze if you have more than one, so be careful. The Morning Glory Fizz has taken a few turns along the years, as far as ingredients go, and on occasion you see it without the fruit juice, or without the absinthe or Pernod (used when absinthe wasn't legal here in the ol' U.S.A.), but I like this lineup. You'll appreciate it the next time you wake up woozy.

Ice cubes

1½ ounces **Scotch**

1 ounce **absinthe** or **Pernod**

1 ounce **Simple Syrup** (page 12)

½ ounce **freshly squeezed lemon juice**

½ ounce **freshly squeezed lime juice**

1 **egg white**

Chilled club soda

1. Fill a cocktail shaker halfway full with ice cubes. Add the Scotch, absinthe, simple syrup, lemon juice, lime juice, and egg white. Shake exceptionally well (I know it's morning, but rise to the occasion).

2. Fill a highball glass halfway full with ice cubes. Strain the mixture into the glass. Top with club soda, stir well, and watch the morning come into focus.

✖ *A Warning: As this contains a raw egg, don't serve it to the elderly or to those with compromised immune systems.*

⬆ *A Note: Here and there you'll see this made with bourbon instead of Scotch. I think the Scotch goes well with morning's significance (according to some, this is the most important drink of the day), but if you have only bourbon and need a bracer, it'll work dandy in Scotch's place.*

Morning Star

The Morning Star—sounds pure, doesn't it? As if it were a bright light over the horizon that you glimpse after staying up all night making a hard decision. You know you made the right one, because there it is, that one perfect star, coming to greet you. Maybe the Morning Star isn't the perfect drink, but it is darn fine, and a good choice as your liquid accompaniment in these sorts of momentous but happy up-all-night situations, as it has **a resolute but touchingly friendly nature**, with a mingling of Scotch, port, cream, and club soda. Plus, like most drinks with "morning" in the title, it contains an egg (see Morning Glory Fizz, opposite page, for further evidence). It may be true (though I have my doubts) that not every situation needs a specific drink to go with it, but life-changing situations often do. Remember that, and the Morning Star, the next time you've stayed up and wrestled out a considerable question. I'll bet you'll be glad for it.

Ice cubes

1½ ounces **Scotch**

1 ounce **ruby port**

1 ounce **heavy cream**

1 **egg**

Chilled club soda

1. Fill a cocktail shaker halfway full with ice cubes. Add the Scotch, port, cream, and egg. Shake really well (you'll appreciate stretching out those limbs after the long night).

2. Fill a highball glass three-quarters full with ice cubes. Strain the mix over the ice. Top with club soda. Stir well, if thoughtfully.

A VARIATION: There's another Morning Star recipe I've seen that uses rum, simple syrup, sherry, and an egg white. For significant situations, it doesn't seem as sincere as the above recipe, which is modified from one I found in Jacques Straub's 1914 book *Drinks*, if that history helps as you make your own history.

❌ *A Warning: As this contains a raw egg, don't serve it to the elderly or to those with compromised immune systems.*

New Orleans Buck

I go back with the Buck family. Back to at least 9:30 on the night of June 17, 1996. From the Orange Buck to the Nordic Buck to the New Orleans Buck, and even the matriarch, the plain Gin Buck, all the family members are welcome at my celebrations. They show up and instantly improve the party, thanks to their effervescence, their bursts of citrus, their quick repartee, their lovely and sturdy base, and their adaptability, as the Buck family fits in both at last-minute shorts-and-T-shirt wingdings as well as at more planned-out short-sleeved-collared-shirts and flowery-dress brunches. The New Orleans Buck goes especially well with a slightly spicy brunch, as the dark rum base dances well with piquant dishes.

Ice cubes

3 ounces **dark rum**

2 ounces **freshly squeezed orange juice**

2 ounces **chilled ginger ale**

Lime wedge for garnish

Lime slice for garnish

1. Fill a highball glass three-quarters full with ice cubes. Add the rum.

2. Carefully add the orange juice and the ginger ale at the same time. This way, neither important ingredient gets jealous. Stir briefly.

3. Squeeze the lime wedge over the glass, then let it join the mix. Garnish with the lime slice.

A Note: This version of the Buck a bit too buck-y for you? It's okay to drop the rum down just a bit, I suppose, but keep the ginger ale and orange juice in equal amounts, or else things will get ugly.

VARIATIONS: As mentioned, there are a number of Bucks worth trying. For an Orange Buck, substitute gin for rum, and for a Nordic Buck, sub in vodka. For a classic Gin Buck, make it with gin and no orange juice.

A Warning: I feel I've warned everyone in America about this, but I want to warn you, too (just in case). After a couple of Bucks, partakers will probably start slipping phrases such as "Buck you" and "That's bucked up" into their conversation. Which means you probably should, too.

"As he **warmed up under the influence** of Randulf's old Jamaica rum, he forgot both his internal malady and his anxieties for his soul."

ALEXANDER L. KIELLAND, *Skipper Worse*

Northside Special

If, when hearing the name Northside Special, you think of a possible snowstorm ripping down the mountains to drop heaps of flakes on your town, then you need to step back, take a deep breath, and reroute your thinking. Because the Northside Special is **a tall, bouncy, cooling combo**, but it isn't bitterly cold, and it tends to shine as an accessory to a beach party—maybe one where you need the right drink as you show off that cute new swimsuit that ties around the neck to promote even tanning, or those rad new swim trunks with the octopus on them.

Ice cubes

2 ounces **dark rum**

2 ounces **freshly squeezed orange juice**

1½ ounces **Simple Syrup** (page 12)

¼ ounce **freshly squeezed lemon juice**

Chilled club soda

1. Fill a Collins glass three-quarters full with ice cubes. Add the rum, orange juice, simple syrup, and lemon juice. Stir once.

2. Fill the glass almost to the top with club soda. Stir well, and remember, there's no snow on the horizon.

⬆ *A Note: I've heard tell of this made sans lemon juice, but I feel that it should be included if at all possible, to keep that flirty orange juice in check.*

O Happy Day

Don't fret, those of you who know of my singing prowess. I'm not going to profane the song that shares this border-crossing refresher's name by belting it out full force every time I'm serving it. It does deserve the vocalized adulation, though. Maybe you, if you have the pipes, should **do a refrain when consuming**. I'll just hum along loudly between sips.

Ice cubes

2 ounces **Canadian whisky**

1 ounce **Heering cherry liqueur**

Chilled **ginger ale**

Lemon slice for garnish

1. Fill a highball glass three-quarters full with ice cubes. Add the whisky and cherry liqueur. Stir briefly with a conductor's baton or long spoon.

2. Add enough ginger ale to almost fill the glass. Stir a bit more.

3. Squeeze the lemon slice over the bubbling ginger ale, then drop it in.

⬆ *A Note: Cherry Heering is a Danish cherry liqueur that's been made from all-natural ingredients— including Danish cherries—since 1818.*

Ponce de León

The first governor of Puerto Rico, a comrade of Christopher Columbus on his second voyage to the New World, probably the first Old World-er to discover Florida, generally a busy late-1400s/early-1500s kind of guy, Ponce de León is, and rightfully so, remembered most for his desire for—and failure to find—the fountain of youth. He tried hard, too, with multiple expeditions (or at least that's what the history books say), yearning as so many do for a few more hours on planet Earth. Here's the saddest part: If he had been able to hang around a couple hundred years longer, he would have discovered this drink, which is named after him. This drink won't make you stop aging, but it will, when taken in the right amount with the right friends and loved ones, help you **enjoy the time you have** even more. And that, according to this humble deckhand, is so much more worthwhile than searching for a nonexistent fountain.

Ice cubes

1 ounce **Cognac**

½ ounce **white rum**

½ ounce **Cointreau**

½ ounce **freshly squeezed grapefruit juice**

Chilled brut Champagne or **sparkling wine**

1. Fill a cocktail shaker halfway full with ice cubes. Add the Cognac, rum, Cointreau, and grapefruit juice. Shake well.

2. Strain the elixir into a cocktail glass. Fill the glass not quite to the top with the Champagne. Serve with a youthful grin.

⬆ *A Note: This was originally served in a saucer-style Champagne glass, which, unfortunately, you don't see much of behind the bar anymore. I've placed it in a cocktail glass here, to have the more wide-open personality it would have had in a saucer-style glass. If you have that type of Champagne glass, though, use it and call me so I can partake, too.*

Presbyterian

The Presbyterian first became a hit during secular and nonsecular box dinners, those events where eligible ladies would arrive with a piping-hot homemade meal (in a box, I presume), and where the eligible fellas would then bid on individual box dinners—and the chance to eat it with the lady who made it. The Presbyterian came into play when the fellas decided they needed a bidding booster to get their courage up, but didn't want to be seen hitting the courage straight out of the bottle. A tall, invigorating drink named after a religion could be seen as safe. Well, that's the story I'm telling. What you need to know is that if you're at a summer dinner of any kind and need to boost your courage to **enter into a rapport** with a certain lady or fella, and don't want to get it straight out of the bottle, treat my story as fact and follow in its footsteps with a Presbyterian.

Ice cubes

1½ ounces **bourbon**

Chilled club soda

Chilled ginger ale

Lemon twist for garnish

A Note: On occasion, the Presbyterian (also called the Pres behind a few dancehalls) has been made with 7UP instead of ginger ale. My choice is ginger ale, but serving it with 7UP certainly isn't a sin.

1. Fill a highball glass three-quarters full with ice cubes. Add the bourbon.

2. Gently add equal parts club soda and ginger ale to the glass at the same time, filling it almost to the top. Stir about 6 times (the stirring also helps with the courage).

3. Garnish with the lemon twist.

Roffignac

Here it is, duchesses and dukes, a nonchalantly regal concoction that turns a hot-weather fête from flat to *fantastique*, that **transforms guests from fuddy-duddies** into fabulous, that adds a delightful dollop of fizzy fun (or what the French might call *un plaisir pétillant*), and that shows you off as the host or hostess who knows how to live right.

Ice cubes

2 ounces **Cognac**

½ ounce **raspberry syrup**

Chilled club soda

1. Fill a highball glass three-quarters full with ice cubes. Add the Cognac and syrup. Stir with flair.

2. Fill the glass with club soda, and stir again.

⬆ *A Note:* *This can be made with grenadine or red Hembarig instead of raspberry syrup. I think raspberry syrup stands out more than grenadine, and red Hembarig isn't easily found, but do what you have to.*

Rum Rascal

Ah, you rascal, you. Slipping in a little dark rum with a little lime and pineapple juice, a touch of that Caribbean favorite orange curaçao, and a blast of bouncy ginger ale to **create a tropical tonic** that fits like sand on a beach into a swaying and smooth party, even one that's miles inland, one that only gets to approximate the tropics, one where the closest body of water is the ice that's melted in the ice bucket. Remember, any place is a good place for a party, if you have the right state of mind. The rascal state of mind, that is.

Ice cubes

2½ ounces **dark rum**

1 ounce **orange curaçao**

1 ounce **fresh pineapple juice**

½ ounce **freshly squeezed lime juice**

Chilled ginger ale

1. Fill a Collins glass or large goblet halfway full with ice cubes. Add the rum, curaçao, pineapple juice, and lime juice. Stir, but without sweating it.

2. Top the glass off with ginger ale, almost to the top. Stir again.

A VIRGIN VARIATION: Omit the rum and curaçao, and add 2 ounces freshly squeezed orange juice and 1 ounce simple syrup (page 12). Call it the Little Rascal.

⬆ *A Note:* *If this Rascal is too naked for you, garnish with a lime slice, two pineapple chunks, or a combination of those two fruits.*

Saratoga

It's fitting, I think, that a cocktail like this shares its name with a significant battle from the American Revolution that is usually referred to in the singular, but that actually took place over two different battles (the Battle of Freeman's Farm and the Battle of Bemis Heights), which were actually 18 days apart. Why so fitting? Because there are also multiple versions of the Saratoga drink, though usually referred to under the one name (only sometimes with a #1 or #2 tacked on). Of the versions out there, one **shines like a rocket's red glare** for me, because of its interesting-but-well-combined list of ingredients (brandy and a little pineapple juice, maraschino, and Angostura), and because of its final coup de grâce: two splashes of club soda.

Ice cubes

2 ounces **brandy**

1 ounce **fresh pineapple juice**

½ ounce **maraschino liqueur**

2 dashes **Angostura bitters**

Chilled club soda

1. Fill a cocktail shaker halfway full with ice cubes. Add the brandy, pineapple juice, maraschino liqueur, and bitters. Shake well.

2. Strain into a cocktail glass. Top off with two splashes of club soda.

A VARIATION: Want to go a completely different, no-bubbles route? Mix up 1 ounce apple brandy, 1 ounce sweet vermouth, ½ ounce Dubonnet Rouge, and ½ ounce freshly squeezed orange juice. You could still call it a Saratoga, but I don't think it has the same oomph.

A VIRGIN VARIATION: Want the Saratoga without an army backup? I've seen yet a third version that contains just 1 ounce freshly squeezed lemon juice, ½ ounce Simple Syrup (page 12), and 2 dashes Angostura bitters over ice in a highball glass, topped with ginger ale.

The Settler

I've watched my fair share of the show *Little House on the Prairie* (spending formative years in Kansas is my excuse, but to be straight I also just watched the episode with the raccoon named Jasper, who becomes a pet for a while, about an hour ago). Never in any episode, though, did I see Pa Ingalls sit back, light his pipe, and have Ma or one of the girls bring him a drink quite this refined yet merry. Blackberry wine? Sure. Cognac and crème de cassis and carbonation? Sadly, no. Does that mean you shouldn't have this when watching the family come to grips with various frontier and townie issues? Nope. It just gives you one more reason to be glad you're watching it, and not living it.

Ice cubes

2 ounces **Cognac**

1 ounce **crème de cassis**

Chilled club soda

1. Fill a highball glass three-quarters full with ice cubes. Add the Cognac and crème de cassis.

2. Top the glass off with club soda. Stir with a whittled tree branch or hickory stick.

Sleepy Head

"Hey, Sleepy Head," those bright-eyed-and-caffeine-buzzed people call out as you lean languidly against a wall. Go ahead, enjoy the moment, laugh at those rushing by while drinking a Sleepy Head, happy in your knowledge that life is meant to be sipped and savored and not just passed through.

1 **orange wheel**

5 to 6 **fresh mint leaves**

Ice cubes

2 ounces **brandy**

Chilled club soda

Orange twist for garnish

A Note: All this fruit too much for your sleepy teeth? It's okay to strain the mix out of the cocktail shaker (you'll have to add ice to the glass first) instead of pouring it. The proper name for this version is Sleepy Smile, though.

1. Add the orange wheel and the mint leaves to a cocktail shaker. Using a muddler or wooden spoon, muddle the fruit well.

2. Fill the cocktail shaker halfway full with ice cubes. Add the brandy. Shake, but don't feel the need to wake up too much.

3. Pour the contents of the shaker (ice and all) into an old-fashioned glass. Fill the glass with club soda, and stir briefly.

4. Squeeze the orange twist over the glass and drop it in.

Snow Ball

Watch out! Watch out! The Snow Balls are flying, chilling out (and I mean that in the actual temperature-dropping way, not the "you need to calm down" way) any in their path who want to **whoop it up without boiling over**, providing a frothy balance to a sizzling afternoon. They do take some shaking (much like their condensed counterparts take some packing), so don't think there isn't any sweat involved. The results are more than worth it, though—so chill out.

Ice cubes

2 ounces **brandy**

1 ounce **Simple Syrup** (page 12)

1 **egg**

Chilled ginger ale

1. Fill a cocktail shaker halfway full with ice cubes. Add the brandy, simple syrup, and egg. Shake very well.

2. Fill a Collins glass three-quarters full with ice cubes. Strain the well-shaken mix over the ice.

3. Top the glass off with ginger ale. Stir, but calmly.

❌ *A Warning: As this does contain a raw egg, it shouldn't be served to the elderly or to those with compromised immune systems.*

Spring in Your Step

When March 20 rolls around every year, don't you feel like skipping down the lane, even if it's raining, or snowing, or hailing, or cold enough that winter doesn't seem to be ready to leave anytime soon? If you don't, and therefore need a little outside push to have you believing that spring has in fact sprung, and that **before long flowers will be bursting** into bloom, then try inviting your spring posse over to share in a big round of Spring in Your Steps, and watch how soon the season changes. That nasty old winter will be far behind you in the rear view before the second glass is poured. You know, now that I think of it, the first day of spring should be a national holiday, and the Spring in Your Step should be its official drink. Let's lobby together and make it happen.

Ice cubes

1½ ounces **rye**

½ ounce **freshly squeezed lemon juice**

½ ounce **Citrónge**

½ ounce **Simple Syrup** (page 12)

Chilled club soda

Orange slice for garnish (optional)

1. Fill a highball glass halfway full with ice cubes. Add the rye, lemon juice, Citrónge, and simple syrup. Stir briefly with a long green spoon (or a silver spoon—but pretend it's green).

2. Fill the glass almost to the rim with club soda. Stir again, briefly, with that long spoon.

3. Garnish with an orange slice if necessary (depending on how much spring you want to take in at this early-season sitting).

⤴ *A Note: Citrónge is an all-natural orange liqueur from Mexico, which uses a combination of sweet Jamaican oranges and bittersweet Haitian oranges, along with a neutral grain spirit and pure cane sugar. The result is a liqueur that has layers of orange flavor, changing as it crosses your tongue.*

Tip Top

Never has a drink so lent itself to happy viewpoints, a jolly stance, and a jaunty reply than when a bash-thrower asks a consumer (a.k.a. guest) how everything's going. The answer inevitably mirrors this classy-yet-gallivanting drink, because it's nigh impossible for anyone with a Tip Top in hand to not feel tiptop. The only worry is that those drinking Tip Tops will be so outwardly hunky-dory that they might cause any melancholy souls to leave the merrymaking—though, now that I think about it, they weren't much of an addition anyway.

Ice cubes

1½ ounces **brandy**

½ ounce **Benedictine**

½ ounce **freshly squeezed lemon juice**

½ ounce **Simple Syrup** (page 12)

Chilled brut Champagne or **sparkling wine**

1. Fill a cocktail shaker halfway full with ice cubes. Add the brandy, Benedictine, lemon juice, and simple syrup. Shake jovially.

2. Fill a highball glass halfway full with ice cubes. Strain the amusing mix over the ice and into the glass.

3. Cheerily but carefully (there's no need to bring a cloud into all this sunshine with spilled bubbly), fill the glass with Champagne. Stir, again carefully.

"She had another pull of rye that would have knocked me kicking. **She might have been drinking water** for all the effect it had. Her stomach, I thought, must have been installed by the Bethlehem Steel Company."

HAROLD Q. MASUR, *Suddenly a Corpse*, 1949

Vick's Zither

Vick, pally, I'm not sure who you are, or how a drink with your name ended up in a little bound volume called *Ronrico's Official Mixtro's Guide*, put out in 1954 by the folks at Ronrico rum to advertise their liquors with recipes (a common practice at one time), but I'm thankful you and your zither made it. The combination named after you features a fine and graceful mingling of rum, apricot brandy, and citrus, **a mingling that brings a refined panache** to evening gatherings in the summer, the type of gatherings I think you would like, and might play your zither at, sitting on a wicker lawn chair under a cherry tree.

Ice cubes

1½ ounces **dark rum**

½ ounce **apricot brandy**

½ ounce **freshly squeezed lemon juice**

½ ounce **Simple Syrup** (page 12)

Chilled club soda

Orange slice for garnish

Maraschino cherry for garnish

1. Fill a cocktail shaker halfway full with ice cubes. Add the rum, brandy, lemon juice, and simple syrup. Shake well.

2. Fill a highball glass halfway full with ice cubes. Strain the mix into the glass. Top off with club soda. Stir, but be considerate about it, for Vick's sake.

3. Garnish with an orange slice and a cherry. Attach them together (if you think they'll be lonely) with a toothpick.

⬆ *A Note: All that fruit making you feel less delicate and more drama-queen? Drop down to just an orange slice if you must.*

⬆ *A Second Note: All that thanks for Vick and his zither above almost made me forget: Thanks also to Anthony Mamunes, who originally owned the copy of* Ronrico's Official Mixtro's Guide *that I'm now in possession of. It's still in great shape.*

Support Your Local- and Worldwide-Cocktail

You look like a keeper. You're oodles of kicks, you clench your fists only in joy, as when a bosom companion buys you another Bosom Caresser (page 146) or other cool imbibable, and you aren't slow to buy a round for the fellas and fillies your own self. Among the best of the bunch of facets of your personality (if not *the* best) is that you like learning more about cocktails and other drinks, and want to keep the cocktail-learning and revolution charging forward. What to do, though—you may ask yourself, on occasion, after a couple of drinks—to offer your support? I'm here to suggest the following ideas.

1. Be creative, by trying new things. A good way to do this (and I hope this doesn't sound too self-promoting) is to pick up cocktail books that catch your eye and dive right into the recipe section. Then introduce your friends to said books and recipes when you're slinging the drinks at home.

2. Listen to your bartenders, both professional and home-style. Once you find a good pro or become pals with a home pro, step into the mode of asking for a "bartender's choice" and see what delights are brought forth (check out the chapter of the same name on page 55, too). But always, always make sure the bartender isn't so busy as to have it be an imposition. And, this should go without saying, but I'll say it: Always, when out, tip well. Those folks are working hard for you.

3. Get a membership to the Museum of the American Cocktail: www.museumoftheamericancocktail.org. This nonprofit organization is "dedicated to preserving and celebrating the history and culture of the American Cocktail," and you'll dig both being a member and supporting those very cocktails that give you so much joy. Don't forget to visit the permanent collection in New Orleans, too.

4. Take a trip down to Tales of the Cocktail, which happens in July and which is "a culinary and cocktail festival [that] allows the connoisseur or amateur to fully experience (taste, see, and learn about) cocktail culture in New Orleans and around the world." You'll be surrounded by folks who have the same cocktail interest as you, and that's worth cheering about. Drink in the details at www.talesofthecocktail.com.

Washington's Wish

Now, I wouldn't make such a bold statement as to assert that this lively liquid assemblage is going to automatically be "first in big parties, first in small parties, and first in the hearts of party-goers everywhere," as one famous saying has it. George Washington himself, history says, did have a soft spot for the Washington's Wish. (I think the cherry and apple-y flavors **went straight to his heart**, not to mention the brandy warming him up on those cold Mount Vernon nights.) And if it's good enough for the first president of the United States, that's quite an endorsement.

Ice cubes

2 ounces **brandy**

¾ ounce **Apfelkorn**

½ ounce **grenadine**

Chilled brut Champagne or **sparkling wine**

Maraschino cherry for garnish

1. Fill a cocktail shaker halfway full with ice cubes. Add the brandy, Apfelkorn, and grenadine. Shake patriotically.

2. Strain the mixture into a Champagne flute, and top with chilled Champagne. Stir with a thin spoon three times.

3. Sensibly drop the cherry into the glass (sensibly or you'll spill, which would be a sad affair—no lying).

A Note: Apfelkorn is a German apple liqueur, slightly sweet but with a full apple taste.

A Second Note: All history books that have George Washington talking about his love for this drink are, from what I can tell, out of print. Or, he didn't actually say it. But I'm pretty sure that if he were here, and you served him one of these, he'd smile widely, showing every one of his presidential teeth.

Dim the Lights, Chill the Cocktails

Maybe you're decked out in a gray gabardine three-piece number that you save for such intimate evenings,
or maybe it's a more modern Dior getup and wingtips shined so shiny. Or maybe you're slipping that perfectly shimmery black spaghetti-strap sheath on, the one that goes down low enough, but not too low, or a silhouette number in crimson. Maybe you're taking it a bit lower in key, with slightly roughed-up dungarees and a hip tee, or white short shorts (but not too short—you need to sell it a bit) and a spring-y tank. Or, maybe you'll go my favorite smooth style, with an early 1960s Monte Carlo after-dark vibe, all big sunglasses, laughter, and a bouncy skirt. Hmm, so many choices, and you haven't even decided what music to have on when your paramour comes through the door. At least, thanks to this chapter, you have a choice of drinks that'll fit any occasion.

Any romantic occasion, that is, because on the following pages you'll be able to choose from a cooing assortment of lovers' lovely elixirs (all scaled for two, because it takes two to tango). We have potions ideal for cozy celebrations *à deux* on the couch with a little mellow music or a classic Hepburn/Tracy flick (the Ambiance, for example, or the Sweet Dream). There are also drinks perfect for outdoor afternoons when you and yours are skipping through a field of strawberry flowers, having a picnic on a checkered cloth, flying a smiling kite, or curling up like cats under a tree. (May I suggest the Highland Fling, the Wildflower, or the Blossom?)

Wait, you say, what about a long moonlit hand-in-hand amble over a short bridge that's spanning a trickling creek in our favorite park, as the grass lightly bends in the light breeze and the stars turn the water into a milky way? Well, if it were me, I'd be bringing along a Lover's

Moon or a Paradiso. And what about those more flirtatious evenings that might not end up at the end of an aisle with crying bridesmaids and blushing groomsmen on either side—can't we have fun, frisky drinks? My barroom-eyes maker, let me introduce you to the Dalliance and the Brace Up.

But, I can hear the slyer one or two of you asking, what about those romantic moments that aren't maybe quite as sweet, but are maybe a little more, um, sexy—those where there might somehow be a fluffy rug in front of the fireplace and a few diaphanous garments that might not stay in place for long, or those when there's a riveting game of strip Quiddler being played? Don't these moments deserve drinks, too? Indeed, and that's why we also have the Bosom Caresser, the Temptation Cocktail, and the Natural.

And that's just the beginning of our trip into the cocktail tunnel of love. Oh, and if you're still sweating the music, a little tip: You can't go wrong with Al Green (if you want to go classic) or The National Trust (if you want a little modern musical mood magic).

Six Movie Bars to Visit

Many want to be in pictures, and some (like me) just think it'd be a kick to visit some famous fictional movie bars, starting with (or finishing at) these five.

1. Terminal Bar, _Who Framed Roger Rabbit_. The customers may be down and out, but they sure stick up for the 'toons. If only a "shave and a haircut" weren't so deadly.

2. Mos Eisley Cantina, _Star Wars_. Sure, it's a bit tough, and they don't let droids in, but wow, those futuristic drinks are out of this world.

3. The Winchester, _Shaun of the Dead_. Need to escape the horde of zombies crawling the streets outside? Or solely want to enjoy the interesting customers? This one's a good spot for both.

4. Hartner's Paints and Varnishes, _The Roaring Twenties_. Okay, you have to get past the actual paint store first, but once in the backroom speakeasy, you'll get Gin Bucks and James Cagney.

5. The Velvet Onion, _The Mighty Boosh_, season three. Admittedly, this is a TV show, but it's BBC, so you have to watch it on DVD like a movie. In the Velvet Onion, find far-out musical stylings, fashion, and lovable freakiness.

6. The Charles's living room bar, _The Thin Man_. Learn how to shake from Nick Charles, watch Nora drink six Martinis, and pet Asta, one of the movies' most lovable mutts.

Ambiance

The lights are dimmed, or perhaps off altogether, replaced by a number of candles (some pillars on the mantle, some tea lights on the table), the throw pillows are thrown with modest disarray on the couch, that book with the lovely pictures of rural France is angled on the coffee table's top, the music is subdued, but with **a touch of mysterious intrigue** in it (Chicago's own Aerial M perhaps, or a touch of Chopin's nocturnes, or, if a slight upbeat is needed here and there, the British group the Cinematic Orchestra), and you, you're wearing that ideal off-black outfit, relaxed but with a hint of sexy. This would be perfect, if only you had a drink to match the mood. Well, now you do. **Serves 2**

Ice cubes

4 ounces **Cognac**

2 ounces **Benedictine**

1 ounce **Simple Syrup** (page 12)

2 **lemon twists** for garnish (optional)

1. Fill a cocktail shaker halfway full with ice cubes. Add the Cognac, Benedictine, and simple syrup. Shake well, but not so well that you go outside of the room's current state of mind.

2. Strain equally into two cocktail glasses and garnish each with a lemon twist if that fits the atmosphere. Serve with only the hint of a smile.

"It was by now eleven and after, a disheveled mass of tortured napkins, sprawled flowers, **glassware tinged with repeated refills** of red wines and white; Champagne and kirsch and little upright thimbles of Benedictine for the ladies, no two alike at the same level of consumption."

CORNELL WOOLRICH, *Waltz into Darkness*, 1947

Bedroom Eyes

While both may be precocious and have just what it takes to make a pro blush (so to speak), I'm not sure Bette Davis's eyes are exactly the same as bedroom eyes. For one, I don't think there's a drink named after them. And for two, bedroom eyes are much more personal, and a touch harder to fake because of it (when that right person is giving you their specific bedroom eyes, you know it, and feel those happy goose bumps start to rise). This drink is also hard to fake, because it has to be made with real apricot liqueur. Apricot schnapps or apricot syrup are too sugary—track down the good stuff, serve it in this smooth mix to that special someone giving you bedroom eyes, and thank me at the wedding. **Serves 2**

Ice cubes

4 ounces **dark rum**

2 ounces **apricot liqueur**

1 ounce **crème de cacao**

1. Fill a cocktail shaker halfway full with ice cubes. Add the rum, apricot liqueur, and crème de cacao. Shake well, while focusing on those eyes.

2. Strain equally into two cocktail glasses. Garnish each with nothing but a look.

4 Matrimonial Mixes

Dum dum da dum, dum dum da dum . . . just humming the beginning of the wedding march brings a vision of white dresses with long trains, smiling faces, lots of blooming flowers, and a scrumptious cake—not to mention tears—to my eyes. Tears of happiness, of course, because this special couple is serving one or two or more of the following.

1 Blushing Bride (page 145)

2 Sweet Dream (page 171)

3 Lalla Rookh (page 115)

4 Lover's Moon (page 161)

Between the Sheets

It's a strange twisty fate that this drink has had, though I suppose one somewhat to be expected with its amorous title, as it's probably always going to be thought of first as a silly amalgamation constructed by collegians who want every beverage to have a come-on of a name, in hopes that the object of their attraction might be amused. But, actually, it's a well-balanced concern, one that has been around the bar for quite a while (at least since Patrick Gavin Duffy's 1934 *Official Mixer's Manual*), shaking up brandy and rum together with a few friends. Remember when ordering or making this up for that gentleman or lady across the way with whom you'd like to flirt a little (in a liquid manner): You have history on your side between those sheets. **Serves 2**

Ice cubes

1½ ounces **brandy**

1½ ounces **dark rum**

1½ ounces **Cointreau**

1 ounce **freshly squeezed lemon juice**

½ ounce **Simple Syrup** (page 12)

2 **lemon twists** for garnish

1. Fill a cocktail shaker halfway full with ice cubes. Add the brandy, rum, Cointreau, lemon juice, and simple syrup. Shake in a manner that's suave, yet sophisticated.

2. Strain the sheets equally into two cocktail glasses. Squeeze a lemon twist over each glass, and then let those twists slide right into the drink.

A VARIATION: I believe it's best to get Between the Sheets with rum and brandy, but there have been past occasions where the party's only brandy-based. Try it, if you're rum deficient, and see if the results are as silky.

Black Pearl

Even if a certain movie franchise highlights a ship of the same name, this is not a pirate reference in the least (argh, you'll need to visit the chapter called Dark Drinks That Go Bump in the Night for that, page 183). The Black Pearl is an exquisite arrangement that you should serve to your favorite elegant other on special occasions (especially anniversaries of first kisses, surprise birthday celebrations, and alternate Fridays). **Serves 2**

Ice cubes

2 ounces **Cognac**

2 ounces **Tia Maria liqueur**

Chilled brut Champagne or **sparkling wine**

2 **maraschino cherries** for garnish

1. Fill a cocktail shaker halfway full with ice cubes. Add the Cognac and Tia Maria. Shake as if you were diving for a Tahitian black pearl (the rare ones).

2. Strain the mix into two Champagne flutes or white wine glasses. Carefully fill the glasses with Champagne, almost to the top. Drop a cherry into each glass (also carefully), or spear them with a toothpick and balance them on top of the glasses.

> ⬆ *A Note: Tia Maria has a deep coffee taste that's miraculous in this drink. The exact recipe for Tia Maria, like most liqueurs, is a closely guarded secret, but the ingredients include Jamaican coffee, vanilla, sugar, and a cane-based spirit.*

Blossom

Isn't it a delicious fact of nature how love can bloom? Sometimes it starts with a bang, but often it starts slowly, slowly, opening itself up first to a friendly stage, then opening more over time as those roots start to take hold. Then you're in the middle of this amazing flower-like situation, where every day is a special glance, or a touch like a firecracker, or a realization that life, after all, is wonderful. It's a delicious fact, also, that there's a drink that goes with that realization. **Serves 2**

Ice cubes

4 ounces **dark rum**

1 ounce **freshly squeezed lime juice**

1 ounce **fresh pineapple juice**

1. Fill a cocktail shaker halfway full with ice cubes. Add the rum, lime juice, and pineapple juice. Shake well (hey, you're glowing).

2. Strain the love into two cocktail glasses. Serve with a kiss.

What Makes It a
Maraschino (Cherry, That Is)?

You might think (because it would be the first obvious notion) that the maraschino cherry serving as a garnish in many cocktail recipes was a Marasca cherry (the same cherry whose fruit and pits are used to make maraschino liqueur—see page 150). And, if you'd lived a hundred years ago, you'd be right. It was during that time, and earlier, when all cherries sold under the moniker "maraschino" were actually Marasca cherries, preserved in maraschino liqueur.

But today, cherries found under the maraschino name tend to be a lighter-colored example of the species, most often Royal Ann but also the mighty Rainier, that have been dyed red and preserved in sugar syrup. This change happened gradually, but the final push to storing cherries in something other than alcohol occurred during that old enemy of all right-thinking people: Prohibition. An Oregon professor named Ernest H. Wiegand wanted to polish up a reliable brine solution, though supposedly he said that it had nothing to do with the fact that alcohol was illegal at the time. By 1940, the FDA defined them as "cherries which have been dyed red, impregnated with sugar, and packed in a sugar sirup flavored with oil of bitter almonds or a similar flavor."

Today, if you're looking for maraschino cherries, find a brand that promises organic cherries and runs lighter on the preservatives and heavier on the natural ingredients. (Look for some at Princess Pickled, www.princess pickled.com, including Tillen Farms All-Natural Merry Maraschinos, which you can also find at www.tillenfarms.com.) You might also try looking in high-end liquor stores for Luxardo maraschino cherries, which are made from Marasca cherries.

If you want to try, you can easily pack your own cherries in maraschino liqueur (though you'll probably have a hard time finding fresh Marasca cherries and will have to use Royal Ann or Rainier). Just fill a jar almost all the way with the cherries, then cover them with the liqueur. Let sit for two weeks, then taste one. If it's not quite sweet enough, pour off a little liqueur (and by "pour off" I mean "into a drink") and add some simple syrup (page 12). Stir, let sit for two more weeks, then start using them. In the liqueur, they'll stay good for at least six months.

Blushing Bride

Ah, that's a sight to behold: A bride genuinely blushing in this day and age makes one feel sappy from the toes of those rented tux shoes up to the top of the cake. Be sure and **run over to that open bar** (I'm guessing it's that kind of a wedding—or hoping so, for your sake) and order her up a Blushing Bride. You may have to walk the bartender through it (and don't forget to tip), though, as he or she may not have heard of it, or may have heard tell of a different version. (I've seen a drink of this title made with as far-reaching ingredients as peach schnapps and Champagne or Chambord and vanilla vodka.) If you want to stay on the bride's good side, and not turn that blushing to a quick bit of temper, I suggest sticking with the following. **Serves 2**

12 **fresh raspberries**

6 **lime wedges**

Ice cubes

4 ounces **Cognac**

2 ounces **vodka**

1 ounce **Simple Syrup** (page 12)

1. Put the raspberries and 4 of the lime wedges into a cocktail shaker. Using a muddler, wooden spoon, or stiletto-heeled bridesmaid's shoe, muddle well.

2. Fill the cocktail shaker halfway full with ice cubes. Add the Cognac, vodka, and simple syrup. Shake in a celebratory manner.

3. Strain the mix equally into two cocktail glasses. Garnish each with a remaining lime wedge.

Bosom Caresser

Hey, you, don't start thinking that because you sidle up in that fancy western shirt with the shiny buttons and present one of these frothy mergers for that sweet gal or guy you've had your eye on since the party began (no matter how late in the evening) that said presentation entitles you to start getting handsy. That's going to end with the drink on your head, as opposed to in anyone's mouth, and you'll look idiotic besides. Give one of these enticing (and enticingly named) tipplers without any secondary motives outside of your love of giving good drinks, though, and who knows what might happen. Serves 2

Ice cubes

4 ounces **brandy**

2 ounces **orange curaçao**

1 ounce **grenadine**

2 **egg yolks**

1. Fill a cocktail shaker halfway full with ice cubes. Add everything else (except your wandering hands). Shake really well, for at least 10 seconds.

2. Strain the caresser into two glasses (you could call the glass the caressed in this situation), making sure both get their fair share.

⬆ *A Note: Though it seems to be more fabric and less fantastic, in* Crosby Gaige's 1941 Cocktail Guide and Ladies' Companion, *he calls this the Brassiere.*

✖ *A Warning: As this contains raw eggs, you shouldn't serve it to the elderly or to those with compromised immune systems.*

Four for Festive Anniversaries

It's a joy to celebrate the day wedded bliss began, but sometimes tough to know the perfect gift. Having the ideal drink to go along with the celebration, though, is now much easier—at least for the following four anniversaries:

Eighth: In modern times, this one matches up with linens, making a Between the Sheets (page 141) a fine fit.

Eleventh: Though your relationship isn't tarnished, I still suggest a Rusty Nail (page 43) here—as it is, in the traditional sense, the steel anniversary, and nails are (well, the nonliquid kind) made of steel.

Twelfth: This is a bejeweled or be-pearled commemoration, so you know it's going to be sparkly. This is why a Black Pearl (page 142) is the ideal bubbling accompaniment.

Fiftieth: The golden anniversary should have a celebratory beverage befitting its legacy. The Golden Lady (page 108) is the perfect pick.

Brace Up

Here and there (and at certain ages and for certain folks, everywhere), romance can be daunting. Say you spot a special someone in the corner who looks a touch like Natalie Portman, or a bit like a young Johnny Depp, depending on your perspective and degree of movie star worship (if you have none, let's agree instead to say that the person in question is what the kids might call a "hottie"). Walking up to that lovely sometimes seems more significant a task than scaling Everest—with a potentially colder response. My advice, young romantic? A quickly sipped Brace Up. After that, remember that lovely is **probably a bit shy**, and would probably like a Brace Up, too. **Serves 2**

Ice cubes

4 ounces **brandy**

1 ounce **anisette**

1 ounce **Simple Syrup** (page 12)

½ ounce **freshly squeezed lemon juice**

4 dashes **Angostura bitters**

⌃ *A Note: Anisette is (as you might guess) an anise-flavored liqueur that's slightly sweet, and usually has a lower alcohol content than other liqueurs.*

1. Fill a cocktail shaker halfway full with ice cubes. Add the brandy, anisette, simple syrup, lemon juice, and those dashes of bitters. Shake well, while thinking of the right words to say (keep it simple).

2. Strain the mixture equally into two cocktail glasses. Drink up and start walking.

A VARIATION: There's a modified version (perhaps it's even the progenitor of this version) called a Bracer that adds 1 egg and a splash of soda (at the end) to the recipe. I feel an egg and soda combo is a bit much for a nervous stomach to handle (and prefer the vigor of the above without it). If you need a higher level of sustenance, add them.

Caribbean Bloom

A rummy shout-out to the sweltering honeymoon spot south of the American continental coasts, the Caribbean Bloom—besides having a peppy floral taste—helps the new couple get over any trepidation about appearing on sandy beaches in skimpy bathing suits (or less, depending on the beach and the mood). Wait a minute, though—don't forget that high-SPF sunscreen before **taking the drinks to the beach,** or the bloom won't be one of romance, but of sunburn, which dampens honeymoon affections but quick. **Serves 2**

1 teaspoon **dried hibiscus flowers**

4 **lime wedges**

2 teaspoons **granulated sugar**

Cracked ice

4 ounces **dark rum**

1. Add the hibiscus flowers, lime wedges, and sugar to a cocktail shaker. Using a muddler or sturdy wooden spoon, muddle well.

2. Fill the cocktail shaker halfway full with cracked ice. Add the rum. Shake very well, for at least 15 seconds.

3. Strain the mix into two fancy cordial glasses.

⬆ *A Note: Having problems tracking down hibiscus flowers? Try your local gourmet shop, or online at www.dandelion botanical.com.*

A VIRGIN VARIATION: Worried about drinking and swimming? Substitute fresh pineapple juice for the rum, and call it a Caribbean Bud.

Maraschino Liqueur

Without a doubt, I love the maraschino liqueur. Some of my pals even say I love it too much, as I tend to reach for it first when putting together a new drink (well, after the base liquor) and talk about it in such cooing tones. And I do love the taste, and how well even a mere drop or two plays with other ingredients, bringing its own flavor but also pushing notes from those other ingredients to new heights. But I also feel it's been somewhat maligned over the past, oh, 50 years, due to its name being identical to that of a certain bright garnish. This has led unsuspecting folks to mix a little sweet maraschino cherry juice into recipes that call for maraschino liqueur.

This, *mon ami*, is a definite no-no. Maraschino liqueur is made from the fruits and pits of the Marasca cherry, in a process such as a fruit brandy would be made, distilled before having just a touch of cane sugar added. The time taken to make the liqueur, as well as the addition of the pits plus the fruit, ends in a deliciously dry product, one that has some cherry flavor, sure, but also undercurrents of almonds (it's the pits that do it) and a unique nature that's all its own. If you want cherry syrup, use the juice of the maraschino cherry, maybe even adding a little of your own simple syrup. But if you want the refined and sublime taste of maraschino liqueur, be sure you get the right bottle.

Several different maraschino liqueurs are available, though the best known currently is probably Luxardo, which boasts a clear, crisp taste and is easy to find because of the large patented green glass bottle, wrapped up nicely in a hand-fitted straw holder. Luxardo maraschino is aged for two years in Finnish ash vats after it's distilled, but before it's diluted a bit and mixed with cane sugar.

Dalliance

Babies, sometimes you have to slow life down a bit, forget about the numerous beeping noises from phones and other electronic devices, forget about work and those harebrained meetings, forget about the family, forget even about the fantastic books out there you think you have to read, forget everything except that special someone, and have a little dalliance (which means both the frivolous spending of time and a playful flirtation—how amazing) with him or her, where you lie around on a couch, or in a park, and say silly things in a soft voice, maybe run a finger lightly on a collarbone, maybe a little hand-holding, and maybe (even if it's already a perfect afternoon) a few of these drinks to make the moment complete. **Serves 2**

Ice cubes

3 ounces **brandy**

2 ounces **maraschino liqueur**

1 ounce **freshly squeezed lemon juice**

1 ounce **fresh pineapple juice**

2 **maraschino cherries** for garnish

1. Fill a cocktail shaker halfway full with ice cubes. Add the brandy, maraschino liqueur, lemon juice, and pineapple juice. Shake well.

2. Add a maraschino cherry to each of two cocktail glasses. Strain the mix into the glasses, making sure an equal amount gets into each. There's no reason to ruin the Dalliance with selfishness.

"The cook was there with blackened face, seated on the beautiful chintz sofa by the side of Mrs. Raggles, to whom she **was administering Maraschino**."

WILLIAM MAKEPEACE THACKERAY, *Vanity Fair*

Debutante's Dream

Did you know that *debutante* comes from the French and means "female beginner?" If a female reading this has just come of age (drinking age, that is) and is dreaming of that first drink, which will be the beginning of her lifelong love of cocktails and highballs and punches (oh, my!), then please, for your sake (it is your night), let me warn you that this is a rather strong first drink, one you should take only in a single dose.

If, on the other hand, you're having a mock cotillion as a chance to pounce around with pals (or even one singular pal whom you've always wanted to see in a ball gown), wearing lots of white and satin gloves and dancing terrifically formally for the first two dances while munching on small finger sandwiches, then you can take your Dream in multiple doses. Be wary, though, of having a few while attired in that long dress—the possibility of tripping goes up as the Debutante's Dreams go down. **Serves 2**

Ice cubes

2 ounces **brandy**

2 ounces **bourbon**

2 ounces **freshly squeezed orange juice**

½ ounce **freshly squeezed lemon juice**

1. Fill a cocktail shaker halfway full with ice cubes. Add the brandy, bourbon, orange juice, and lemon juice. Shake well (but don't spill on those immaculate gloves).

2. Strain the dreamy mix equally into two cocktail glasses. If the cocktails don't seem fancy enough, garnish each with a single camellia.

Highland Fling

I found this Scottish affair in an excellent little book called *A Guide to Pink Elephants*, volume 2 (Richards Rosen Associates, 1957), a book given to me by my pal Lisa Ekus, who is a sparkly bon vivant of the best variety (as well as being a first-rate media trainer, agent, and overall exceptional person to know). I'm not sure she's had an actual Highland fling (the kind that involves falling for a lady or gentleman in a kilt), but I know she enjoys a happening cocktail and happening cocktail party as much as anyone. So, if you're going to serve these up at your next wingding, send her an invite—she's the kind of guest that makes any bash better. **Serves 2**

Ice cubes

4 ounces **Scotch**

2 ounces **sweet vermouth**

4 dashes **orange bitters**

1. Fill a cocktail shaker halfway full with ice cubes. Add the Scotch, vermouth, and bitters. Shake Scottish style (which means well).

2. Strain the mix equally into two cocktail glasses.

⬆ *A Note: This simple yet strikingly satisfactory mixture works with many Scotch varieties. I like a blended number that has character, with flavors that combine interestingly with other ingredients, something like Johnny Walker (Red or Black) or Famous Grouse.*

⬆ *A Second Note: I suggest using Regan's Orange Bitters No. 6 in your Fling, if you don't want it— and you—to become a "Flung."*

⬆ *A Third Note: Sure, this is close to a Rob Roy (page 40), but it's the little differences that make flings sparkle.*

Honey Bee

If you'd like, sing the following flitting lines to a wannabe honey while constructing this drink: "Oh, the Honey Bee is a sweetish drink, but not as sweet as you. It has a kick of dark, dark rum, but it won't make you blue. Its touch of lime is certainly fine on a summer ev-en-ing, but without you, it's not as true, and has a terrible sting." Now, if that doesn't **bring props by the bucketful** from your prospective paramour, then you'd better try a dance next time—one where you mimic the patterns of mating bees, perhaps? **Serves 2**

Ice cubes

4 ounces **dark rum**

1 ounce **freshly squeezed lime juice**

½ ounce **Benedictine**

1 ounce **honey**

A Note: *If you can get a good organic clover honey, then your song will sound even better. But whatever honey you use, make sure it's pourable. If it's too thick, heat it very briefly in the microwave.*

1. Fill a cocktail shaker halfway full with ice cubes. Add the rum, lime juice, and Benedictine. Shake well.

2. Strain the Honey Bee into two cocktail glasses, getting an equal amount in both. Slowly drizzle the honey equally over each drink. You'll get a little buildup at the bottom of the glasses, but that's a sweet treat you both can enjoy.

A VIRGIN VARIATION: Omit the rum and Benedictine, double the lime juice, triple the honey, and add 2 ounces heavy cream to the shaker in step 1. It will be a stinger-less bee, but a good dessert.

Hoop La

It's reassuring to me (and to you, too, one would imagine) that people have been prancing and romancing by bringing the Hoop La on dates since at least 1930, as that's when Harry Craddock, who was known to be quite a charmer (well, at least that's my recollection from 1930), published *The Savoy Cocktail Book*, where I discovered this mix. Not for a first date, mind you, where you want to take things calmly and a little slower—the Hoop La is ideal for the date where you've become close enough to the one dated to know that he or she, much like you, wants to kick up those heels in dancehalls or hallways. I believe this may be the sixth date, but then again, it may depend on the daters. Such calls only the two involved can make for certain. **Serves 2**

Ice cubes

3 ounces **brandy**

2 ounces **Cointreau**

2 ounces **Lillet Blanc**

1 ounce **freshly squeezed lemon juice**

2 **orange twists** for garnish (optional)

1. Fill a cocktail shaker halfway full with ice cubes. Add the brandy, Cointreau, Lillet, and lemon juice. Shake jauntily.

2. Let loose the Hoop La into two cocktail glasses, sharing fairly. Garnish each, if you desire, with an orange twist.

Lillet

A fortified wine, Lillet has movie and literary credits to its credit, thanks to an appearance in *Casino Royale*, both the book and the Daniel Craig movie. (No quibbling about the "literary" here—Ian Fleming's main character is pretty indelible. Or, if you do disagree about espionage fiction, at least don't let it lean you away from the Lillet.) In the book, firstly, Mr. Bond orders up a Kina Lillet Martini, instantly naming it the Vesper after his double-agent lady love. (See how creative he was? Take note, and impress the lads and ladies, by never just calling a drink a "blah-blah Martini.") Bond instructs the bartender to make it with "three measures of Gordon's, one of vodka, half a measure of Kina Lillet." The 1953 novel's famous drink reappears in the movie of the same name 53 years later, with the same ingredient list.

This repeating is nice, but it does date the movie a bit (or, I should say, confuses the dates of the movie, as there are other parts that are obviously meant to suggest the present time period), because Kina Lillet stopped being produced in 1986. Originally developed in 1887 by Paul and Raymond Lillet and released in the Bordeaux region of France in 1895, Kina Lillet was a quinine-heavy white wine-based mixture that contained a doughty dose of bark from the Peruvian Kina Kina tree (often called the Cinchona), which led to the name. In 1986, the quinine was reduced, leaving us with a lighter Lillet, but one that still holds its place as a slightly orange-flavored ingredient in mixed drinks like the Hoop La (opposite page) and on its own, or chilled over a little ice with a lemon or orange twist (flaming the orange twist over the Lillet was a craze in the 1950s—and is still fun today). There have been other variations, including Lillet Dry, created especially for the English market, and Lillet Rouge, created in 1962.

Lady Godiva

Surely you and yours do not have to ride around town shirtless while sipping these to protest a raise in rent, or a recent toll hike, or a difficult-to-bear tax increase on alcohol, in homage to the original noblewoman who shares this breast-baring beverage's name. But if you need to **prove a smaller point** (perhaps your beau or belle put a toll on the use of the DVD player) and want to trot around your own yard in the altogether on a horse or just acting like you're on a horse, while consuming your influence's namesake cocktail, well, I think that's a very honorable—if potentially chilly—idea. **Serves 2**

Ice cubes

3 ounces **dark rum**

2½ ounces **sweet vermouth**

1 ounce **apricot liqueur**

½ ounce **grenadine**

½ ounce **freshly squeezed lemon juice**

⬆ *A Note: Want to impress the beaus and belles at the bar? When ordering one of these, bring up the fact that the phrase "peeping Tom" supposedly originates with the real Lady Godiva, and a man—named Tom, naturally—who was said to have snuck a look-see at her when she was taking her famous ride. His peeking is said to have cost him his sight.*

⬆ *A Second Note: Don't get confused by the Godiva-ing and put in apricot syrup instead of apricot liqueur. These, shirtless one, are different animals.*

1. Fill a cocktail shaker halfway full with ice cubes. Add everything else, except your shirt (at least keep it on until after the drink-making is done, so as to reduce stickiness). Shake well, in a galloping motion.

2. Strain the mix into two cocktail glasses, working hard to ensure a fair pour. (Which reduces hurt feelings and the need to protest, and thus perhaps keeps clothes in place for a while. Whether you think that's a good thing, I can't say.)

A VARIATION: I've seen a completely different version of this drink that has brandy, triple sec, lemon juice, lime juice, and sugar in it. I like the above recipe better (the double citrus plus sugar seems to me to be a recipe for itchiness and a slight sting, considering that you may be less than fully dressed by the second or third drink), but if you want to try something new, be my guest.

The Late Caress

I've done my research (some of it hands-on, because I care about you, dear readers), and talked to a few bar-bound biologists, a number of only-slightly-befuddled-by-highballs physicists, a handful of tipsy chemists, and even one astrologist who had just finished his second Fair Skies (page 104), and not a one of them could tell me with any real equation or theory to back it up why this lovely drink is not nearly as lovely as lightly tracing your fingers along the inner arm, or collarbone, or back of the neck, of that person who makes you happiest by walking into a room when the evening's winding down and you're both a little sleepy, but **happy, oh so happy**. I can't guarantee you'll be happier with a late caress while having a Late Caress, but I can say that it won't ruin the moment. **Serves 2**

Ice cubes

3 ounces **rye**

2 ounces **Frangelico**

1 ounce **freshly squeezed orange juice**

1. Fill a cocktail shaker halfway full with ice cubes. Add the rye, Frangelico, and orange juice. Shake well.

2. Strain the mix equally into two cocktail glasses. Garnish with a look that leads to caressing.

⬆ *A Note:* *For those caressing: Please, don't caress directly after shaking this drink. Those fingers are cold—let them warm up a little.*

⬆ *A Second Note:* *Frangelico, the liqueur that comes in a monk-shaped bottle complete with rope belt, has been painstakingly made for more than 300 years in the Piedmont region of northern Italy, using wild hazelnuts combined with a number of other natural ingredients.*

Lover's Moon

That big ol' white ball in the nighttime sky sure wrangles loads of credit for **instigating a lot of starry eyes**, as well as a number of held hands, deep and unforgettable kisses, proposals, and broadly amorous behavior. I'm glad, then, to be able to introduce you to an imbibable that celebrates this celestial object's place in passionate and tender schemes. Does the Lover's Moon have the same persuasive powers as the moon? Have a couple, and you'll know the answer without even having to look out the window. **Serves 2**

Ice cubes

3½ ounces **bourbon**

3 ounces **macadamia nut liqueur**

2 ounces **heavy cream**

2 **maraschino cherries** for garnish

1. Fill a cocktail shaker halfway full with ice cubes. Add the bourbon, macadamia liqueur, and cream. Shake well.

2. Add a cherry to each of two cocktail glasses. Strain the mix into the glasses, making sure each gets its full share. Sure, the cherries will vanish for a minute, but like the moon, they'll reappear.

The Natural

I agree with you, fast talker, so there's no need to argue: This nature-monikered mixture could easily slide into a chapter about baseball drinks (following up on the fine book and movie of the same name), or could scare up in a chapter about spookier drinks (much like the chapter in this very book titled Dark Drinks That Go Bump in the Night, page 183). Without arguing, though, I state my belief that while it's a touch strong, it also has an underlying sweetness that belongs in this chapter with other sweetheart mixes. With that firmly in mind, I consider it in the "au naturel" motif, meaning: Serve it when you're celebrating a state of undress. As I'm having one now, you can see why I'm so against arguing the point. **Serves 2**

Ice cubes

4 ounces **dark rum**

2 ounces **brandy**

1½ ounces **freshly squeezed lemon juice**

1 ounce **orgeat syrup**

1 ounce **grenadine**

2 **maraschino cherries** for garnish (optional)

1. Fill a cocktail shaker halfway full with ice cubes. Add the rum, brandy, lemon juice, orgeat, and grenadine, quickly but carefully. Shake well.

2. Strain equally into two cocktail glasses. If it feels naked without a garnish, add a maraschino cherry to each glass.

⬆ *A Note: Orgeat is an almond-flavored syrup, available in many gourmet and grocery stores.*

Nuit de Noces

I'm a humongous Champagne and sparkling wine fan. I could bathe in it and be awfully happy; maybe you could, too. (Hey, hey, relax, I'm not asking to share a bath—get your mind out of the bubbly gutter.) Even with this lively love, I think if there really *is* a darn fine drink named after the wedding night, a drink that's individualistic, pleasing to the palate, containing an underlying oomph, and first chronicled in Crosby Gaige's *Cocktail Guide and Ladies' Companion* (circa 1941), you should sub it in for the traditional wedding beverage—the nightcap for the newly espoused couple, if for no one else. That way, you can save the Champagne for bathing. **Serves 2**

Ice cubes

4 ounces **dark rum**

1½ ounces **freshly squeezed lime juice**

1 ounce **pure maple syrup**

Crushed ice

1. Fill a cocktail shaker halfway full with ice cubes. Add the rum, lime juice, and maple syrup. Shake well.

2. Smoothly fill two champagne flutes with crushed ice. Strain the mix into the glasses, over the ice.

A VARIATION: No crushed ice around the honeymoon suite? Feel free to strain these into cocktail glasses sans ice, and don't worry about a cloud descending.

"With knowing art, she presents a sovereign formula for that night of nights when **we would all like to do our best**."

CROSBY GAIGE, *speaking about Jeanne Owen, who gave him the above recipe*

Paradiso

I don't want to dwell on my man Dante (or ever have to answer for calling him "my man Dante") too much, but drat it, this blended beauty is named after the ultimate reward in his *Divine Comedy*, one of the tiptop literary works in history. Not to mention the *Paradiso* being underlined by his love for his Beatrice. Maybe you don't know even one stanza of the long poem; that's okay. You should know, though, that if you find your Beatrice (or your Dante, for that matter), you should plug in that blending machine, make a couple of Paradisos, and say a few sweet poetic words, without waiting around for some future right moment. That right moment is now. **Serves 2**

2 cups **cracked ice**

4 ounces **dark rum**

4 ounces **heavy cream**

2 ounces **freshly squeezed orange juice**

2 **orange slices** for garnish

1. With an eye skyward, add the ice, rum, cream, and orange juice to a blender. Blend well.

2. Pour the Paradiso equally into two large cocktail glasses or goblets. Garnish each with an orange slice.

Parisian Blonde

You Continental rascal you, sporting that shiny white tuxedo (leaving the bow tie rakishly askew) or shimmery ball gown and making with smatterings of chatter that allow everyone to know that, yes, you've spent some time recently on a yacht in Monte Carlo, and for that matter, you've been idling away the winters at a small chalet in the Alps, and yes, those are bona fide diamonds, and can you bide some time for a little baccarat? No, sadly, you can't. You have a date with a Parisian Blonde (or two). **Serves 2**

Cracked ice

3 ounces **dark rum**

2 ounces **orange curaçao**

2 ounces **heavy cream**

1. Fill a cocktail shaker halfway full with cracked ice. Add the rum, curaçao, and cream. Shake well, but in a jet-setting manner.

2. Strain the mix into two cocktail glasses, making sure that each gets an equal amount.

⏏ *A Note:* A quick à votre santé *to Matty Simmons, author of* The New Diner's Club Drink Book *(Signet, 1969), the book where I first viewed the Parisian Blonde.*

Quickie

Who says love has to be all long, leisurely walks in the park under benign oak tree branches, watching rabbits frolic in the forest, gazing with fingers entwined while the red-winged blackbirds wing their unhurried way across the blue skies? That's nice and valid, and makes for a dandy closing movie montage. However, sometimes love has to be rapid and **muss up your hair a bit**, and possibly happen in a short amount of time, maybe in an elevator (well, that happened in a movie, at least). Here's a substantial drink ideal for honoring those hasty demonstrations of your and your partner's feelings, because they're worth celebrating, too. **Serves 2**

Ice cubes

3 ounces **bourbon**

2 ounces **white rum**

¾ ounce **triple sec**

2 **maraschino cherries** for garnish

1. Fill a cocktail shaker halfway full with ice cubes. Add the bourbon, rum, and triple sec. Shake thoroughly but, well, quickly.

2. Strain the mix equally into two cocktail glasses. Drop a cherry into each glass, and serve with a satisfied smile.

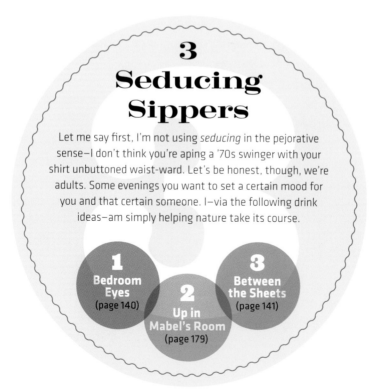

3
Seducing Sippers

Let me say first, I'm not using *seducing* in the pejorative sense—I don't think you're aping a '70s swinger with your shirt unbuttoned waist-ward. Let's be honest, though, we're adults. Some evenings you want to set a certain mood for you and that certain someone. I—via the following drink ideas—am simply helping nature take its course.

1
Bedroom Eyes
(page 140)

2
Up in Mabel's Room
(page 179)

3
Between the Sheets
(page 141)

Rumba

Hello to all Carole Lombards and George Rafts, let's see you cut that rug as they did in the 1935 movie that shares this cocktail's name—a movie that sadly wasn't quite as successful as this drink will be when you serve it up cold between songs at your next dance party, which might just be a dance party for two due to the Rumba's hip-swinging sensuality. Once you kick off the rumba-ing, I'm guessing your natural rhythms will guide you, but picking which Rumba to drink might be a touch more difficult. See, everyone wants to put their own spin on a Rumba, so there are several to choose from. I like this recipe because it **taps its toes in rip-snorting fashion**, and sometimes I need encouragement to approach the dance floor. You could tag-team Pernod in for the gin, though, and not be far from a tasty sipper. You could also (as I've seen) remove the lemon juice, getting even closer to the rip-snorter side. Or, you could follow these instructions and focus more on cutting said rug. **Serves 2**

Ice cubes

4 ounces **dark rum**

2 ounces **gin**

1 ounce **freshly squeezed lemon juice**

1 ounce **grenadine**

1. Fill a cocktail shaker halfway full with ice cubes. Add the rum, gin, lemon juice, and grenadine. Shake well, and don't forget to swing those hips.

2. Strain the mix into two cocktail glasses, making sure that each gets an equal share.

"I want to make loud, rude noises. **I want to spill things** and push chairs over. After all, I'm a human being and I like to act like one occasionally."

DIANA HARRISON (CAROLE LOMBARD), *Rumba*, 1935

Soother

There are nights when the sole romantic act should be to comfort. Listening to your sweetheart unload a few choice phrases about bad coworkers, calling up the pizza delivery place so as not to dirty up the kitchen, maybe watching that particular evening soapy show you don't like and not making fun of it for once, keeping the dogs or kids or fish **more peaceful than usual**, and making up a steady stream of Soothers to take those cares away. Hey, it can't be roaring fires, bearskin rugs, and Bedroom Eyes (page 140) every night. **Serves 2**

Ice cubes

2 ounces **brandy**

2 ounces **dark rum**

1 ounce **orange curaçao**

1 ounce **freshly squeezed lime juice**

1 ounce **apple juice**

1 ounce **Simple Syrup** (page 12)

1. Fill a cocktail shaker halfway full with ice cubes. Add the brandy, rum, curaçao, lime juice, apple juice, and simple syrup. Shake well, but quietly.

2. Strain the soothing mix into two cocktail glasses, equally.

Four Drinks I Wish I Had Named

Those who know me know that I tend to get, how shall I say it, a little exuberant over good cocktails I'm introduced to (blathering on and on to whoever is within earshot). On the flip side, though, I do tend to get a little down-in-the-tooth (not so much to ruin an evening, 'cause that would be, as the kids say, wack) when having a good or even darn decent drink that has been poorly named. I'm not sure why, exactly, but the lack of creativity in naming makes me sad, as bartenders, both at home and out and about, tend toward imagination in other areas. Luckily, this poor-naming trend (adding "-ini" or "-olitan" to everything instead of coming up with a real name is perhaps the most egregious example) is on the wane, as proved by these finely made, and finely named, drinks.

1. The Search for Delicious (page 85)
2. Black Feather (page 58)
3. Polynesian Donkey (page 84)
4. Sweet Louise (page 88)

Summer Dream

In his famous eighteenth sonnet, when he lays down the immortal line "and summer's lease hath all too short a date," Shakespeare perhaps wasn't exactly referring to a coquetry that happened in those hotter months between him and a fair lady, an ardent connection that slid smoothly past light flirtation into something a trace more serious, a Mercury-rising *affaire d'amour* that—for at least as long as those months lasted—seemed more important than the sun. As these adoring concerns are, sadly, like this drink, over much too soon, his line does hit the romantic nail on the head, though—showing again why Will S. was the master. **Serves 2**

3 **orange slices**

2 **peach slices**

Ice cubes

4 ounces **bourbon**

2 ounces **Campari**

1 ounce **Simple Syrup** (page 12)

1 ounce **freshly squeezed lemon juice**

1. Add the orange and peach slices to a cocktail shaker. Using a muddler or wooden spoon, muddle well.

2. Fill the cocktail shaker halfway full with ice cubes. Add the bourbon, Campari, simple syrup, and lemon juice. Shake really well, if a little wistfully, for at least 15 seconds.

3. Strain the dream equally into two cocktail glasses.

A VARIATION: Want a more cluttered drink? After step 2, instead of straining into cocktail glasses, pour the whole shebang, ice and fruit and every sad last word, into two large goblets. Rename it the Disordered Dream.

⬆ *A Note: Campari is a lovely red-hued Italian apéritif made from a secret arrangement of herbs and spices, with a result that's somewhat bitter and amazingly tasty.*

Five Suggestions for Successful Parties

1. Serve drinks that match the seasonal temperament. For example, in winter, serve drinks that are "warmers"—either actually warm or hot in temperature, or ones that have a serious helping of that warming fortitude, both of which will take off a newly arrived guest's chill. On the flip side, in summer, be sure that the first drink offered is extra-cool and bubbly, to beat the heat.

2. Think about offering one or two (or three) signature drinks, which you reference from the first e-mail, e-vite, phone message, or handwritten invite (the last still has the most class, by the way). This generates the idea that your affair is going to be more special than a run-of-the-mill evening. Also, it allows you to focus more, instead of trying to have every possible drink for everyone.

3. Proper planning prevents poor performance. I received this bit of advice in a fortune cookie, and I've never forgotten it, as it's perfect for party prep. I take it two ways. First, that it's always a good idea to have a little more of the crucial ingredients on hand for your signature cocktails than you think you'll need. Someone always shows up with a guest or cousin. If you end up having too much, you've started to stock your bar a little more fully (never a bad thing). Second, make up whatever garnishes and such that you can beforehand, so that you don't spend all night chopping. Obviously, not a long time beforehand (you don't want anything drying out), but work some things out early, and relax more later.

4. Always have the number of a good taxi company or two on hand. Even in cities where cabs are as plentiful as D-level celebrities, it doesn't hurt to have a number of reliable numbers. I'm not saying your pals are lushes, but it's always better to be a little safe than to have a dented fender (or worse).

5. Most important suggestion of all—a rule, even, for your parties: Never forget that, even as the hostess or host, you should have fun, too. Really. If you're not having fun, then what's the point of throwing a party, anyway? So pick a couple of good drinks, prepare a little, and then relax, enjoy, and give yourself a little "cheers."

Sweet Dream

If you were a bartender (of the home or pro variety) and had dressed to the nines (even wearing those too-tight-but-oh-so-fashionable boots) for a 2:00 A.M. date, or you were serving a *très chic* customer who caught your eye on a slow Friday night at work and wanted to bring said customer a singular sipper past the midnight hour, one that would cause you to be remembered fondly, wouldn't you maybe think calling it the "Sweet Dream" was a suave idea? Here's the hard news: You wouldn't be the only one, as there are multiple variations on this particular theme. Use this recipe next time and save yourself the trouble of making something up. (But between us, you can say you did make it up. I won't tell.) **Serves 2**

Ice cubes

3 ounces **Cognac**

2 ounces **Kahlúa**

3 ounces **heavy cream**

1. Fill a cocktail shaker halfway full with ice cubes. Add the Cognac, Kahlúa, and cream. Shake well.

2. Strain the mix into two cocktail glasses, ensuring that both have an equal amount.

A VARIATION: Want to go a totally different route to dreamland? There's another Sweet Dream containing 1 ounce white rum, 1 ounce gin, 1 ounce apricot brandy, and ½ ounce pineapple syrup, shaken and strained.

A SECOND VARIATION: Once, I saw a drink wearing the Sweet Dream moniker consisting of gin, Cointreau, and orange juice. Which is, of course, a Sweet Patootie, but that's a mistake that can be forgiven.

Temptation Cocktail

A fairly stiff mix, this could have easily served as proxy for the apple in the Garden of Eden (there's no snake involved in it, but there is a twist, which can take on a snake-like appearance). No worries, though, about getting kicked out of paradise when consuming. Unless you insist on having more than three Temptations, after which (depending on Temptation tolerance) you may begin behaving in a devilish manner that gets you booted from your *tête-à-tête*, which I'm guessing resembles a paradise. **Serves 2**

Ice cubes

3½ ounces **rye**

1 ounce **orange curaçao**

1 ounce **Pernod**

1 ounce **Dubonnet Rouge**

2 **orange twists** for garnish

1. Fill a cocktail shaker halfway full with ice cubes. Add the rye, curaçao, Pernod, and Dubonnet. Shake well.

2. Strain the combination into two cocktail glasses (resisting the temptation to give yourself extra—share and share alike). Garnish each with an orange twist.

⬆ *A Note: At one point in our drinking history, this was made with both an orange and a lemon twist. The lemon addition seems almost too much temptation for me, but if you have lemons, give it a whirl.*

⬆ *A Second Note: Dubonnet is a French wine that's been fortified with herbs, spices, and quinine. There are two versions: Blanc, made with white wine, and the slightly sweeter Rouge, made with red wine (that's the version bringing the persuasion here).*

"I remember, for example, being taken to see a neurotic Frenchman who was staying there with his wife, and vividly recall Sunday morning in his suite, the wireless resounding to a clergyman's voice reading the Lesson, **while we drank Pernod, and a Pekingese tried in vain to seduce a monkey**."

ANTHONY POWELL, "A Bottle of Wine at the Cavendish," *The Complete Imbiber* 6, 1963

Three Wishes

I wonder how much a chance encounter with a djinn or genie changes depending on when in our lifetime it happens? When young, the wishes are probably more pure and more selfish in a way (I wish I had a lot of chocolate, for example), and then they become more conquering wishes (I wish I could be as good a b-ball player as Michael Jordan, or I wish I were as rich as ol' King Croesus). What wishes, though, come out when older? Perhaps they become simpler (beyond the obvious wish for more time). A wish, for example, to **re-spend that one perfect spring day** with that one perfect someone, just one more time, lying lazily under the sun and sipping this lovely cocktail along with those last minutes of sunlight and love. Not a bad wish at all, I think.

Serves 2

Ice cubes

4 ounces **dark rum**

2 ounces **Rhum Clément Créole Shrubb**

1 ounce **amaretto**

1. Fill a cocktail shaker halfway full with ice cubes. Add the rum, Créole Shrubb, and amaretto. Using a spoon or other long stirring device, stir well.

2. Strain the mix equally into two cocktail glasses. Wish away.

⬆ *A Note: Rhum Clément Créole Shrubb is an orange-flavored liqueur based on a sugarcane (as opposed to molasses) rum from Martinique. It combines rum with bitter orange peels and spices to create a crisp liqueur that's not overly sweet.*

Ti Penso Sempre

If you're someone like me (and I think you are), who loves drinks—both fresh and classic—you have on occasion taken a hand at making up your own. And then, **when everything came together perfectly**, taken a hand at naming said mixture. If you're like me in another way (you love books of most shapes and sizes), some names are drawn from books you've read and enjoyed that seem to couple up kindly with the mix. That, drinking-and-reading pals, is the case here, as I found the name for this lovely, sweet, and powerful cocktail in a book I was reading at the time I first made the drink. The book was Meg Mullins's first book, *The Rug Merchant*, which is a romance novel deep with beauty and sadness. Though the story takes place in New York, the phrase *ti penso sempre* is Italian, just like one of the drink's ingredients, Aperol, a light, mildly bitter apéritif. **Serves 2**

Ice cubes

3 ounces **brandy**

2 ounces **Aperol**

1 ounce **Simple Syrup** (page 12)

2 **orange slices** for garnish

1. Fill a cocktail shaker halfway full with ice cubes. Add the brandy, Aperol, and simple syrup. Shake well.

2. Strain the mix equally into two cocktail glasses. Garnish each drink with an orange slice.

⌃ *A Translation: What does the name of this drink actually mean? "I always think of you." And know that I do.*

Tropical

Young lovers mulling over matrimonial materials, lean in close so I can whisper in your ears. There's a reason sultry islands make such homey honeymoon spots after weeks of wedding stress (well, let's admit it—getting hitched can be dotted with hitches). And it's not just the fact that palm-treed paradises promise a little sweatiness, leading to the amount of clothing worn on a steamy beach weighing usually a little less than a feather (though that's a good reason, too). It's more because the frolicking fruity drinks doled out in the tropics taste so swell and tend toward having a healthy helping of rum in them. Which is **what every honeymoon needs**. Serves 2

1 **fresh pineapple round**

1 ounce **Simple Syrup** (page 12)

Ice cubes

4 ounces **dark rum**

1½ ounces **freshly squeezed lime juice**

1 ounce **grenadine**

1. Add the pineapple round and the simple syrup to a cocktail shaker. Using a muddler or wooden spoon, muddle well.

2. Fill the cocktail shaker halfway full with ice cubes. Add the rum, lime juice, and grenadine. Shake really well, even if it's a tad stifling.

3. Pour the contents of the shaker equally into two white wine glasses or goblets. Toast to your good fortune.

A Note: If this seems too chaotic with all that pineapple plopping around in there, strain after step 2 into two cocktail glasses, instead of pouring.

A Second Note: I've seen a number of versions of this drink that are completely different. If you want your honeymoon to be a success, stick with the above and then send me a thank-you card.

A VIRGIN VARIATION: Skip the rum, and after you pour the shaker out in step 3, top the drink off with chilled club soda. It won't be the same, but it'll sure cool you down.

"What should I do but **drink away** the heat and troubles of the day? In this more than kingly state, Love himself shall on me wait."

THEOGNIS

Quotes from the Classics

There's been a lot said about drinking, about drinks, about liquors, liqueurs, wines, beers, and mixers, and about drinkers. But here are five quotes from five classic cocktail books that you may not have heard (and if you have, they're good enough that I'll bet you'll be happy to hear them again).

1. "An efficient bartender's first aim should be to please his customers, paying particular attention to meeting the individual wishes of those whose tastes and desires he has already watched and ascertained." –Jerry Thomas, *The Bar-Tender's Guide or How to Mix Drinks*, 1862

2. "It should be understood, however, that no matter whether these drinks be made at the club, café, or your private house, it is only by using the best quality of goods that proper and satisfactory results can be obtained." –Jacques Straub, *Drinks*, 1914

3. "Before closing this dissertation on the products of the American School of Drinking, one must say frankly that so far as chemistry and logic are concerned, it would seem that either has had little to do with the formulas of most cocktails." –Albert Stevens Crockett, *The Old Waldorf-Astoria Bar Book*, 1935 (reprinted 2003)

4. "In a less heroic generation, however, it must be recorded that few demands are received across the bar of the Stork for cocktails until after the sun has crossed the proverbial yardarm at noon. Public taste in restoratives, pick-me-ups, and simple old-fashioned drinking for pleasure runs more to longer and taller drinks and less to the concentrated essence of life to be encountered in cocktails." –Lucius Beebe, *The Stork Club Bar Book*, 1897 (reprinted 2003)

5. "I have developed a certain mature philosophy about the use of alcohol that I would like to pass on to any ear that is willing to listen. . . . After a day of toil, it brings relaxation; it promotes wit and conversation; it stirs the circulation of the blood and sends the crimson stream hurrying to the assistance of flagging organs." –Crosby Gaige, *Cocktail Guide and Ladies' Companion*, 1941

← Up in Mabel's Room

Up in Mabel's Room, the story goes, and the ballad goes, and the limerick goes, and the epic poem goes, and the little ditty goes, and the bildungsroman goes, and the anecdote goes, and the fable goes, and the canzone goes, and the hearsay goes, up there when the door's closed and the lights are dimly lit, there's **a helpful helping of rye**, a squeeze of grapefruit juice, a smooch of honey, and a whole lot of rumpled clothes. What else? I can't tell you, now can I? You'll have to find out on your own. That's just the way it goes. **Serves 2**

Cracked ice

3 ounces **rye**

1½ ounces **freshly squeezed grapefruit juice**

1½ ounces **Simple Syrup** (page 12)

1. Fill a cocktail shaker halfway full with cracked ice. Add the rye, grapefruit juice, and simple syrup. Shake exceptionally well (you have to live up to the legend, after all).

2. Strain into two cocktail glasses, making sure each receives an equal amount. Then shut the door. Garnish with an almost knowing look.

Whisper

Shhhhh . . . keep your voices muffled. This needs quiet (like a first declaration of love) and is between us only, so speak in soft tones directly into each other's ears or cocktail shakers. The secret? After a few Whispers we'll be talking in very loud voices, as the drink is a hearty combination of whisky and the vermouth cousins, not the fluffy tipple you might expect, which is why I wanted to keep us subdued right now. Later, I promise **nothing but lovely noise**. **Serves 2**

Ice cubes

3 ounces **blended Canadian whisky**

2 ounces **sweet vermouth**

2 ounces **dry vermouth**

1. Quietly fill a cocktail shaker halfway full with ice cubes. Add the whisky and vermouths. Shake well.

2. Strain the Whisper into two cocktail glasses.

"This cocktail is very easy to make and is **a great favorite** in the West Indies."

HARRY CRADDOCK, writing about the Whisper in
The Savoy Cocktail Book, 1930

Wildflower

Forget about the sad, lesser-known song by one-hit wonder Skylark that shares its name with this naturally named drink, and instead think about a picnic, where you and yours (you "free and gentle flower"—wait, there's that song again) are surrounded by buttercup, goldenrod, and maybe a dollop of western wood lily. Idyllic, isn't it? Well, it can **transform into another level of idyll** if you pack along some liquid Wildflowers to go along with that cinematic scenic-ness. It takes a dash of panache and planning (and some good Tupperware, or an insulated container for ice)—but if it makes it easier, introduce the grapefruit juice and the grenadine before leaving the house by putting them in one container, then bring your Scotch along in a flask. One cocktail shaker later, your Wildflower cocktail will be blooming like the surroundings. **Serves 2**

Ice cubes

4 ounces **Scotch**

2 ounces **freshly squeezed grapefruit juice**

1 ounce **grenadine**

1. Fill a cocktail shaker halfway full with ice cubes. Add the Scotch, grapefruit juice, and grenadine. Shake well.

2. Strain the mix equally into two cocktail glasses. I would say garnish each with an actual wildflower, but unless you're a naturalist specializing in edible versus inedible flowers, that is a dangerous proposition. Nothing kills a picnic like a little poison.

Yokohama Romance

Now then, everyone in the room take five and dwell on your original Yokohama Romance. Wait, you say you've never had a Yokohama Romance, either of the drink variety or of the actual girl-meets-boy-in-the-capital-of-Kanagawa-Prefecture variety? I say, it's high time you did. And, since you probably aren't going to jump onto a plane this instant (**more romantic power to you** if you do), let's focus on the drink, which I picked up from Charles H. Baker's *The Gentleman's Companion*, Volume 2: *Exotic Drink Book* (Crown, 1946; Volume 1 being devoted to exotic cookery). Mr. Baker traveled the world eating, drinking, and romancing (that's a touch of supposition, but the three go together so aptly) so that we today could eat, drink, and romance in finer fashion. Thank his spirit boisterously. He says about the Yokohama Romance: "Concocted by one Toyama, No. 1 bar-boy at a Tokyo night spot called 'Romance' cabaret." Thank Toyama boisterously now, too. **Serves 2**

Crushed ice

3 ounces **Cognac**

1½ ounces **cherry brandy**

1 ounce **freshly squeezed lime juice**

½ ounce **Rose's lime juice**

1. Fill a cocktail shaker halfway full with crushed ice. Add the Cognac, brandy, and lime juices. Shake well.

2. Strain into two cocktail glasses, sharing equally.

A VARIATION: Mr. Baker says that this is also awfully romantic when made in a blender. If it's a hot day, give it a spin.

Zoom
A concoction called "Zoom" may not pop up like a daisy when dwelling on drinks that delight on a day when you're deliciously trying to deploy a match between you and that dolled-up hotness in the corner (well, unless you're thinking about the hot early-1990s Midwestern rock band Zoom). Wait, though, and hear me out. Doesn't the heart, during that moment when you first make eye contact with said hotness, start zooming around inside you? And after that first tentative kiss, aren't the energy bursts zooming around your brain? And when you take those even more amorous steps, doesn't even your skin feel slightly like it's zooming at every moment? As the French might say, *je pense que oui*. All of which, especially when adding in the drink's lick of honey, make the Zoom equal to one sexy evening. **Serves 2**

Ice cubes

4 ounces **brandy**

1½ ounces **heavy cream**

1 ounce **clover honey**

1. Fill a cocktail shaker halfway full with ice cubes. Add the brandy, cream, and honey. Shake thoroughly, for at least 20 seconds, to ensure proper zooming.

2. Strain the mix into two cocktail glasses.

A VARIATION: One could, if it helps the mood, make one's Zoom with Cognac, bourbon, or dark rum (in place of the brandy, naturally).

Dark Drinks That Go Bump in the Night

The night is long and treacherous. There are many twists and turns in the road you're walking, under trees with noose-like branches, and rickety buildings with boarded-up windows through which a solitary pale and sickly light trickles through, like the glare off an eye that's about to be covered by a Black Hood. And what's that noise in the distance? A banshee's howl with an avian bent, a harbinger of a night that gets darker and blacker? It must be the Crow wandering about with his murderous flock. Is there someone back there, back there in the shadows, trying to sneak up and trap you with an Artist's Special?

It looks a shade simian, but muddy and dragging a bit, with looping arms and a scent that's hard to place—could it be a Dirty Monkey? Or, when slithering out of the shadows and into the alley's entry, it could be that it's not simian in the least, it was just those clouds causing the horrific illusion. But, then, what is it? Or who? And is that a cowl, or cape, rustling in front of its, or his, or her mangled face, right above the silver chain tracing around the chest, with some sort of pendant, or emblem, or . . . wait, it's a Serpent's Tooth! And it's not any old person, it's a Warlock, walking the streets at midnight. Be brave and follow him, and hope for a Brainstorm that leads you out of this endless evil-seeming evening.

Now you're not sure what it is you're following—the night, the mystery, or the drinks—and has the creature in front of you shortened somehow? It almost looks the size of a Leprechaun, and it's walking with a stumbling gait, almost as if it were going in circles, or stuck on a Quarter Deck. No, no, it's drawing circles on the ground, or shaking some sort of metallic container filled with liquids, shaking, shaking . . . oh no, I think it's trying to call up a Demon of Destiny! You'd better duck into the one open door, ignoring the carousing noises, but when the door swings open you realize you've stumbled upon a Gaslight Tiger, and in the corner, a Dutch Charlie's on the table, and you're heading right for it.

About this time, you'd better hope there's somewhere to put your feet up. You've entered a dark and deadly place, albeit an often refreshing one that you may never want to leave once you've properly met the inhabitants. Sure, they're a potentially dangerous lot, but they may also end up being your best bar pals. You may never want to leave this bloodcurdling place, where you're surrounded by drinks that go bump in the night.

Five More Obscure Facts to Bring Up at the Bar

If the facts on page 37 didn't cement your reputation (what as, I'm not prepared to venture a guess on), then dive into the bubbly facts below next time you feel the need to show off your skill and knowledge.

1. In the 1800s, rum was often used by hair stylists, as it was thought to be perfect for keeping hair healthy and clean, while brandy was thought be a great hair strengthener. Salons were much more fun then, too.

2. Most wordy people know that "The quick brown fox jumps over the lazy dog" is thought to be a singular sentence in English, one that uses all the letters of the alphabet. But at one time (and maybe in some spots to this day), typesetters used another sentence that shares that same trait: "Pack my box with five dozen liquor jugs."

3. Fishermen and fisherwomen beware: There's a law in Ohio that makes it illegal to get a fish drunk.

4. At one point in the 1600s, thermometers used brandy instead of mercury.

5. Napoleon carried Cognac on all of his campaigns. But, sadly, he used it mostly for sanitation purposes.

Artist's Special

Of the many and sundry creepy and kooky creatures in this chapter, is there anything more chill-inducing than the "artist?" *Brrr*, I feel goose bumps rising even as I say the word. Whether it's chopping off an ear, running wild in the streets with paintbrush or pen in hand, or, scariest of all, making you think about the world through a written or visual medium and thereby think about your place in the world, which could lead to a lot of introspection and general deep thinking, those artist types can be **a tad dangerous to sit by** at the bar. If you *do*, however, find yourself in this position, or are entertaining one at home, I suggest serving a few of these, and quick. The Artist's Special has been known to placate even the nuttiest creative genius.

Ice cubes

2 ounces **bourbon**

1½ ounces **dry sherry**

½ ounce **freshly squeezed lemon juice**

½ ounce **grenadine**

1. Fill a cocktail shaker halfway full with ice cubes. Add the bourbon, sherry, lemon juice, and grenadine. Shake well.

2. Strain into a cocktail glass that has had the splattered paint wiped off of it.

⬆ *A Note: This drink was originally made with groseille syrup instead of grenadine. Groseille is made from red currants and seems to be available only in remote parts of the United Kingdom. If you'd like to try making your own, add 2 cups fresh red currants to a large glass container (one that has a good lid). Using a muddler or large wooden spoon, muddle the currants well, until as much juice as possible has been forced out. Then add 3 cups Simple Syrup (page 12). Stir well, seal, and let sit for 3 days. Strain through a fine-mesh colander or sieve into a pitcher, and then pour into bottles. Keep in the fridge like regular simple syrup.*

"This is **the genuine 'Ink of Inspiration'** imbibed at the Bal Bullier, Paris."

HARRY CRADDOCK, writing about the Artist's Special in *The Savoy Cocktail Book*, 1930

Bayou

I know, I know, crocodiles are a brutal level above their broad-snouted brethren, the alligator, in the ferociousness department. The American alligator is usually content to relax in its lair, coming out and roaring a bit during mating season (and really, who doesn't do a little of that?) and snacking only rarely on swimming tourists. Still, when taking a boat trip through the watery highways and byways of the Louisiana bayou and seeing those alligator eyes peeking out at water level, I wanna head straight for land, and take my time consuming a few Bayous while leaving the actual swamp, and the gators, far behind. Call me chicken if you must; I won't feel bad. You're the one stuck on a boat while I'm sipping a juicy, rummy delight.

Ice cubes

1½ ounces **dark rum**

1 ounce **freshly squeezed orange juice**

1 ounce **grenadine**

½ ounce **freshly squeezed lime juice**

1. Fill a cocktail shaker halfway full with ice cubes. Add the rum, orange juice, grenadine, and lime juice. Shake well, but watch out for that tail—that's how they get you.

2. Strain the mix into a cocktail glass, and serve while watching for any beady eyes that might be watching you.

A VIRGIN VARIATION: Omit the rum, and take the orange juice up to 2 ounces. After shaking and straining, add a good splash of ginger ale, and title it Crocs' Day Off.

Black Hood

Eerily it hovers in the distance, for a dark moment behind a cloud, then around the brick corner's edge, then **in a streetlight's shadow** . . . is it an executioner's hood? The covering cowl of a demon from the ninth plane? A headdress hiding a headless honcho come to hand out some heavy harm? Regardless, it seems the evil thing is getting closer and closer, but the street's so dark, and you can feel it back there, closer, closer—you'd better start running, it's almost got you, oh no, no, noooooo. Wait, what's that? It wasn't a salivating nighttime specter, but a rye-based drink? Then what's the hubbub about?

Ice cubes

1¾ ounces **rye**

1 ounce **Grand Marnier**

¾ ounce **Benedictine**

Lemon slice for garnish

1. Fill a cocktail shaker halfway full with ice cubes. Add the rye, Grand Marnier, and Benedictine. Shake fearlessly.

2. Strain into a cocktail glass. Squeeze the lemon slice over the glass, and then drop it in. Serve hoodless.

⬆ ***A Note:*** *Benedictine is an herbal liqueur containing 27 secret herbs, spices, and arcana of a mystical nature. Remember, though, it's always consumed in the name of doing good deeds.*

3 Hellacious Hits

I'm not weighing in seriously on any deep theological questions here, but I am saying that if there is an afterlife possibility that includes a lot of evil-doing folks, these are the drinks on the menu (or, they could be on the menu in a bar that Homer Simpson visits on one of his stops in the cartoon underworld).

1 Serpent's Tooth (page 219)

2 Black Hood (above)

3 Demon of Destiny (page 198)

Benedictine

Peer through the mists of time and you'll find that Benedictine's history matches its mysterious herbal taste like
a truly monastic monk matches up with his long robe
and contemplative demeanor. Benedictine's distinctive
flavor—one that is a crucial component in a number of
drinks, but also enjoyable on its own on occasion over ice,
or combined with brandy to make a B&B—comes from its
list (a secret list, as you might expect) of 27 ingredients.
We know there is angelica, hyssop, juniper, myrrh, saffron,
aloe, arnica, and cinnamon, but how much of each? And
what other this-and-thats are contained in what proportions passed from generation to generation? Finding that
out is a hazy proposition, indeed.

It's only right, considering that the recipe was lost for
many years. Gather round (with a glass of Benedictine
in your hand, in a chalice-type vessel, I would hope) and
hear the saga of Dom Bernardo Vincelli (first called Dom
Bernar), who, while living at the Abbey of Fécamp, gathered a number of herbs and spices and plants from around
the world in order to create a healing brew—one that
became a hit with any who had it. Then (cue the timpani),
during the French Revolution, a nobleman bought the
recipe, put it in his library for safekeeping (seems chancy,
but books are often a clever hiding place), and then in the
revolution's tumult, lost the recipe. And it stayed lost.

In 1863, an intrepid and praiseworthy fellow by the
name of Alexandre le Grand uncovered a book of spells in
which he found the secret recipe (a true treasure). Real-
izing that here, in front of him, was an ingredient list of
merit and might, he worked hard, deciphered and made
the recipe, balanced it out a bit, made a few more batches,
sipped and sipped, realized it was a hit, and called it Benedictine. And we, many years later, are all the better for it.

Bobby Burns

Earlier (in the Artist's Special, page 185, to be exact) there was a reference made (by me, to be exact) about the scariness of artists. I include poets with artists. Quoting phrases of their own and of those giants who came before them after a few rounds, writing very serious scribbles on bar napkins, and then going home to type away, to create poems that, once read, can never be forgotten. That's a bit scary. I'm not saying that Bobby Burns, the famous Scottish poet from the latter 1700s, was the first to follow along this poetic path, though he did like his drinks, and did write some poems that have been read for hundreds of years. I'm not even saying this drink was named after him (it could have been a cigar salesman who was known to buy a round for the folks who used to prop up the legendary Waldorf-Astoria bar). I'm just asking you to watch out for poets (and, to help you know how to recognize one, I suggest investing in a few good books by poets) and suggesting that this drink will charm most of them.

Ice cubes

2½ ounces **Scotch**

1 ounce **sweet vermouth**

¼ ounce **Benedictine**

Lemon twist for garnish

1. Fill a cocktail shaker halfway full with ice cubes. Add the Scotch, vermouth, and Benedictine. Shake like an inspired poet (which is a bit rowdily, I must admit).

2. Strain the mix into a cocktail glass. Squeeze the lemon twist over it and let it float into the glass.

"O Whisky! **soul o' plays an' pranks**! Accept a Bardie's gratefu' thanks!"

ROBERT BURNS, *"Scotch Drink"*

Brainstorm

Here's a hearty toast to the mad scientists and demented doctors in the house (Victor Frankenstein, quit hiding under that light shade), with your unruly hair, your blinking and sputtering and brightly flashing machines, your eyes that tend to go this-a-way and that-a-way, your poor stooped sidekicks, and your schemes and dreams and love of lightning storms—weather explosions that mirror those going off in your mind as you put together creatures, robots, and oftentimes evil machines in your attempts to take over the world. But world domination can't happen like a finger snap. And if you don't take time to stop and smell the cocktails, is it even worth it? Why not, this once, come into the party's main room and set the plotting aside with the coats in the bedroom? Then you can consume a Brainstorm for once, instead of having it consume you.

Ice cubes

2 ounces **Irish whiskey**

1 ounce **sweet vermouth**

¼ ounce **Benedictine**

Orange twist for garnish

1. Fill a cocktail shaker halfway full with ice cubes. Add the whiskey, vermouth, and Benedictine. Shake in a manner befitting a mad scientist.

2. Strain the mix into a cocktail glass. Squeeze the orange twist over the glass and drop it in.

Cameron's Kick

Who is the mysterious Cameron, and why is his kick so renowned amongst the great kickers (and those who've been kicked)? A stranded orphan from Toledo, raised among ninjas? Or one whose name is **spoken in whispers** because in 1989 he took out a window half a block away in the Hays, Kansas, kickball tourney? Here's a thought: The next time you have a couple of imaginative pals around, serve a tray of Cameron's Kicks, and have everyone come up with their own explanation for Cameron and his miraculous kick. Whoever has the finest (or funniest) legend gets a free drink.

Ice cubes

1½ ounces **Scotch**

1½ ounces **Irish whiskey**

¾ ounce **freshly squeezed lemon juice**

¾ ounce **orgeat syrup**

1. Fill a cocktail shaker halfway full with ice cubes. Add the Scotch and Irish whiskey (at the same time, to avoid bruised feelings), then the lemon juice and orgeat. Shake well—but no kicking.

2. Strain the mix into a cocktail glass.

⊙ *A Note: Orgeat is an almond-flavored syrup, which earns its keep mainly with the Mai Tai (page 32). It's available in gourmet shops, some grocery stores, and the occasional coffeehouse.*

Corpse Reviver

No one ever throws séance soirees anymore (if anyone in the room now says "they don't throw them any less," you might need this very libation sooner than you think), where **the room is illuminated** by a glowing crystal ball or a few dim wall sconces, and a drink-maker crouches at the head of a table in flowing robes, or a turban, or a gray wig and pointy hat, mumbling and kicking the table's legs, maybe tinkling a few bells via threads wrapped around those toes, tossing some slates, thumbing a Ouija board, and, as séance tradition dictates, making Corpse Revivers for all and sundry.

Ice cubes

1½ ounces **brandy**

1½ ounces **applejack** or **apple brandy**

¾ ounce **sweet vermouth**

1. Fill a cocktail shaker halfway full with ice cubes. Add the brandy, applejack, and vermouth. Shake as if you were trying to free yourself from a sealed coffin.

2. Strain the reviving mixture into a cocktail glass. Serve happily.

Creole Cocktail

A number of drinks use the word "Creole" in their monikers, or have throughout history, and I can understand why: The word sounds so nice on the tongue when set alongside "cocktail," and Creole cooking's piquant personality **could drive any expeditious bartender** toward wanting to create a combination whose notes pair perfectly with the cuisine's. Perhaps even more will be created, by those few who haven't read this, or who are willfully ignoring it (you know who you are). If you'd rather follow my advice than go off willy-nilly on your own, then I suggest the following recipe (or, in a pinch, the variation below it).

Ice cubes

1½ ounces **rye**

1 ounce **sweet vermouth**

¼ ounce **Benedictine**

¼ ounce **Amer Picon**

Lemon twist for garnish

1. Fill a cocktail shaker or mixing glass halfway full with ice cubes. Add the rye, vermouth, Benedictine, and Amer Picon. Using a long spoon, stir really well.

2. Strain the above assortment into a cocktail glass. Twist the lemon twist over the top, then let it join up.

🔼 *A Note: Amer Picon is a bitter French apéritif with orange accents. It's hard (if nigh impossible, depending on where you are) to round it up in the United States, at least at this moment, but things are changing rapidly in the cocktail world, so by the time you read this, Amer Picon may be in your local Quik Shop. Try searching around on the Internet for it, or pick up a case in France and then send me a bottle when you get stateside.*

A VARIATION: Not as tasty, but not bad in the least, the Creole Cocktail #2 is made by stirring together over ice 2 ounces bourbon, ½ ounce orange curaçao, and 2 dashes each of Angostura and Peychaud's bitters, then straining the mixture into a cocktail glass that has been rinsed with a few drops of Pernod.

Crimson Slippers

I choose to believe there's a hidden mystery by Dame Agatha (Christie, that is) called *The Crimson Slippers*, where mercurial and Belgian (not French) detective Hercule Poirot must solve the multiple murders (seems there's almost always more than one) circling around two single clues: a pair of comfy slippers with a tiny bloodstain on the toe, and a cocktail glass containing the remains of a bitter-ish combination aglow with a deep red hue. Naturally, if there isn't a yet-to-be-discovered Agatha manuscript with this title out there—perhaps in a trunk in the back corner of the attic in an English country house—then I guess you're going to have to write that mystery. Once it's an international publishing phenom, though, I'll expect you to buy the next round.

Ice cubes

2 ounces **dark rum**

1 ounce **Campari**

½ ounce **triple sec**

Dash of **Peychaud's bitters**

Lime wheel for garnish

1. Fill a cocktail shaker halfway full with ice cubes. Add the rum, Campari, triple sec, and bitters. Shake well.

2. Strain into a cocktail glass (being sure not to spill on any manuscripts lying around).

3. Squeeze the lime wheel over the glass and drop it in without any mystery.

Crow

Caw, caw, caw, those black doom-callers on wings circle above battlefields, track and field tournaments, and the occasional revelry that has pitched its tent long after midnight. Beware the crows at this hour and, while warnings are being issued like salty snacks, beware drinking the Crow at this hour, as it's a powerful bit of legerdemain in its own right. Though the drink won't circle around you, discussing whether to eat you if you're slumping on a couch (as the actual crows might), you still should have your hawk, your hound, and your true love around to protect you. It never hurts.

Cracked ice

2½ ounces **blended whiskey**

½ ounce **freshly squeezed lemon juice**

½ ounce **grenadine**

1. Fill a cocktail shaker halfway full with cracked ice. Add the whiskey, lemon juice, and grenadine. Shake, but watch the sky.

2. Strain into a cocktail glass. Drink, because tomorrow we may have a terrible headache.

"**You'll crow**, all right."

IRVIN S. COBB, writing about the Crow in *Irvin S. Cobb's Own Recipe Book*, 1934

Dark Mountain

The ominous mountain was there, in the distance, and as we walked up to it, it seemed to blot out the horizon and become more than a natural feature, nearly alive in our minds as it loomed, taunting us, daring us to attempt the long, rocky trail up to the summit, through treacherous passes and snow-speckled sides, around boulders, and past packs of wandering wolves, cold and hungry after the long winter. The implacable mound stood there, watched us, and waited. And we? We realized that it would be much more fun to **stay at the base of that big old hill** and make and drink a bunch of Dark Mountains instead. Who wants the hassle of climbing when you could be drinking with friends, anyway?

Ice cubes

1 ounce **dark rum**

1 ounce **freshly squeezed orange juice**

½ ounce **vodka**

½ ounce **Tia Maria**

Lemon twist for garnish

⤴ **A Note:** *Tia Maria is a coffee-flavored liqueur available, and beloved, worldwide.*

1. Fill a cocktail shaker halfway full with ice cubes. Add the dark rum, orange juice, vodka, and Tia Maria. Shake well.

2. Strain this non-gloomy mountain into a cocktail glass. Twist the lemon twist over it and let it descend into the drink.

A VARIATION: There is, in some tomes, a "Mountain" that uses white rum. But, as I found out during one expedition, dark rum does wonders.

A Drinker's Blogosphere

It's a swell time to have a drink and a computer. Just don't spill your drink on your computer. Do, though, use your computer to search out information on new recipes and nutty videos about cocktails and, especially, other cocktail connoisseurs who share your interests and might be fun to have a drink with (if only digitally). Start with these fine blogs and work your way through the wide Internet cocktail world.

1. The Cocktail Chronicles: www.cocktailchronicles.com
2. LUPEC (Ladies United for the Preservation of Endangered Cocktails) Boston: lupecboston.com
3. Jeffrey Morgenthaler: www.jeffreymorgenthaler.com
4. Beachbum Berry's Grog Blog: blog.beachbumberry.com
5. Cask Strength: caskstrength.wordpress.com

Demon of Destiny

Let's see, there's Choronzon, of the abyss. The half-human giants, the Nephilim. Lempo, who here and there doubles as a Finnish swear word. Jason Blood, the Demon, who sometimes fights for good and sometimes evil, depending on the year and the comic book. And then there's the demon that causes your computer to crash right before you saved that document, and the demon who always makes you spill a soda in your lap at the precise precious moment that twinkly-eyed him or her is walking by, and (most ferocious of all) the demon who induces the last drops of maraschino liqueur to somehow disappear when you're about to make this supernatural (thought not malevolent) beverage. You, brave one, can defeat this last demon—always buy a backup bottle. I have faith in you.

Ice cubes

1½ ounces **bourbon**

¾ ounce **sweet vermouth**

½ ounce **absinthe**

¼ ounce **maraschino liqueur**

¼ ounce **freshly squeezed lemon juice**

Lemon twist for garnish

1. Fill a cocktail shaker halfway full with ice cubes. Add the bourbon, vermouth, absinthe, maraschino liqueur, and lemon juice. Shake the demons away.

2. Strain into a cocktail glass, twist the lemon over the glass, let it drop into the glass, and sip, sip, sip.

⊕ A Note: Absinthe, though long unavailable, is back on these shores. If you can't seem to find it, be sad. Then substitute Pernod and feel a touch less sad.

"Any boy who loves **cobras, toads, and apes** can't be all bad."

GOMEZ ADDAMS, *The Addams Family*

Dirty Monkey

Bad monkey! Bad! Quit throwing those bananas around the room, wearing my underpants on your head, scratching the dog with your little monkey claws, spilling rum on your golden-tasseled red vest, leaving the icebox open and us without any ice . . . aw, who am I kidding? I can't stay mad at a simian. Come here and let's cuddle.

1 ounce **Cognac**

1 ounce **dark rum**

1 ounce **Coole Swan liqueur**

⟳ *A Note:* Coole Swan is a premium Irish cream liqueur that's becoming more available by the day. Thankfully.

1. Add the Cognac to a cordial glass that holds at least 3 ounces. Carefully (over a spoon if necessary to avoid mixing) pour in the dark rum. The two should be stratified.

2. Carefully pour the Coole Swan into the glass (again, over a spoon if necessary). The three monkeys should be separate, until they mix when being consumed.

Dutch Charlie's

The idea of running into a fella named "Dutch" gives me the shivers, especially if it happens on the waterfront, or in an alley, or even in a smoky bar—it's one of those names that implies scarred knuckles at the least, and the leading role in a popular book of crime nonfiction at the most. Charlie, on the other side of the coin, seems like a good time. I can relax with Charlie, even make a friendly wager over a game of Kemps (a card game that isn't, sadly, named after onetime basketball player Shawn Kemp). Put them together (in this drink unveiled for me first in Jacques Straub's 1914 book *Drinks*) and I'm happy, if still a touch wary. Adopt the same attitude, and your evening's sure to shine.

Ice cubes

1½ ounces **rye**

1 ounce **Dubonnet Rouge**

1 ounce **sweet vermouth**

2 dashes **Angostura bitters**

1. Fill a cocktail shaker halfway full with ice cubes. Add the rye, Dubonnet, vermouth, and bitters, saying each out loud as you add them to make both Dutch and Charlie happy. Shake well.

2. Strain into a cocktail glass. Garnish with a playing card (but keep an eye out while doing it).

Enchanted Field

Perhaps, lovey-dovey one, you believe this witchy mix should be in the Dim the Lights, Chill the Cocktails chapter (page 137), with such lovelorn natural luminaries as the Highland Fling (page 153), the Lover's Moon (page 161), and the Wildflower (page 180), picturing a slightly fuzzy field through which people roam in various states of flowing and falling-off clothing, with a wisp of fairy dust in the air. This, I'll admit, sounds dreamy. But not every enchantment lives up to our romantic notions (as the anti-romantics in the audience will point out). There've been many a witch who's been more than happy to lay an evil spell on a field in an attempt to wreak havoc. Which is why when you're taking part in **a fantastic adventure**, you always, always, always (saying things in threes is always the way in these types of adventures) need to have a flask or Thermos brimming with this drink. It's a cure for field-type curses, and it restores the idyllic scene faster than you can say, "Well, my pretties."

Ice cubes

1½ ounces **rye**

1 ounce **freshly squeezed orange juice**

½ ounce **Strega**

¼ ounce **Simple Syrup** (page 12)

Orange twist for garnish

1. Fill a cocktail shaker halfway full with ice cubes. Add the rye, orange juice, Strega, and simple syrup. Shake magically (while watching for broomsticks).

2. Strain into a cocktail glass. Twist the orange twist clockwise over the drink, then let it sink in.

Gaslight Tiger

All right, see, we're meeting up at midnight, ya get me? And then we're going to pack choppers, shine our shoes, load up in your flivvers, and head over, see, to the Gaslight Tiger, and we're gonna track down this drink, so don't get sidetracked by any gams (or dames or drugstore cowboys). Ya get me? Good, 'cause I'm not sure I do, completely, but if you're drinking a Gaslight Tiger, then you should be wearing a mop at least.

¼ ounce **Pernod**

Ice cubes

3 ounces **bourbon**

1 ounce **Dubonnet Blanc**

Lemon twist for garnish

⬆ *A Note: According to* Esquire's What Every Young Man Should Know *(Random House, 1962), where I discovered this recipe, you'll want to make sure you don't get too zozzled, because at one point this mix was supposed to be an aphrodisiac, and you'd hate to miss the chance to find out with your sheik or sheba if the rumors are true, no matter what year you're talking from.*

1. Pour the Pernod into an old-fashioned glass. Swirl it around so it completely coats the inside of the glass.

2. Fill the glass three-quarters full with ice cubes. Add the bourbon and the Dubonnet. Using a shiv or a spoon, stir well.

3. Twist the lemon twist over the glass, then let it fall on in.

Ginger Smash

This sounds positively Hulkish (Hulk smash!), but I don't think it really requires you to talk about yourself in the third person, or even to smash anything at all. Well, except for a few mint leaves and some fresh ginger. And, as it's so refreshing, you will somewhat **smash the sweatiness** out of a summer's day when drinking it. That's a good kind of destruction.

5 **fresh mint leaves**

1 teaspoon **granulated sugar**

½ ounce **freshly squeezed lemon juice**

1 teaspoon **minced ginger** (or ginger extracted from a garlic press)

Ice cubes

1½ ounces **brandy**

Dash of **Angostura bitters**

Chilled club soda

Chilled 7UP or **Sprite**

1. Place the mint, sugar, lemon juice, and ginger into a cocktail shaker. Using a muddler or long wooden spoon, muddle well.

2. Fill the shaker halfway full with ice cubes. Add the brandy and bitters. Shake well.

3. Fill a Collins glass halfway full with ice cubes. Strain the mix into the glass. Top it off with equal portions of club soda and 7UP.

⊕ *A Note: I modified this smash from a recipe by Jeremy Sidener (who knows many, many things about refreshing beverages). In his recipe he suggests VSOP brandy but doesn't specify a particular bitters. I've gone with Angostura here, but experiment and let us know how it works out.*

Green Room Cocktail

The green room may be filled with plants (whose plant-y nature is calming) or actually be painted green (as green is such a mellowing color, unless it's like a neon leaf of lettuce—that color could keep you up all night if you painted a room with it), but either way, when you're getting prepared to make your big debut in the theatre or on a daytime talk show, **the best way to stop those butterflies** twittering in your stomach and those daymares of tripping on stage, or falling into Oprah's lap, is to sip a Green Room in the green room.

Ice cubes

1½ ounces **Cognac**

1 ounce **dry vermouth**

½ ounce **orange curaçao**

1. Fill a cocktail shaker halfway full with ice cubes. Add the Cognac, vermouth, and curaçao. Shake thoroughly, but be loose about it, and let the tension flow out instead of in.

2. Strain the calm mix into a cocktail glass, and drink between deep breaths.

Hunter

"Hunter" has an ominous, trapped-in-a-snowy-woods-being-chased-by-a-madman-who-only-wants-to-hunt-the-most-dangerous-game: man! kind of a ring to it. But in this case, the hunting was much friendlier, as it involved my helpful cocktailing wife, Natalie, hunting down a book for me last time she was in Mexico: *Cocteles*, by R.S. Peysson. Though it takes a little translating, it's utterly worth it when you find a simple treasure like this drink.

2 ounces **bourbon**

½ ounce **cherry brandy**

½ ounce **freshly squeezed orange juice**

¼ ounce **anisette**

1. Fill a cocktail shaker halfway full with ice cubes. Add the bourbon, cherry brandy, orange juice, and anisette. Shake well (but not like a madman).

2. Strain into a cocktail glass. Garnish with a very small arrow.

Iollas's Itch

It's funny (in the curious sense, not the George Burns sense) how this strong/sweet/herby/fruity amalgamation carries the name of Iollas, who was the son of the viceroy of Greece and who at one point was thought to have carried to Alexander the Great a poison that supposedly killed him. This murderous story has been derided as inaccurate and ridiculous—hence the "funny" earlier. Also, this drink isn't poisonous in the least, so that's a bit odd. On the antique flip side, though, Alexander was thought to have brought the apricot to Greece, and there is apricot liqueur in here. It's quite a historical and alcohol-laden pickle we're in, one that could cause us to "hmm" and "umm" in professorial fashion from dawn until dusk if we'd let it. But how about we let history lie still for a second, make the drinks, then go put on some togas and talk about it?

3 **fresh mint leaves,** plus 1 **fresh mint sprig** for garnish

Ice cubes

2 ounces **rye**

¾ ounce **apricot liqueur**

¾ ounce **sweet vermouth**

1. Rub (carefully but firmly, as you want to expel the oils in the leaves) the 3 mint leaves all around the inside of a cocktail glass. Then discard them.

2. Fill a cocktail shaker halfway full with ice cubes. Add the rye, apricot liqueur, and vermouth. Shake forcefully (as if you were about to conquer Mesopotamia).

3. Strain into the minty glass from above. Garnish with the mint sprig.

King Cole

You know (c'mon, you aren't *that* old) the key lines having to do with this particular king: "He called for his pipe, and he called for his bowl, and he called for his fiddlers three." Since most bars and many homes are now smoke-free, you may have to skip the pipe, but the bowl of course refers to the drink below (which **you can't skip in the least**), and the three fiddlers refers to the traveling musicians that everyone has at parties. Right? Or, just put some fiddling-style music on the CD player, if you're afraid of traveling musicians (as I've known some, I can understand the fear). It's not known who exactly the famous nursery rhyme refers to, but it is known that in Patrick Gavin Duffy's *Official Mixer's Manual* (of 1940), this is constructed with "gum" syrup. In the revised edition of Mr. Duffy's *The Bartender's Guide* (the Pocket Books edition of 1971, specifically) it's made with plain "sugar syrup." If you're feeling adventuresome, or feeling as if you want your King Cole 1940s-style, you can construct gum syrup in the back-in-the-day manner, thanks to David Wondrich, who printed up the recipe (which he unearthed in the *Gentleman's Table Guide*, from 1871) in his fine book *Imbibe!* (Perigee, 2007). See the note below for the breakdown.

1 **pineapple round**

1 **orange slice**

Ice cubes

2 ounces **bourbon**

½ ounce **Fernet-Branca**

¾ ounce **Simple Syrup** (page 12) or **gum syrup** (see A Note)

1. Put the pineapple round and orange slice in a cocktail shaker. Using a muddler, wooden spoon, or scepter of some sort, muddle the fruit well.

2. Fill the cocktail shaker halfway full with ice cubes. Add the bourbon, Fernet, and simple syrup. Shake exceedingly well (or you'll have the ghosts of the authors of all books mentioned above after you—and maybe the live Mr. Wondrich, too).

3. Strain into a cocktail glass.

A Note: Mr. Wondrich says: "Dissolve 1 lb. of the best white gum arabic in 1½ pints of water, nearly boiling; [take] 3 lbs. of white sugar or candy; melt and clarify it with half pint of cold water, add the gum solution and boil all together for two minutes." Mr. Wondrich suggests making sure the gum arabic is food safe, and suggests melting the sugar and water over a low flame, instead of melting the sugar first, as our sugar is better (in so many words). He seems completely trustworthy in these matters, so I'd follow his advice.

Fernet-Branca

I'd like to believe (if I don't sound too much as though I'm serving up some political posturing like so much faux pork) that I'm a builder, and not a divider. Though one liqueur I love, Fernet-Branca, sadly can't say the same. Its bitterness, which is sharp and in your face and wonderful, doesn't win over everyone in a room, much less everyone in a bar, especially on that first sip. Strong personalities may always have this effect on folks (take famous British comedian and TV star Matt Berry, for example). It's probably always been this way to a point, since 1845, when Fernet was created by Maria Scala (who through marriage became Maria Branca) as a medicine in Milan, Italy. It's still considered to have medicinal benefits, especially by those in the land of its birth, and it is thought to be one of the best remedies for alleviating the pain from eating a little too much. It's also a great ingredient in drinks, serving up a wide assortment of accents when mixed (akin to many of the bitters mentioned on page 224).

What brings out this bitter and sometimes party-wedging taste? It's a secret recipe (natch) kept by the Fratelli Branca company (which is overseen by members of the original Branca family)—a recipe containing 27 ingredients from 4 different continents, including aloe, gentian root, rhubarb, gum myrrh, red Cinchona bark, galanga, zedoary, and saffron. Whew. There are two versions—one that's sold in Italy, and one we get over here—and the reach of this latter *amaro* (as Fernet is a type of Italian amaro, or bitters) has stretched around the world. (It's a special hit in Argentina, where it's consumed with Coke. Really.) If you haven't tried it, get over the fear and give it a whirl solo, over ice, or in a cocktail. If you've tried it, and got that bitter face and never tried it again, give it another shot, for me. Maybe in a Stomach Reviver Cocktail (page 225)?

Kitchen Sink

The extensive ingredient list here does not, I say, *does not* include an actual kitchen sink. This isn't a sideshow, y'all, and I don't expect you to gnaw on porcelain, or 18/10 stainless steel, or whatever those wacky kitchen designers are making sinks out of today. Neither do the instructions have you making this drink *in* an actual kitchen sink, as this would be ridiculously dangerous, unless you have a sink without a garbage disposal. The "Kitchen Sink" is only a name. Remember that.

Cracked ice

¾ ounce **rye**

¾ ounce **gin**

¾ ounce **apple brandy**

¼ ounce **freshly squeezed lemon juice**

¼ ounce **freshly squeezed orange juice**

½ ounce **Simple Syrup** (page 12)

1 **egg**

1. Fill a cocktail shaker halfway full with cracked ice. Add the remaining ingredients. Shake rapidly and thoroughly.

2. Strain into a large cocktail glass. Garnish with nothing (especially not a faucet, which is dangerous to teeth).

✖ *A Warning: This does contain a raw egg, so be sure your egg is fresh. And this shouldn't be served to guests who are elderly or who have compromised immune systems.*

Leatherneck

Sounding a little icky, *Leatherneck* is indeed an honorable slang term referring to a member of the Marines (it comes from the high leather collars worn to ward off sword blows to the neck). You might decide snappily that this drink would be one, then, that was especially tough, a battle to get down, or at least one that left you feeling as if you'd survived a day of Marine boot camp. But, as in many cases, **the name is tougher than the mixing**, as this one's a snap to make and a taste sensation. You may end up saluting its simplicity, even. Hey, wait, maybe that's the connection.

Ice cubes

2 ounces **rye**

¾ ounce **orange curaçao**

½ ounce **freshly squeezed lime juice**

1. Fill a cocktail shaker halfway full with ice cubes. Add the rye, curaçao, and lime juice. Shake like a Marine.

2. Strain into a cocktail glass. Salute. Drink.

Freshness Is Bestest

Maybe you aren't the kind of the person who says "bestest" when sending out your party invites, and maybe you aren't the kind of person who even sends party invites, instead going for a more laissez-faire approach to swashbuckling soirées. Even if these points get checked in your personality profile, you should still always follow the "fresh" rule, meaning you'll want to use freshly squeezed juices, even in the early A.M., and even if you have a minor case of lemon squeezer's shoulder or orange juicer's elbow (here's where pals come in handy). In the same vein, don't bother with cream that's gotten old and bold enough to open itself, or with a bottle of club soda whose fizz has fizzled. Be fresh with your mixers, and become a party-throwing legend. Or, if you aren't the kind of person who wants legendary status, simply be happy in the fact that you're consuming much better drinks.

Leprechaun

I feel a bit sick to my stomach (wait, wait, not from the drink, which is a balanced affair, **fine for afternoons and dinners of state**) to admit that when I hear "Leprechaun," I think of a murderous movie character spun out into numerous (far too numerous) sequels, and not of a mischievous fairy shoemaker who may play a trick or two, but who certainly won't strangle you with a telephone cord. Where did it all go wrong? I'm not sure, but I know that I'm going to have a couple more of the beverage Leprechauns, in hopes of realigning my mind. You do the same, if you're in the same sad predicament.

Ice cubes

2 ounces **Irish whiskey**

1 ounce **freshly squeezed lemon juice**

½ ounce **Simple Syrup** (page 12)

2 dashes **Angostura bitters**

1. Fill a cocktail shaker halfway full with ice cubes. Add every remaining ingredient (but don't think of them as sequels). Shake well enough to drive the movies sharing this mix's moniker out of your mind.

2. Strain into a cocktail glass. Serve without a movie reference.

5 For the Four Corners

Go global with your get-up-and-go beverages-or at least give a shout-out to spots this-a-way and that-a-way the next time you're shaking and straining or stirring and sipping with these five hits.

1 Northside Special (page 121)

2 Caribbean Bloom (page 148)

3 Parisian Blonde (page 164)

4 Shanghai Cocktail (page 219)

5 Southstreet (page 266)

Leviathan 477

As a Biblical beast (as well as a beast mentioned in many other ancient and historic books), it makes a big dollop of sense to have a strong Scotch toe-curler carry the name "Leviathan." But where, mystery buffs, does the "477" originate from? From my bits of research, it's not the name of a Bible verse with the big beastie in it, nor does it seem to be a specific reference to the Talmud or the Blake or Milton poems, or other literary works (though there is a 477-page book about Thomas Hobbes, who wrote a book called *Leviathan*, but that seems too remote). Admittedly, it could be a singular page notation. (I sure haven't had the time to check each and every printing of each and every book that uses the word—I mean, if I did that, how would I be able to test these drinks for you, dear reader?) Even David Embury, who is a man of many opinions, says nothing at all in his book *The Fine Art of Mixing Drinks* (Doubleday, 1948) about this particularly monstrous combination of ingredients. Which leads me to this: If you can tell me what the "477" refers to (and I'm sure it's something simple, because that's the way it goes), your next liquid Leviathan 477 is on me.

Ice cubes

2 ounces **Scotch**

1 ounce **freshly squeezed lemon juice**

1 ounce **freshly squeezed orange juice**

½ ounce **Simple Syrup** (page 12)

1. Fill a cocktail shaker halfway full with ice cubes. Add the Scotch, lemon juice, orange juice, and simple syrup. Shake like a beast.

2. Strain into a cocktail glass.

Limbo

One way out of thinking that serving this blended beauty at your next warm-weather affair might leave some consumers a smidge depressed is to bypass the religious connotations (where limbo isn't as bad as a few other spots, but is a decidedly somber place) and the psychological connotations (limbo as that general "blah" state between a couple of more interesting possibilities) and focus on limbo as a popping party game. To do this, have the limbo pole as near to the entrance of your yard as possible. That way, guests arriving are set on the right limbo reference from the get-go. Oh, and serving them one of these right quick helps, too. **Serves 2**

2 cups **cracked ice**

4 ounces **dark rum**

1 cup **peeled and cubed papaya**

1 cup **coconut milk**

1. Place all of the ingredients in a blender. Blend well.

2. Pour into two large, peppy goblets and serve to two folks who know where they're going.

⬆ *A Note:* *Coconut milk shouldn't be confused with the sweeter, syrupy crème de coconut. If you find this isn't quite sweet enough, though, you could add an ounce of the latter. But I'm not sure that's going to get you to the right place.*

Oriental

One of the many, many tiptop traits about cocktails, and highballs, and punches, and drinks of every sort and size is that they frequently come accompanied by splendid stories. This is one of my favorite cocktail stories, and one I've told before. But it's so good, I'm going to tell it again, using the version in Harry Craddock's steadfast 1930 *Savoy Cocktail Book*: "In August, 1924, an American engineer nearly died of fever in the Philippines and only the extraordinary devotion of Doctor B. saved his life. As an act of gratitude, the engineer gave Doctor B. the recipe of this cocktail."

Ice cubes

1½ ounces **rye**

¾ ounce **sweet vermouth**

¾ ounce **orange curaçao**

½ ounce **freshly squeezed lime juice**

1. Fill a cocktail shaker halfway full with ice cubes. Add the rye, vermouth, curaçao, and lime juice and shake like a lifesaver.

2. Strain the mix into a cocktail glass. Serve with a story. (If you've already told the above while making the Oriental, then you'll have to make up another. Start your storytelling engines now.)

Quarter Deck

Just because I mix my rum with a few choice ingredients, don't for a Caribbean second doubt my pirate cred (though I am much more of a friendly pirate type, who likes to say "argh" and wear a red floppy hat and fake gold doubloon necklaces and swill Quarter Decks while splashing around the kiddie pool in the backyard). It's not as if I've stopped talking about "me booty" or saying "yo ho ho." Before making me walk the mythical plank, make up one of the swillers below. Then, if you're not swayed, I'll hand over my hat.

Ice cubes

1½ ounces **dark rum**

1 ounce **mead**

½ ounce **freshly squeezed lime juice**

Lime slice for garnish

1. Fill a cocktail shaker halfway full with ice cubes. Add the rum, mead, and lime juice. Shake well, me hearty.

2. Strain the mix into a cocktail glass or goblet (if the latter seems more pirate-y). Garnish with the lime slice.

⊙ *A Note: Mead is a wine variant made most often from honey, water, and yeast, at a brewery called a meadery or a mazery. Look for it at your local large liquor emporium.*

Rattlesnake Cocktail

Hey hombre, was I a-hearin' you right? Mah ten-gallon hat was pulled a bit low over mah twenty-gallon head and I wasn't sure I heard you proper, cowpoke. But if I did get what you said rightly over the barroom's click and clatter and the rufflin' and shufflin' of the cards, and the swish-swish of the saloon girls—did you call me a lowdown rattlesnake just now? Wait, what's that? You offered to buy me a Rattlesnake—an anise-y, bitter-y, tangy spread built on a backbone of rye? Well, pardon me, that's a horse of a different color. I think you and I may end up waltzin' off into the sunset. **Serves 6**

Ice cubes

9 ounces **rye**

3 ounces **freshly squeezed lemon juice**

3 ounces **Pernod**

4 dashes **Peychaud's bitters**

1. Fill a large cocktail shaker halfway full with ice cubes. Add the rye, lemon juice, Pernod, and bitters, with a tip of that big hat. Shake well. (Need I say, in a rattling motion? I didn't think so.)

2. Strain the mix equally into six cocktail glasses or boot-shaped cordials. Drink with pardners.

⬆ *A Note: You'll notice this is for six folks. There's a justifiable reason: You always need to have at least five with you, because Rattlesnakes are a bit sneaky. And it's better to be safe.*

⬆ *A Second Note: Don't have a large cocktail shaker? Make this in a pitcher instead. Watch for the ice when straining, though.*

Rum Cobbler

When spending that last wish on a hot day for a Rum Cobbler, the fear is that you end up with a deranged shoemaker (using "rum" in the usually British secondary definition of "presenting danger") chasing you down cobblestone alleys with a giant sewing awl in one hand and a strange glint in the eye, as opposed to an old, seldom-seen drink that takes a peck of stirring but **ends with icily lovely results**. With this in mind, be really clear to the genie that you want the *drink* when making that wish.

Crushed ice

1½ ounces **Simple Syrup** (page 12)

3 ounces **dark rum**

Orange twist for garnish

Orange slice for garnish

Fresh mint leaves for garnish

1. Fill a goblet three-quarters full with crushed ice. Add the simple syrup first, and the rum second.

2. Stir really well—the key to the Cobbler is stirring until the outside of the glass gets frosty to the touch. Once the chill has descended, garnish with the orange twist, orange slice, and mint leaves.

VARIATIONS: There are many Cobblers that are fun to try. For a first little variation, substitute orgeat (an almond-flavored syrup) for the straight simple syrup in the above recipe. Or, why not exchange the rum for gin, whiskey, applejack, brandy, Champagne, or even sherry? You could even try replacing part or all of the simple syrup with a liqueur, such as using half maraschino liqueur and half simple syrup with gin, or adding different fruits at the end. The key (as mentioned above), though, is to stir until it gets frosty, and always add the sweeter ingredient first.

Scofflaw Cocktail

What a fine word *scofflaw* is, the way it slides off your tongue in a devil-may-care manner, wearing a tailored suit and scuffed-up shoes. It matches this drink (with its sporting of balanced and well-groomed but twisty flavors) to a Model T, and matches the Prohibition-era criminal element it's associated with as well. Here's a fact to slide out at the bar when introducing some pals (maybe those who like to pretend to be a little outside the law themselves by getting out of jail free when playing Monopoly, or by hooking into the video system for a Grand Theft Auto marathon) to the Scofflaw Cocktail. The word came into use during a competition held in 1923 to find the best word to describe those lawless folks who drank illegally made booze. In modern parlance, *scofflaw* is generally dangled over any lawbreaker. It does come together nicely, though, much like a well-planned robbery of the last doughnut brought into work for your cubicle-mate's birthday.

Ice cubes

2 ounces **rye**

1½ ounces **dry vermouth**

½ ounce **freshly squeezed lemon juice**

½ ounce **grenadine**

2 dashes **orange bitters**

Lemon slice for garnish

1. Fill a cocktail shaker halfway full with ice cubes. Add the rye, vermouth, lemon juice, grenadine, and bitters. Shake well, though not criminally (which would mean spilling).

2. Strain into a large cocktail glass and garnish with the lemon slice.

"Jock, the genial bartender of Harry's New York Bar, yesterday invented the Scoff-law Cocktail, and it has **already become exceedingly popular** among American prohibition dodgers."

HARRY AND WYNN (Harry McElhone and Wynn Holcomb), *Barflies and Cocktails*, 1927

Serpent's Tooth

I can hear the wizened wizard whispering, "The ways of the Serpent's Tooth, my knock-kneed apprentice, are varied and tie us into a world of magic, from the deep vales where the Irish brew to the sweet vermouth made by Italian enchanters to the caraway conjurors with kümmel in their cast-iron caldrons, aided by the occult powers of lemons, and the wizardly herbs and spices known as Angostura, rising out of the mist to make one helluva good drink." And now I've passed the spell on to you.

Ice cubes

1½ ounces **Irish whiskey**

1 ounce **sweet vermouth**

½ ounce **kümmel**

½ ounce **freshly squeezed lemon juice**

3 dashes **Angostura bitters**

1. Fill a mixing glass or cocktail shaker halfway full with ice cubes. Add the whiskey, vermouth, kümmel, lemon juice, and bitters. Stir well with a long spoon or wand (as long as the wand is 18/10 stainless steel).

2. Strain into a large cocktail glass. If you feel a garnish is needed, float a glittering snake eye on top (I get my snake eyes at the local magic store, the Kwickie Cadabra).

Shanghai Cocktail

In towns as varied as Port Townsend, Washington (now an artist and vacation spot), Astoria, Oregon (where the movie *Goonies* was filmed), and San Francisco, California (home of novelist Andrew Sean Greer), roaming "crimps" used to lure unsuspecting fellas into becoming sailors through trickery, cajoling, and knocks to the noggin. One minute you're contemplating picking up a gewgaw to take back home to Ma, the next you're being woken by waves and the snoring of the world's biggest cabin mate—victim to this process called "getting shanghaied." Today, you may be shanghaied by a local in these same locales, but the result has you ending up with a hand-painted ashtray or pirated DVD. Less dangerous, but still not involving this cocktail one bit. Which is just sad.

Ice cubes

1½ ounces **dark rum**

½ ounce **freshly squeezed lemon juice**

½ ounce **anisette**

½ ounce **grenadine**

1. Looking over your shoulder (it pays to be watchful), fill a cocktail shaker halfway full with ice cubes. Add the rum, lemon juice, anisette, and grenadine. Shake warily.

2. Strain into a cocktail glass. Garnish with a healthy dose of caution and skepticism.

Sir Henry Morgan

I found this simple tickler in *Here's How: A Round-the-World Bar Guide* (Signet, 1957–not the *Here's How* cocktail book with wooden covers, by the way), and was a touch intrigued by the name, and especially by the description, which states that it was named for a pirate who became governor. Hmm, the Henry Morgan I know (historically, that is), was a government-okayed privateer, then pirate, who was famous in his own time for intense brutality in his quest for gold and riches (popping eyeballs, hanging people by parts they'd rather not be hung from, and such), and who is (ironically, when you think about it) famous now for being an international party guy marketing figure and rum logo: Captain Morgan. Perhaps another Henry Morgan did follow the path mentioned in the above book, but my guess is the author had a few of these and confused Henry with his uncle Edward (who was lieutenant governor of Jamaica at one point). I can't blame the author too much, if that's the case. I've almost confused myself, and am just now pouring my first Sir Henry Morgan of the night.

Ice cubes

2 ounces **dark rum**

1 ounce **sweet vermouth**

2 dashes **Angostura bitters**

Lime slice for garnish (optional)

1. Fill a cocktail shaker halfway full with ice cubes. Add the rum, vermouth, and bitters, and shake well.

2. Strain into a cocktail glass. If you feel a garnish is needed (or fear that your guests might go on a pirating, or marketing, rampage), a lime slice is the best route.

Sookie Cocktail

Ruff, ruff, growl, growl . . . uh-oh, could it be a black and tan dog rocketing up the alley and around the recycling bins, a dog thick in the chest and with paws the size of small steaks, a glint in its eye, now past the neighbor's oddly windowless white van, and around that old tin can and the empty bottle of Maker's Mark, closer now, wait, it's a Rottweiler? And the tongue's hanging over those big, big white teeth . . . what's going to happen? It's almost here!

Oh, wait, it only wants a belly rub, and a scratch behind the ears? Whew.

That, dog lovers, is exactly how this drink operates. It appears strong and tough and a tad dangerous to those not in the know, and then trots nearer and nearer, but once it reaches you, you'll realize **the drink just wants that belly scratched**, and maybe, just maybe, will end up being your best pal.

Ice cubes

2 ounces **Maker's Mark bourbon**

¾ ounce **macadamia nut liqueur**

½ ounce **freshly squeezed orange juice**

1. Fill a cocktail shaker halfway full with ice cubes. Add the bourbon, macadamia liqueur, and orange juice. Shake like a dog jumping for joy.

2. Strain the Sookie into a cocktail glass. Start scratching (or drinking).

↑ *A Note: Kahana Royale Macadamia Nut Liqueur is constructed from an assortment of exotic natural flavors and roasted macadamia nuts. If you've got a sweet tooth, try it not only in this drink, but also poured over ice cream. That's living, y'all.*

Stockholm Tar

Shady, boy-o, shady. That's what I used to call any man, woman, or beast who came up to me when the sun was down and the lights were low and whispered in a raspy, rusty jangle, "Can you set me up with the Stockholm Tar?" Could be drugs, could be a formula for a new illogical weapon of massive power, or could be a viscous smuggled-in substance destined to stick to shoe soles. I wanted nothing to do with it. Until that fateful day when a crusty old salt took me aside and laughed at my dread. He whispered two phrases: "pine tar" and "rum drink," and my life changed forever. First, I wondered if George Brett (ex–Kansas City Royal, famous for being accused of having too much pine tar on his baseball bat and then throwing a fit) knew that "Stockholm tar" was another term for pine tar; second, I wondered if he knew it was the name of a drink; and third, I wondered if we were in a bar together, would he buy me one? Let's hope so.

Ice cubes

1½ ounces **dark rum**

½ ounce **freshly squeezed lime juice**

½ ounce **cranberry juice cocktail**

½ ounce **Simple Syrup** (page 12)

¼ ounce **maraschino liqueur**

Lime slice for garnish

1. Fill a cocktail shaker halfway full with ice cubes. Add the rum, lime juice, cranberry juice, simple syrup, and maraschino liqueur. Shake well (you want to ensure it doesn't get a tar-like appearance).

2. Strain the mix into a cocktail glass. Garnish with the lime slice (and, if serving to Mr. Brett, a small baseball bat).

⬆ *A Note: Maraschino liqueur is not the dregs of that old jar of maraschino cherries that's been in your fridge for a year. Serve that, and you may end up getting tarred.*

A Bounty of Bitters

It brings tears of joy to my eyes that I can even write the above title, "A Bounty of Bitters," without being somewhat sarcastic, because until recently we suffered from a paucity of bitters, with only Angostura—and on occasion, in the right locales, Peychaud's—being available. In some local hooch parlors you couldn't even get those, but lately, this bitters deficiency has been attacked with an eye toward remedying it. (And, by the way, saying "bitters deficiency" is in no way a slur on either of the above brands. *Au contraire!* Both Angostura and Peychaud's are bastions of bitters in the cocktail world for a very good reason: They work wonders.)

See, at one point in time, people had access to a wider variety of bitters—meaning liquid elixirs containing a long list of secret ingredients, including herbs, spices, plants, roots, and more that have been infused or distilled into a liquor base. Then, the bitters drought happened. The past few years, though, has seen a resurgence of bitters, with the two mentioned above being more available, but also with a host of new bitters showing up in drinks and in stores, including Regan's Orange Bitters No. 6 (which is a delicious throwback to a time when orange bitters were stocked behind every bar), the Fee Brothers line of flavored bitters (which have been around a bit, but are now much more available), and even newer bitters entries, like those from The Bitter Truth and Bittermens. Angostura has now come out with an orange bitters, and many bars are making their own house bitters to add something extra to cocktails.

I was lucky enough to go to a "bitters party" hosted by Andrew Bohrer at Seattle's 22 Doors, along with a host of tip-top bartenders, bar scribes such as Robert Hess, and drinking devotees like Husky Boy Jeremy Holt. Every attendee brought homemade bitters, with a list that covered chocolate bitters, grapefruit bitters, and much more. The beauty of it is that each of the bitters adds its own imprint to a drink, bringing out the best in other ingredients as well as introducing its own flavors and personality. Can you switch bitters in a drink (say, subbing in an orange one for Angostura because your corner store stocks only orange)? Sure, but the drink will taste different, and become a different drink. So, take advantage of our bitters renaissance, and start bitters-ing.

Stomach Reviver Cocktail

By Godfrey, I love this cocktail. I mean, it's not that I've been known for overeating (though not for undereating, either) or overimbibing (though, between us, I do take a wee tipple here and there), those proclivities that may lead to a smidge of rumbling and grumbling in the tummy. I just love the name of this cocktail. And the taste. And how it's nice to **wake up to after a night of overindulging**. (Well, I had to admit it sometime, right? Just to keep us on the up-and-up.)

Ice cubes

1½ ounces **brandy**

1 ounce **kümmel**

½ ounce **Fernet-Branca**

2 dashes **Peychaud's bitters**

1. Fill a cocktail shaker halfway full with ice cubes (do it gingerly if you're, um, slightly under the weather, as they say). Add the brandy, kümmel, Fernet, and bitters, and shake in the best manner you can.

2. Strain the mix into a cocktail glass. Garnish with good will toward yourself and your fellow man.

⬆ *A Note: Fernet-Branca, for many, is an acquired taste. It's an Italian bitter drink (perhaps the most bitter Italian amaro) that traces its considerable roots to 1845. The secret recipe boasts 27 herbs and spices, including luminaries from across the globe, such as aloe, gentian root, rhubarb, gum myrrh, red Cinchona bark, galanga, zedoary, and saffron. Don't be afraid of the Fernet, though—you'll grow to love it like a favorite Italian shirt.*

⬆ *A Second Note: Kümmel traces its legacy back to 1575 in Holland, where it's said Erven Lucas Bols created it. It floats out a mix of caraway, cumin, and fennel flavors and is consumed solo as well as in mixed drinks.*

Tartan Swizzle

I see you wallflowers out there, hugging the dancehall's walls, worried about your steps and your shoes (thinking they may rebel and trip you as you set off for that opening dance), chewing that bottom lip ever so slightly because of your lack of knowledge of those modern steps. I was with you, once. Then my pal Jeremy Holt (the Husky Boy) told me about the Tartan Swizzle, a dance so **wild and extemporaneous** that no one can do anything but applaud as you're cutting that crazy rug. Wait, wait, before you head to the floor to bring it (as the kids say), I should tell you that Jeremy also served me up a gang of Tartan Swizzles before convincing me to start the dance of the same name. I suggest you take that route, too, before getting all Baryshnikov.

Ice cubes

2 ounces **Scotch**

1½ ounces **freshly squeezed lime juice**

¾ ounce **Simple Syrup** (page 12)

2 dashes **Angostura bitters**

Crushed ice

Chilled club soda

~~~~~~~~~~~~~~~~~~~~~~~~~~~~

⬆ *A Note: The Husky Boy suggests a lighter Scotch here, such as Dewar's, J&B, Cutty Sark, or Clan MacGregor. You should rely on him.*

1. Fill a cocktail shaker halfway full with ice cubes. Add the Scotch, lime juice, simple syrup, and bitters. Shake, but in dancer fashion.

2. Fill a Collins glass three-quarters full with crushed ice. Stir the ice briefly to chill the glass, then strain the mixture from the shaker over the ice.

3. Fill (a lot of filling here, which is good, because it provides energy for dancing) the Collins glass almost to the top with club soda. Stir a bit, to get a little frothiness.

A VARIATION: Swizzles can be made with other base liquors (they're a whole family of dancing drinks). Try rum or gin, and see if that gets your toes tapping.

Thumper

A deadly, deranged rabbit, upset about a lack of primetime billing in the next nature blockbuster? Or the actual name of the next headline-grasping horror movie, turning critics all twitchy because of its peg-legged killer? Or the new game filling the nation with glee that involves "thumping" your ex-boss (or current one, if you're on the way out) with a giant plastic thumping device? Or a drink that **packs a wallop** of brandy mixed with Tuaca (supposedly created for Italian Renaissance thumper Lorenzo de' Medici) and other subtleties? The last definition is the one in this dictionary.

Ice cubes

2 ounces **brandy**

1 ounce **Tuaca**

½ ounce **sweet vermouth**

Lemon twist for garnish

1. Fill a cocktail shaker halfway full with ice cubes. Add the brandy, Tuaca, and vermouth. Shake well. Thumpingly well.

2. Strain into a cocktail glass. Twist the lemon twist over the glass and drop it in.

5 Tailgating Triumphs

Are you ready for some tailgating? I sure am—and (between us) I'm not the hugest sports fan ever. But the tailgating? The tailgating I can get behind, every time. A bunch of buddies, an outdoor buffet of handheld and fried and potentially unhealthy foods, and an assortment of sporty drinks? That's a little chunk of heaven. If you find your tailgating lacking in the last part of that list (the sporty drinks), score with the following mixes.

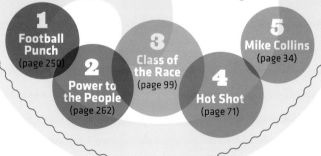

1 Football Punch (page 250)

2 Power to the People (page 262)

3 Class of the Race (page 99)

4 Hot Shot (page 71)

5 Mike Collins (page 34)

Ward Eight

What the world needs now is more Ward Eights. No matter your political perspective, I hope we agree on this salient issue (unless you're riding an early 1900s Prohibitionist ticket, in which case maybe you should just shut this book before you get your long johns bunched). With an equilibrium of rye, sweet, and sour, it should be beyond politicking—a drink bringing us back together in these hard times, a drink that can be served on Wall Street and Main Street. You see, even I **start sounding like a county speechwriter** when I haven't had enough Ward Eights. This is why politics is dangerous business, and why some folks whipped up the first Ward Eight at Boston's Locke-Ober restaurant to trumpet in liquid form Mr. Martin Lomasney's election as the Eighth Ward's representative in the 1898 state legislature.

Ice cubes

2 ounces **rye**

1 ounce **Simple Syrup** (page 12)

¾ ounce **freshly squeezed lime juice**

¼ ounce **grenadine**

Orange slice for garnish

Maraschino cherry for garnish

1. Fill a cocktail shaker halfway full with ice cubes and no double talk. Add the rye, simple syrup, and lime juice. Shake well.

2. Add the grenadine to the shaker, and shake twice more, giving a nod to Washington (the city or state).

3. Strain the mix into a goblet and garnish with the orange and cherry (politicians get hungry).

A VARIATION: Another popular recipe for this political favorite is also worth trying. Omit the lime juice and simple syrup, and add ½ ounce each of freshly squeezed orange juice and lemon juice. I learned my eights on the above recipe, but I'm not going to campaign against the variation either.

Warlock

If you're hanging out, on an October evening perhaps, **when the owls are circling**, watching the not-so-famous 1989 Julian Sands movie *Warlock* while listening to the not-so-famous German metal band Warlock, and at the same time reading comics featuring (usually in a back-page second story) the Marvel character Adam Warlock (once known spookily only as "Him"), then I believe you have either a short attention span or the ability to pay attention to many types of media at once. Whichever it is, pour a Warlock to indulge yourself in yet a fourth media type: the magical cocktail.

Ice cubes

1½ ounces **brandy**

¾ ounce **Strega**

½ ounce **limoncello**

½ ounce **freshly squeezed orange juice**

Dash of **Peychaud's bitters**

⬆ *A Note: Limoncello, if you don't know, is an Italian lemon-based liqueur, available under many brands and one of the finer things in life.*

1. Fill a cocktail shaker halfway full with ice cubes. Add the brandy, Strega, limoncello, orange juice, and bitters. Shake sorcerously (but not so much that you call down a demon or some such creature who might take the drink).

2. Strain into a good-size cocktail glass or a mug made of dragon's hide. Garnish with a plastic pitchfork (in case you want to fly around like a warlock without risking the injury a full-size pitchfork might bring).

Strega

Sometimes, after a particularly long day, I'll come home, put a few ice cubes in a glass, add a few ounces of Strega, and let the witch (which is what *strega* means, in Italian) cast her spell on me, taking my cares away. Other times, when I've had an especially nice day (like when I read that Heather Bouzan wrote in Boston's *Stuff@Night* magazine, "A.J. Rathbun, we'd kill to buy you a drink"), I'll come home and let the witch make my enjoyment of the moment even more enjoyable. See, when a liqueur's as good and as memorable as Strega is, it's like a part of the family.

Strega was first made in 1860 by Giuseppe Alberti, whose father was a grocer, giving Alberti easy access to many herbs and spices. Together, they decided on the name "Strega," both a testament to the liqueur's magic and to the witches who supposedly gathered around Benevento, Italy, where the Albertis lived. Strega is still made in the same factory today, though the factory has been expanded and refined and is also now used to make the unforgettable Strega nougat and Strega-filled chocolates. (Make tasting some of these a goal.) The key to the liqueur's taste is the same, too. It's made with 70 herbs and spices from countries worldwide, including wild mint that grows only along the rivers of the former Samnite territory, and the inclusion of saffron, which gives Strega its distinctive golden color. It's also matured in oak barrels to let the flavors gel. The recipe, which combines these many aspects of Strega, is, naturally, a closely guarded secret.

Since 1947, the company has also given out the Strega Prize for literature in Italy, one of the most prestigious prizes for fiction. If you're a bit adventuresome, visit the Strega factory itself, and see the famous walnut tree that still stands in the factory courtyard, and that witches once were said to dance around. There, you can sip this most magical liqueur where it's made. Once that happens, though, you'll be under this liquid witch's spell forever.

Whizz Bang

Holy moley, words change almost as much as drinks. Whizz Bang (sometimes you see that second "z" dropped, but doesn't that seem uncouth?), for example, started as a phrase used by British and American military in World War I to describe the sounds heard when a German large field artillery piece fired a shell—the *whizz* as it was flying and then the *bang* when it hit. Not friendly in the least. And today? A *whiz-bang* refers to a real go-getter, rising up that corporate ladder three rungs at a time, stepping on anything and anyone to make it. Hmm, if you have to make a choice when having a party populated by Whizz Bangs, I suggest dressing in camouflage (shorts, if possible), playing a round of the card game War, and toasting those ancestors who were in that way-back war, thereby bringing the word, and the drink, back to its roots.

Ice cubes

1½ ounces **bourbon**

¾ ounce **dry vermouth**

¼ ounce **Pernod**

¼ ounce **grenadine**

2 dashes **orange bitters**

1. Fill a cocktail shaker halfway full with ice cubes. Add the bourbon, vermouth, Pernod, grenadine, and bitters. Shake well.

2. Strain into a cocktail glass and give a respectful glance skyward.

A VARIATION: At London's dandy cocktail haven the Lonsdale, they make this with Scotch and absinthe instead of bourbon and Pernod. And it tastes pretty darn swell. Also, at the Lonsdale you can learn that the Whizz Bang was invented by Tommy Burton in 1920 at the Sport's Club of London.

Williwaw

It was a big nor'wester—or was it a sou'easter? Those old salts are tough to understand because of their brandy and cherry brandy intake, their pipes always in place, and the cool caps, which tend to take one's attention away from the story. Anyhow, it was **whishing off the mountains** and dropping snow and ice over the water like a herd of upset bighorn sheep, tearing off tree tops and badly attached neon signs, seeming like it was attempting to turn over houses and humans on its way to overturn boats and sailors. Ah, but there was the safety catch. The humans and sailors were inside, at the Williwaw party, snug and sated. That wind didn't stand a chance.

Ice cubes

1½ ounces **brandy**

1 ounce **cherry brandy**

½ ounce **Simple Syrup** (page 12)

2 dashes **Angostura bitters**

1. Fill a cocktail shaker halfway full with ice cubes. Add the brandy, cherry brandy, simple syrup, and bitters. Shake windily.

2. Strain into a cocktail glass. Serve with a twinkle in your eye.

Monster Mash-up

When I was a young lad, long before coming of age and getting wrapped up in beautiful words and bottles, I was obsessed a bit with the most famous movie monsters (this was before slashers became the norm), such as Frankenstein, the Creature from the Black Lagoon, Godzilla, and Dracula, and even with the less freaky and scary and giant creatures, such as Rodan, the Blob, and the monstrous radiated rabbits in *Night of the Lepus*. If you share this nostalgic or (at least in my case) current affection for these last-century dark creatures, then I suggest matching them up with the following drinks next time you're watching one of them on DVD.

1. Monster: Frankenstein. Drink: Tombstone (page 89)

2. Monster: Creature from the Black Lagoon. Drink: Dark Water (page 102)

3. Monster: Godzilla. Drink: Whizz Bang (opposite page)

4. Monster: Dracula. Drink: Corpse Reviver (page 192)

5. Monster: Rodan. Drink: The Eagle (page 282)

6. Monster: The Blob. Drink: Beach Bubble (page 94)

7. Monster: Giant rabbits. Drink: The Human Factor (page 72)

"One minute she's a blackmailer, cagey as Khrushchev, and the next **she wants to gambol half-naked** on a pile of sawdust like a babe on an absinthe jag."

CHARLES WILLIAMS, *The Hot Spot*, 1953

Zazarac

Be warned, intrepid drinker of dodgy, daunting, daringly creepy, and potentially ruthless beverages. Be very light on your feet, as you're now being introduced to the angriest drink known. (Possibly, that is. I mean, I don't know every single concoction created by every single home and pro bartender, because there are hundreds of new ones a day; right now, as you read this, a bartender in, say, Ithaca, is coming up with a mighty mad mixture). The Zazarac—so, so close in pronunciation to its much, much more famous cousin, the Sazerac (page 45)—has been around in its own right since the 1930s and is still seen in a few obscure spots, but it's not being fêted and bejeweled like that cousin. Dang, this drink says (or would, if drinks could speak), **shaking its liquid hand in the air**. Should you be worried? Sure, a bit. Wanna know the way to pacify the Zazarac, though, and stop the worry? Drink another one—that'll make it happy.

Ice cubes

1½ ounces **rye**

¾ ounce **white rum**

¾ ounce **anisette**

¾ ounce **Simple Syrup** (page 12)

½ ounce **absinthe**

Dash of **Angostura bitters**

Dash of **orange bitters**

Lemon twist for garnish

1. Fill a cocktail shaker halfway full with ice cubes. Add the rye, rum, anisette, simple syrup, absinthe, and both bitters. Shake well (it's okay to be aggressive about it, as the cocktail likes it).

2. Strain into a large cocktail glass. Garnish with that lemon twist.

A Note: This was originally made with gum syrup. Intrigued? See the recipe for the King Cole (page 206) and learn more about gum syrup.

A Second Note: Absinthe is available now in the United States (yay!). If your corner store doesn't have any, check online (at www.drinkupny.com, for example). If you still can't lay your hands on any, substitute Pernod.

Powerful Punches

Gather round your punch bowls, my pals, and let me tell you a tale that changes lives as quickly as some sports stars change teams, a tale that leads to treasures untold and wisdom usually unreached . . . wait, why are you raising your hands? What's that, I don't believe what I'm hearing—you don't have a punch bowl to gather around? You don't even have a presentable pitcher to huddle around? Well, I don't know what to say.

A good punch bowl and one or two good pitchers (maybe an indoor and an outdoor pitcher) come in awfully handy when you want to throw a party, a clambake, a potlatch, or even a box social; host a troop of ten; carouse with a larger cabal; or get into any kind of fiesta with a bigger faction. If you're going to have a bacchanal with all the boys and girls, or a celebration solely with the classiest people from your company, or even have a simple social evening with more than one or two others, you'll find that these easy-to-obtain items will become your best friends.

Luckily, they look nice too, especially a sparkling punch bowl (though a sparkling pitcher is also darn fine) with a big block of ice or an ice ring bobbing in a sea of liquors and liqueurs, some bubbles perhaps, and some fruit. Ladle it up prettily into punch glasses, and listen to the toasts in your honor as they pile in. This chapter is spilling over with punch and pitcher favorites, from working-class groupings like Bring the House Down, Power to the People, and Day-Off Punch to more exotic liquid locals such as Xalapa Punch, Crimean Cup à la Marmora, and Mercurio Punch.

Want to take your party a little farther afield than your current haunt, to make your soiree really travel? Then you might want to whip up a Champs Élysées, a Honolulu Punch, or a Rocky Mountain Punch and take your friends on a tour around the globe (without actually leaving the living room). Get historic with Caesar's Bowl, have a little golden fantasy with the El Dorado Punch, or go for a ride with the Horse's Neck or the Pony Punch. The parties are waiting for you to throw them and ascend into the pantheon of punch and pitcher drink legends. Remember a little simple math, though, when you get to a point where you're throwing bigger and bigger gatherings and you might want to scale up some of the following recipes: A Pin equals 4½ gallons, a Firkin equals 9 gallons, a Kilderkin equals 18 gallons, a Barrel equals 36 gallons, a Hogshead equals 54 gallons, a Puncheon equals 72 gallons, and a Butt equals 108 gallons. Now you're ready for anything.

Bimbo Punch

Here's a toast to serving this **mighty fine mix-up** for a group of pals who want to take back *bimbo* to its Italian roots (where it means a young boy), rerouting a word that took a derogatory turn in the 1920s. With this in mind, drink the Bimbo Punch while recreating with a few rousing rounds of stickball or a couple of games of neighborhood kick the can. You might run slightly slower than when you were ten, but you'll feel younger. **Serves 6**

One 750-milliliter bottle **Cognac**

12 ounces **freshly squeezed lemon juice**

18 ounces **Simple Syrup** (page 12)

10 **lemon wheels**

2 cups **ice cubes**

1. Add the Cognac, lemon juice, simple syrup, and lemon wheels to a small punch bowl or pitcher. Stir well.

2. Let the Bimbo sit for 15 minutes (or longer, even up to an hour). Then add the ice cubes, and stir well. Serve in punch cups or white wine glasses.

A VARIATION: Does using that whole bottle of Cognac in your punch seem too snazzy for an afternoon of kiddie games? Then sub in plain brandy (or, for a little excitement, apple brandy) and don't sweat it.

Blood and Sand

Often made as a single drink, the Blood and Sand also operates agreeably as a punch for many, especially if you're wanting to serve and swill it at a Halloween party, horror movie marathon, or beach masquerade party where attendees are expected to **dress as famous sandy villains** (Bluebeard, for example, or the shark from *Jaws*). If you're punching up your Blood and Sand in these situations, you won't have to pause the movie or worry about upsetting an eye patch, as you might when making many small drinks instead of one large one. **Serves 10**

Ice cubes

9 ounces **Scotch**

9 ounces **cherry brandy**

9 ounces **sweet vermouth**

9 ounces **freshly squeezed orange juice**

10 **orange slices** for garnish

1. Fill a small to medium-size punch bowl halfway full with ice cubes. Add the Scotch, cherry brandy, vermouth, and orange juice. Stir well, with an eye always on the beach.

2. Serve the punch in punch glasses, white wine glasses, or the hollow teeth of a giant shark. Garnish each drink with an orange slice.

"This ancient silver bowl of mine, it tells of good old times
Of **joyous days, and jolly nights**, and merry Christmas chimes
They were a free and jovial race, but honest, brave, and true
That dipped their ladle in the punch when this old bowl was new."

OLIVER WENDELL HOLMES, "On Lending a Punch-Bowl," *Yale Book of American Verse*, 1912

Bombay Punch

A marvelously multifaceted mash-up of mighty proportions, Bombay Punch includes myriad colors, erstwhile boozy friends, fresh faces, a brace of bubbles, a citrus smidge, and lots and lots of love, people. Ladle the Bombay (feel free to drop the "punch" in pleasant company) when you're entertaining a diverse group of pals who aren't afraid to attempt something new, especially if the group includes those **near and dear to you** whom you haven't seen for a while, and especially-times-two if the assemblage has one or two folks who tend to attire themselves in an array of dazzling hues. **Serves 10 to 12**

Ice cubes

10 ounces **brandy**

10 ounces **freshly squeezed orange juice**

5 ounces **maraschino liqueur**

5 ounces **Cointreau**

5 ounces **apricot liqueur**

Two 750-milliliter bottles **chilled brut Champagne** or **sparkling wine**

10 to 12 **orange slices** or **wheels**

1. Fill a large punch bowl halfway full with ice cubes. Add the brandy, orange juice, maraschino liqueur, Cointreau, and apricot liqueur. Using a ladle or large spoon, stir briefly.

2. Slowly (the bubble effect can take out your Bombay if not careful), pour the Champagne into the punch bowl. Again, stir briefly, but this time a bit more slowly.

3. Add the orange slices or wheels, stir once more, and serve in punch glasses, trying to get an orange slice in each glass.

~~~~~~~~~~~~~~~~~~~~~~~~~~~~~~

⬆ *A Note: Maraschino liqueur is a lovely liqueur made from the fruit and pits of Marasca cherries in a distillation process that's akin to how fruit brandies are made. Which means that the juice in the bottom of a bottle of maraschino cherries isn't much of a relative, so don't sub it in, no matter how much it begs.*

Bring the House Down

I've said it before, but it's worth repeating: Working-class heroes and heroines, even at the finest jobs in the land, those where you sometimes don't want to leave, where your boss shows up with bagels once a week, where you come in on vacations to say howdy to the ol' water cooler crowd, even that job (where I'm supposing you roll out with a large roll every month, too) is going to lead you into a bad day, where your computer becomes an evil adversary or where your once-superb manager suddenly becomes a step below subpar. That day, which may come sooner rather than later, is the day you need to **grab your closest worker-bee buddies** and Bring the House Down. **Serves 6**

12 ounces **dark rum**

12 ounces **freshly squeezed orange juice**

1½ ounces **Coco López** (or other cream of coconut)

Ice cubes

Chilled 7UP or **Sprite**

6 **orange slices** for garnish

↻ **A Note:** *Suggest to workers partaking in this refresher that they squeeze the orange slice over the drink before starting, to really forget about that day in the right manner.*

1. Instead of pouring them over bratty electronic equipment, pour the rum, orange juice, and Coco López into a large pitcher or a small punch bowl. With a sturdy slotted spoon, a good whisk, or a large fork, stir everything well, for a few minutes at least (have a workmate help out if you get weary). You want to ensure that the Coco López is dissolved (no reason to make the day any worse, right?).

2. Fill six highball glasses or goblets halfway full with ice cubes. Pour the House Down from the pitcher or ladle it from the punch bowl equally into the glasses.

3. Fill each glass with 7UP, almost to the top, and then garnish each with an orange slice.

Caesar's Bowl

Hail Caesar, friend of the people. Hail Caesar, who I believe invented Caesar's Bowl to celebrate conquering France. Hail Caesar, who, after throwing one legendary Roman party, when talking about the Caesar's Bowl, uttered for the first time the now-famous phrase, "It was made, it was drunk, I was drunk." And also (with this repeated hailing), hail the Junior League of Memphis, who put together the book *Party Potpourri* (the version I have came out in 1988, printed up by Wimmer Brothers–how about a "hail" for them, too?), where I first saw this historical gulper. **Serves 12 to 15, depending on the difficulty of the battle**

One 750-milliliter bottle **dark rum**

12 ounces **white rum**

12 ounces **apricot brandy**

2 cups **fresh pineapple chunks**

8 ounces **fresh pineapple juice**

4 ounces **freshly squeezed lemon juice**

4 ounces **freshly squeezed orange juice**

6 ounces **Simple Syrup** (page 12)

Ice cubes

One 2-liter bottle **chilled club soda**

2 cups **sliced fresh strawberries**

1. Add the rums, apricot brandy, pineapple chunks, pineapple juice, lemon juice, orange juice, and simple syrup to a large punch bowl. With a spoon or olive branch, stir well.

2. Add ice cubes to the punch bowl, until it's about three-quarters full. Smoothly add the club soda (no need to spill the Caesar and cause a historical incident).

3. Add the strawberries, and stir well. Serve in punch glasses, preferably while wearing a toga, and preferably getting a few strawberries in each glass.

Cardinal

I'll take Cardinal, Alex, for one wine glass of punch. Is it a seed-eating family of birds in North and South America, associated in most minds with a bright red coloring? Is it a senior official of the Catholic church who takes part in electing a pope? Is it a navigational term, a train, or a lesser-known Marvel comics villain? Is it a punch that uses two different liquors, a wine, wine's cousin vermouth, two bubbly additions, fruit, and sweetness for **a result that'll make carousing guests coo**? I'll take a glass of that, please. **Serves 10 to 12**

16 ounces **claret**

12 ounces **brandy**

12 ounces **dark rum**

12 ounces **Simple Syrup** (page 12)

4 ounces **sweet vermouth**

1 **ice round,** or **cracked ice**

1 **orange,** sliced

2 cups **fresh pineapple chunks**

One 2-liter bottle **chilled club soda**

One 750-milliliter bottle **chilled brut Champagne** or **sparkling wine**

1. Add the claret, brandy, rum, simple syrup, and vermouth to a large punch bowl. Stir briefly.

2. Add the ice round to the punch, or add enough cracked ice so that the bowl is almost halfway full.

3. Add the orange slices, pineapple chunks, and club soda (slowly on that last one to avoid spillage). Stir briefly again.

4. Add the Champagne (again, slowly), and stir briefly one last time. Serve in white wine glasses.

⌃ **A Note:** *Claret is a red wine from France's Bordeaux region, though the word itself is mostly used in England to refer to this wine, which is usually a dark red wine. Oddly enough, the word comes from a French word,* clairet, *which actually means "pale." This makes sense when you consider that the wine used to be a rosé.*

Champs Élysées

While it may be awfully romantic to wander the most famous street in Paris moony-eyed, **reveling in spectacle and history**, dreaming of the day when you'll pack up and pick up an apartment right there, the fact that it's the second most expensive stretch of real estate known (well, that's the word on the street at least) dampens that dream a dash. Refuse to lose, though, and instead of getting stuffy and sad about it, invite some friends over, put on a CD by French crooner Richard Anthony, insist that every festive friend speak in a bad accent, whip up a pitcher full of the drink that shares the street's sobriquet, and kick back in your very own version of *la plus belle avenue du monde*. **Serves 8**

Ice cubes

12 ounces **Cognac**

6 ounces **green Chartreuse**

6 ounces **Simple Syrup** (page 12)

4 ounces **freshly squeezed lemon juice**

8 dashes **Angostura bitters**

1. Fill a large pitcher halfway full with ice cubes. Add the Cognac, Chartreuse, simple syrup, lemon juice, and bitters. Stir well.

2. Using a spoon (you don't want the ice to slip in), strain the liquid road into eight large cordial or cocktail glasses.

⬆ *A Note: Chartreuse dates back to a scroll given in 1605 to the Chartreuse monks by François Hannibal d'Estrées, marshal for King Henri IV, and was once thought to be a healing elixir (a supposition I still believe in). There are two varieties readily available, yellow and green, and I've seen versions of this recipe with both. I weigh in on the green side here (it's a touch less sweet), but try the yellow if you're so inclined.*

Chartreuse

As shown in modern marvels such as the Irreverent Reverend (page 72) and the Sweet Louise (page 88), Chartreuse is a favorite for many current drink masters and is used in a variety of ways (as well as being enjoyed as a solo sipper). There are four variations of this liqueur: the Elixir Végétal de la Grande-Chartreuse, extra-aged V.E.P. Chartreuse, and the more common green and yellow varieties (the latter two containing a rich herbal taste, with the green having a little more backbone and the yellow being a touch sweeter). Considering how long the story of Chartreuse traces its winding way back into history, it's boozeriffic that this liqueur is still so widely used today.

The story starts, oh, around the 1100s, with the beginnings of the Chartreuse Order of cloistered monks, or Carthusians. About 500 years later (1605 to be exact), the Chartreuse monastery in Vauvert, France, was given a manuscript by François Hannibal d'Estrées (the marshal of King Henry IV of France) titled "An Elixir of Long Life." The manuscript was aged, and in poor shape, and in need of much work to be usable to make this miracle elixir—so much work that the monks didn't begin to actually use it until 1737. Once it was in drinkable shape, they renamed it (calling it Chartreuse Elixir) and begin selling it to the public, at first only in small amounts, and then increasing production and distribution.

Since then, the recipe has been secretly handed down, monk to monk, as the tale is told, with only two monks having the full list of 130 ingredients and quantities at any one time. The list is known to contain an assortment of spices, herbs, leaves, and more, with everything ending up being aged in oak casks. Remember, then, when drinking this healing mixture, that you're sipping hundreds of years of history.

Crimean Cup à la Marmora

Doesn't this sound like a mythical mouthful—something served in a bone goblet at a supernatural ritual, perhaps? In a way, my finding of the recipe for it *was* sort of magical, as I discovered it in a book buried under a stack of *Life* magazines in one of those dusty and lovely used bookstores, the ones with a slim organizational strategy and many nooks and crannies where treasures can be unearthed, if you say the right words, or spin in a circle at exactly 3:30 P.M. The book had a binder whose cover said *The Art of Mixing Drinks* (which is darn close to the David Embury classic *The Fine Art of Mixing Drinks*) but inside it was called, captivatingly, *The Legend of Liqueurs, Wines, and Spirits*. I suppose this could be a subtitle, but I like to think of it as a secret title. Whichever way you play it, it was published by Reilly & Lee in 1961. Mysterious, isn't it?

Serves 8 to 10

Ice cubes

10 ounces **Cognac**

6 ounces **orgeat syrup**

4 ounces **dark rum**

4 ounces **maraschino liqueur**

4 ounces **Simple Syrup** (page 12)

1 **lemon**, sliced

1 **lime**, sliced

One 2-liter bottle **chilled club soda**

One 750-milliliter bottle **chilled brut Champagne** or **sparkling wine**

1. Fill a large punch bowl halfway full with ice cubes. Add the Cognac, orgeat, rum, maraschino liqueur, and simple syrup. Stir thrice clockwise and thrice counterclockwise.

2. Add the lemon and lime slices and stir again three times (either direction is dandy).

3. Add the club soda and Champagne in an enchanted manner (by which I mean slow and steady). Stir six more times (three each way, again—three being a magic number), and serve in bone goblets, of course. Or any goblet used in mystical ceremonies for 100 years or more. Or, any old goblet.

A Note: Orgeat is an almond-flavored syrup relishing its renowned role in the Mai Tai (page 32). It's available in most gourmet stores and online.

Day-Off Punch

Yay! I adore a day off, **forgetting about that persistent persnickety alarm clock**, wolfing down a slice of pizza topped with an egg for breakfast, following it with a doughnut and a glass of chocolate milk (it's a day off from dieting, too, silly), taking those Sookie and Rory dogs (insert your dog or cat or monkey's name as necessary) on an extended neighborhood ambling, watching a few *Addams Family* reruns or some *Mighty Boosh* madness, taking a few naps, putting the weary wanting world far, far in the wayside of the mind, and then whipping up a walloping batch of Day-Off Punch to celebrate—making it at noon, maybe. It *is* a day off, after all. **Serves 8**

Ice cubes

16 ounces **rye**

8 ounces **sweet vermouth**

8 ounces **freshly squeezed lemon juice**

1 **lemon**, sliced

One 2-liter bottle **chilled ginger ale**

1. Fill a punch bowl halfway full with ice cubes. Add the rye, vermouth, lemon juice, and lemon slices. Stir once, without a care.

2. Add the ginger ale to the bowl, but don't rush it (there's no call for spilling). Stir a bit, then a bit more. Serve in punch glasses.

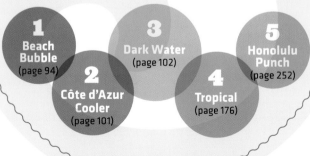

5 Drinks to Bring the Beach Home

Stuck in a Siberian landscape, or don't have time to trek to a real live sandy area on an ocean's edge, or just want to throw a theme party where your pals show up in swimsuits and sunscreen? Serve up one of these five sunstruck beauties and bring the beach to you, wherever you are.

1 Beach Bubble (page 94)

2 Côte d'Azur Cooler (page 101)

3 Dark Water (page 102)

4 Tropical (page 176)

5 Honolulu Punch (page 252)

El Dorado

The legendary city of gold appears (in fantasies, that is) to be a delish theory—a spot of sunny time with some pack mules through the desert, over the mountains, and into a specific secret valley where you uncover a couple of mounds of the pricey yellow stuff. But think it over . . . if it's really a whole city, wouldn't that just devalue the gold, leaving you broken and bitter? That's where being greedy gets you. On the flip side of the personality train, if you're charitable and share your El Dorado in punch form with a number of merrymakers at a bacchanal where the only gold is in the boundless gold lamé outfits and accessories, you'll be a star (and you won't even have to deal with those cranky pack mules).

Serves 10

Ice cubes

16 ounces **whiskey**

10 ounces **dark rum**

10 ounces **brandy**

10 ounces **Simple Syrup** (page 12)

5 ounces **freshly squeezed lemon juice**

1 **lemon, cut into wedges**

One 2-liter bottle **chilled club soda**

1. Fill a punch bowl halfway full with ice cubes. Add the whiskey, rum, brandy, simple syrup, and lemon juice. Stir well, with a gold stirring spoon.

2. Add the lemon wedges and then the club soda to the bowl. Stir well, again, with that shining spoon.

"He had liquor in about any color you could ask for, except **the one I liked best**, standard whiskey brown. I told him no thanks."

GARY WOLF, *Who Censored Roger Rabbit?* (1981)

Football Punch

→

Are you ready for some Football Punch? Now, beerheads, don't get up in arms (I readily down a cold beer, especially on hot days), but I believe that the traditional beer-football duo is, well, a bit dull (please don't tackle me yet) when done over and over. Football fanatics, **make your pigskin bash stand out** from packed crowds, and trust me—you'll score with this punch bowl of glory. See, now aren't you glad you didn't tackle me? **Serves 10**

Ice cubes

One 750-milliliter bottle **dark rum**

16 ounces **apple juice**

10 ounces **sweet vermouth**

5 ounces **freshly squeezed lemon juice**

5 ounces **freshly squeezed orange juice**

Two 25.4-ounce bottles **chilled sparkling apple cider**

2 **apples**, cored and sliced

1. Fill a large punch bowl halfway full with ice cubes. Add the rum, apple juice, vermouth, lemon juice, and orange juice. Stir with a pennant from your team of choice.

2. Add the sparkling apple cider, but in a sustained drive, not in a sprint (meaning, slow and steady wins this game), and the apple slices. Stir well. Serve in punch glasses, mugs, or little plastic footballs.

The Golden Panther

Stalking the wilds of your backyards, patios, balconies, and decks since the days of the Stork Club (or the days of *The Stork Club Bar Book* by Lucius Beebe, published in 1946 and reprinted by New Day Publishing in 2003), the Golden Panther wields a pretty whomping wallop, but still **demands that you retain a general smoothness** (because if you coast past smoothness, you're no longer a panther). **Serves 6**

Ice cubes

6 ounces **freshly squeezed orange juice**

4 ounces **whiskey**

4 ounces **brandy**

4 ounces **gin**

2 ounces **dry vermouth**

6 **orange slices** for garnish

1. Fill a pitcher halfway full with ice cubes. Add the orange juice, whiskey, brandy, gin, and vermouth. Stir well with a long spoon.

2. Using the spoon to keep the ice from slipping out of the pitcher, pour the Panther equally into six large cordial glasses or cocktail glasses. Garnish each with an orange slice and a pantherish look.

Honolulu Punch

It's not just a vacation jubilation for the teeny bikini crowd, or a surfer's suburb, or even a spot solely for Jack Lord to lord over with a badge, justice, and a mighty nice haircut. Hawaiian history dates back to before the East Coast colonies began, as it was settled by Polynesian sailors sometime between 600 and 700 A.D.– sailors who mostly traveled using natural navigation such as stars, skies, and birds. With a toast to these courageous folks, serve this punch up to friends in backyard canoes, or to any group of friends who have a spirit of fearless discovery within them. **Serves 10 to 12**

3 cups **fresh pineapple chunks**

10 ounces **Simple Syrup** (page 12)

3½ ounces **freshly squeezed lemon juice**

20 ounces **dark rum**

10 ounces **brandy**

Block of ice, or **ice cubes** (if your ice store is low on blocks)

Two 750-milliliter bottles **chilled brut Champagne** or **sparkling wine**

1. Combine the pineapple, simple syrup, and lemon juice in a large punch bowl. Stir briefly with an oar, spoon, or ladle.

2. Add the rum and brandy and stir again, intrepidly.

3. Add a block of ice, or fill the bowl halfway full with ice cubes. Stir the liquid around the ice, or around with the ice.

4. Pour the Champagne into the bowl, using as much care as you can. Stir again. Serve in punch glasses.

"Further rounds of drinks were bought and consumed. The Arrowsmith boys declared to each other that they were drunk and made further *sotto voce* observations about the forming bodies of the Wiltshire twins. Mrs. Wiltshire felt the occasion becoming easier as **Cinzano Bianco coursed through her bloodstream**."

WILLIAM TREVOR, *Lovers of Their Time and Other Stories*, 1978

Horse's Neck

The Horse's Neck is straddled in a few ways, but usually in a highball—this is the classic way to **approach a liquid equestrian**. But even the finest rider—one who isn't afraid of jumping the creek, or picking a thorn out of a back hoof—can use a little assistance when a whole flock of folks show up desiring their own drinkable steed at once. In those situations, there's only one way to take the horse by the neck, and that's with the handy aid of a pitcher (a lesser-known training tool, but one used by top trainers). Because there's less chance of spilling with a pitcher, this comes in extra-handy when you're wearing new jodhpurs. **Serves 8**

Ice cubes

16 ounces **Kentucky bourbon**

One 2-liter bottle **chilled ginger ale**

16 dashes **Angostura bitters**

8 **long lemon spirals** for garnish

1. Fill a pitcher or large cowboy boot halfway full with ice cubes.

2. Add the bourbon to the pitcher, and then fill it almost up to the top with the ginger ale.

3. Add the Angostura bitters to the pitcher. Stir nicely.

4. Fill eight highball glasses halfway full with ice cubes, and then drape (sorta like a saddle) a lemon spiral over the edge of each glass.

5. Using a spoon or stirrer to keep the pitcher ice in the pitcher, fill each of the glasses with the mixture.

A VIRGIN VARIATION: To make a virgin variation here is simple, as you just remove the bourbon. It doesn't have the kick, but it's still nice after a long day of riding. And someone needs to pilot the four-in-hand home.

Hot Whiskey Punch

I can almost hear it echoing now, the telltale voice wafting over ice and snow, audible even through earmuffs: "Hot whiskey, hot whiskey, get your hot, hot whiskey here, only two bits a glass, get your hot, hot whiskey here!" Those were the days, with hot whiskey vendors on every other corner from late November until later February—sometimes even into March. And then came the evil, unhealthy, anti-hot-whiskey-ers and their backdoor dealings with Congress, banning hot whiskey sellers from the streets. Didn't they even think about their families? Or about us cold folks walking to and from work and home every day? Didn't they even think? Let this be a lesson: If you don't appreciate your hot whiskey enough, it might just be taken away. **Serves 5 to 10, depending on force of conviction**

16 ounces **whiskey**

10 ounces **brandy**

4 ounces **freshly squeezed lemon juice**

Peel of 1 **lemon**, chopped into 4 pieces

4 cups **water**

1 cup **granulated sugar**

1. Combine the whiskey, brandy, lemon juice, and peel pieces in a punch bowl. Mix slightly.

2. Combine the water and sugar in a medium-size saucepan. Heat over medium-high heat until boiling, stirring occasionally, then reduce the heat to a simmer and cook until the sugar is dissolved completely.

3. Pour the hot syrup (but be wary about it) into the punch bowl. Stir well, and serve in mugs or heatproof glasses.

Little Sister

Little sisters believe they have it bad, but how many siblings have a song sung to them both by Elvis and by country-singer-and-actor Dwight Yoakam, a knock-out novel written with them in mind by the rollicking Raymond Chandler (*The Little Sister*, of course), and a punch pulled together in their honor? No one's going around singing about little brothers, let me tell you, much less pouring out a punch named after us. So, little sisters, listen up: Drink your punch, sing your songs, read your stories, and be glad. **Serves 10 siblings of any kind**

Cracked ice

15 ounces **brandy**

10 ounces **orange curaçao**

5 ounces **freshly squeezed lemon juice**

5 ounces **freshly squeezed orange juice**

5 ounces **grenadine**

5 ounces **Simple Syrup** (page 12)

Two 2-liter bottles **chilled club soda**

1. Fill a punch bowl halfway full with cracked ice. Add the brandy, curaçao, lemon juice, orange juice, grenadine, and simple syrup. Stir well, shaking your hips like Elvis.

2. Being sure not to spill any on the family albums, pour the club soda in slowly. Stir again, and serve in punch glasses.

A VIRGIN VARIATION: Omit the brandy and the orange curaçao, up the lemon juice to 7 ounces and the orange juice to 10 ounces, and (if the mood takes you) sub in a 2-liter bottle of Orange Crush for one of the bottles of club soda. Call it the Little Little Sister.

Four Drinks to Drown Out the Boss's Voice

Okay, sure, some jobs are absolutely perfect: places where you come in with a smile on Monday and greet the boss with an apple (aren't you just the, um, model employee) and then cry on Friday afternoon. Then there are those spots where the boss is yammering at you, taking credit for your work, treating you like a personal shoe scraper, and then pretending to be hurt because you won't buy him or her a double chocolate cookie for the next three-hour pointless meeting. Well, fellow workers, the following four imbibables will help take that boss right out of your mind (and your coworkers' minds, too—it's always good to share with those in need).

1. Bring the House Down (page 242)
2. Day-Off Punch (page 248)
3. Spring in Your Step (page 130)
4. Power to the People (page 262)

Mercurio Punch

Mercurio . . . doesn't that seem like a character Shakespeare cut from a play at the last minute? Mercutio's elder brother? The one who taught him how to swing a sword and wear a fluffy, wide-brimmed, fashionable hat but then didn't make the final draft? I think poor Mercurio needs a stiff drink. Or, if nothing else, a toast with a punch made from a curious list of characters. **Serves 10 to 15**

Block of ice, or **ice cubes**

16 ounces **brandy**

16 ounces **purple grape juice**

8 ounces **Benedictine**

8 ounces **Simple Syrup** (page 12)

One 750-milliliter bottle **red wine** (go for a Cabernet here, one with oomph)

One 2-liter bottle **chilled club soda**

1. Add the block of ice to a large punch bowl, or fill the bowl halfway full with ice cubes. Add the brandy, grape juice, Benedictine, and simple syrup. Stir with a rapier or a spoon (but make it a sharp one).

2. Add the red wine to the cast, and stir again.

3. Smoothly add the club soda, and stir a final time (or maybe a few final times—you want to get it good and combined). Serve in punch glasses.

⊕ *A Note: Does this feel a little light in the garnish area to you? We wouldn't want that, so if this is indeed the case, add 3 cups red grapes (making sure they're well washed) in step 1.*

The Native

Too often, the phrase "going native" is derogatorily toned, as if **assimilating another culture** that you're existing within is a shameful thing. And when that phrase is used in even more slurred tones to refer to someone who's had perhaps a punch cup too many of the Native, and has decided to just sit for a while, well, that's just as shameful. In either situation, can I put it down right here as fact that the one doing the slurring is the one we should pity? Well, I am putting it down. And also assuring you that anyone saying "going native" as a slough-off is definitely not invited back to a party I'm throwing. I hope you adopt the same tactic. **Serves 8**

Ice cubes

8 ounces **dark rum**

8 ounces **white rum**

4 ounces **sweet vermouth**

4 ounces **blue curaçao**

4 ounces **freshly squeezed orange juice**

2 ounces **freshly squeezed lime juice**

2 ounces **Simple Syrup** (page 12)

Crushed ice

8 **orange slices** for garnish

8 **maraschino cherries** for garnish

1. Reveling in your nativeness, fill a large pitcher halfway full with ice cubes. Combine the dark rum, white rum, vermouth, curaçao, orange juice, lime juice, and simple syrup, in no particular order, but making sure they know to get along. With a long spoon or other stirring device, stir well.

2. Fill eight large goblets or other friendly cups with crushed ice (if you don't have crushed ice at hand, cracked ice or even ice cubes work in a pinch).

3. Using a spoon or stir stick to keep ice cubes pitcher-bound, pour the mix from the pitcher equally into the goblets. Garnish each with an orange slice and a cherry.

Nourmahal

The Nourmahal as a group gripper might have first been brought together to commemorate the 240-foot yacht made for noted rich fella William Vincent Astor, a yacht he eventually donated to the Navy. If this is what you'd like to believe, I'm okay with it. Wear either the cravat and blue blazer, reflecting what an Astor might wear while boating, or an outfit celebrating the Navy or Coast Guard (which eventually manned the ship). I, though, like to believe this mix was named after a character in one of the tales told within the poem *Lalla Rookh* (a poem that was also given drink form—check page 115), a tale called "The Light of the Harem." The basics are these: Nourmahal was estranged from her true love, Selim, a prince, and was naturally sad about the sitch. So, as they did way back when, she **rounded up a love spell and appeared** as a masked lute player at a feast being thrown in his honor. Near the end of the evening, she sang her lovely song, at which Selim exclaimed that if Nourmahal had "sung those strains I could forgive her all." At which time she whips off the mask, and lots of hugging and kissing and true-love-proclaiming ensues. Call me sappy, but I'll always go for the kissing and hugging over the money. **Serves 6**

Cracked ice

12 ounces **dark rum**

3 ounces **freshly squeezed lime juice**

12 dashes **Angostura bitters**

Chilled club soda

6 **lime wedges** for garnish

⤴ *A Note: If neither of the above possibilities for the history of this drink gets you or your wingding winging, then feel free to proclaim that the drink was named for the Chocolate Jungle Queen Sticho-phthalma nourmahal, a butterfly found in southeast Asia. I'll bet the drink will taste just as fine.*

1. Fill a pitcher three-quarters full with cracked ice. Add the rum, lime juice, and bitters. Stir six times, either with a long spoon, a gold rudder, or Cupid's arrow.

2. Fill the pitcher with club soda, and stir briefly.

3. Carefully pour the punch into six highball glasses or goblets—be wary of that bubbling soda, though. Neither yachting nor loving appreciates a spilled drink.

4. Garnish each glass with a lime wedge.

Easy-Peasy Savory and Sweet Snacks

You don't have to lay out a spread that would do a famous eater like Henry VIII proud, but it's a shame not to have a few nice snacks to accompany your scrumptious darkly spirited drinks. Especially because the following are a snap to get together, and they earn you a check mark in the "good host/hostess" column.

1. Pizza puffs. Spread a little olive oil, a splash of good bottled marinara sauce, and a slice of mozzarella or generous sprinkling of Parmesan cheese on some biscuits (the kind you buy in the refrigerated section in a tube) that have been cooked almost all the way, according to package directions. Cook a little more to finish the biscuits and melt the cheese, and serve hot.

2. Antipasto instantly. Two kinds of decent cheese, some roasted red peppers or pepperoncini (the hot Italian kind), olives, a little prosciutto or sliceable sausage, and, if feeling fancy, some basil sprigs arranged orderly on a platter, then drizzled with olive oil.

3. Hummus in haste (but still tasty). Add a can of chickpeas, some olive oil, black pepper, lemon juice, and tahini (if at all possible) to a food processor, process, and add a little water to thin and smooth as needed. Just like that. Well, that and some crackers.

4. Chocolate-covered strawberries. Melt a bag of chocolate chips in the double boiler (or one pan over another) on lowish heat (adding a little cream, milk, or butter if it gets too thick), dip in some strawberries, set on waxed paper to cool a bit, and then listen: Those are oohs and aahs from the crowd.

Pony Punch

While it sounds akin to a roundhouse right you'd toss at the backside of some struggling solitary Joe's ear if you were the villain in a 1930s boxing movie ("Watch out, crusher Kosel's winding up for his pony punch"), taking out our hero for not joining up with the syndicate in the back room of a shebeen, this combo isn't villainous in the least. It is a harmonious host of players working together to overcome any jubilee-joiner's reluctance—a reluctance that may seem justified at first glance when looking at everything going into the punch bowl. Contrary to our boxing motif, though, this syndicate of ingredients works via good taste rather than a punch to the noggin. **Serves 8**

Cracked ice

24 ounces **bourbon**

12 ounces **dark rum**

12 ounces **maraschino liqueur**

8 ounces **freshly squeezed lemon juice**

12 ounces **fresh pineapple juice**

24 ounces **cold green tea**

1 **lemon,** sliced

2 cups **fresh pineapple chunks**

1. Fill a punch bowl or large pitcher three-quarters full with cracked ice. Add the remaining ingredients, in the order listed (even though they're working together, there still needs to be an order to things). Stir well.

2. Ladle the punch into punch glasses or other horsey glasses. Be sure each gets ice and fruit as well as liquid. If using a pitcher, forgo the ladle.

⬆ *A Note: This punch, if you were wondering, is not actually suitable for ponies (even if the pony is mob royalty).*

Power to the People

Bump da bump, yea! Bumpity bump da bump, yea! Bump de bump, yea! Bumpity bump de bump, yea! Hold on yo, and let me bounce down the bellowing bass a bit, let me demote the volume a dash, while I reveal all: The bumps are the hips shaking to the beats played when powering up the people, and the "yea's" are emanating from your coterie, **screaming out appreciation** for your beverage-mixing and bash-throwing skills. Feels pretty good to bring that power to the people, doesn't it? **Serves 8**

2 **peaches**, pitted and sliced

2 **apricots**, pitted and sliced

4 ounces **Simple Syrup** (page 12)

Ice cubes

8 ounces **brandy**

4 ounces **freshly squeezed orange juice**

One 750-milliliter bottle **chilled Prosecco**

Orange slices for garnish

1. Combine the peaches, apricots, and simple syrup in a pitcher that can take the decibels. Using a muddler, long wooden spoon, or dancing shoe, muddle the fruit and syrup. You want to muddle to the beat, but also muddle well.

2. Fill the pitcher halfway full with ice cubes, then add the brandy and orange juice into the pitcher's melody. Stir well, but don't stop shaking those hips.

3. Carefully, but rhythmically, add the Prosecco and orange slices. Stir again, well. Serve in wine glasses, getting a slice of orange in each glass if at all possible (you want all the people to be having kicks, right?).

⤴ **A Note:** *Prosecco is an Italian sparkling wine, beloved for its crisp, fruitier-than-Champagne taste, light bubbles, and impeccable dance moves.*

Quintet

If you follow the title's road and share this wine-y punch ("wine-y" in the sense that it contains wine, not that it whines or induces whining behavior—let's get that clear before going a drop further) solely with four faithful friends, bandmates, card players, or rabble rousers, then **be ready for some serious imbibing** and put the car keys down now. I'm not saying you can't take it, but the Quintet could easily serve eight. Which, doing the math, means that each of you five is consuming enough, in reality, for 1.6 people. Which means taking precautions isn't a bad way to start your evening. **Serves 8 or more (or less, following the above guidelines)**

Block of ice, or **ice cubes**

8 ounces **freshly squeezed lemon juice**

8 ounces **freshly squeezed orange juice**

4 ounces **brandy**

4 ounces **dark rum**

One 750-milliliter bottle **chilled white wine** (Riesling works well)

One 2-liter bottle **chilled club soda**

1 **orange**, sliced

1 **lemon**, sliced

1. Add the block of ice to a punch bowl, or fill the bowl halfway full with ice cubes. Add the lemon juice, orange juice, brandy, and rum. Using a spoon or ladle, stir five times.

2. Concurrently (if possible) but being sure not to overflow, add the white wine and the club soda to the bowl. Toss the orange and lemon slices in, and stir five more times. Then five more. Serve in punch glasses, white wine glasses, or any glass with five corners.

⊕ *A Note: This recipe is the outgrowth of one I found in the 34th printing of Patrick Gavin Duffy's* The Bartender's Guide *(Pocket Books, 1971), a book that was revised and expanded by Mr. James A. Beard himself. Now, since I don't have every printing of the book, I can't say for a fact which of these two fine figures we should thank for the Quintet. Which means you should toast both when sipping this.*

⊕ *A Second Note: If you can get it, I suggest the Riesling from Trio Vintners in Walla Walla, Washington—it's a darn fine wine. Look for it at www.triovintners.com.*

Rocky Mountain Punch

Here's to my precious and precocious and pretty pals living on, near, or within shouting distance of (or at least a short truck drive away from) the Rocky Mountains (once-and-future-bartenders Mark and Audra, you'd better be listening). You who look out your windows and **peep at those majestic masses** on the skyline, you who think, "Jeez, how lucky am I to see these every day," and, for that matter, let me also include those of you who have driven past the Rockies and thought, "Jeez, how lucky am I to see these today." The lot of you, listen up: If you really love those mountains, then it's your duty to serve Rocky Mountain Punch in their honor at your next merrymaking. And you don't want to shirk your duty, do you? I didn't think so. **Serves 10**

16 ounces **dark rum**

10 ounces **Simple Syrup** (page 12)

8 ounces **maraschino liqueur**

5 ounces **freshly squeezed lemon juice**

Block of ice, or **ice cubes**

Two 750-milliliter bottles **chilled brut Champagne** or **sparkling wine**

1 **lemon**, sliced

1. Combine the rum, simple syrup, maraschino liqueur, and lemon juice in a punch bowl. Stir well.

2. Add the block of ice to the bowl, or fill it halfway full with ice cubes. Stir again (while meditating on the beauty of nature and ice, naturally).

3. Without haste or overpouring, add the Champagne and the lemon slices. Stir yet a third time. Serve in punch glasses.

⊕ *A Note: Be sure to use maraschino liqueur, and not maraschino cherry syrup, or everyone will doubt your mountain love.*

Southstreet

I never lived on an actual Southstreet, or even a South Street. However, I've occupied them in my own way by serving this kicker at summertime sprees, where its **bubbles and double B's** (brandy and bourbon) helped while away the hours in a felicitous fashion. Isn't it amazing how a particular drink can actually become connected in your mind to a particular place, even when that place is only your own backyard configured in a particular way via the folks who are sharing it with you at that moment? It's this particular phenomenon that allows me to list Southstreet as one of my favorite spots. **Serves 8 to 10 (depending on how wide your street is)**

Cracked ice

15 ounces **bourbon**

8 ounces **brandy**

8 ounces **freshly squeezed lemon juice**

8 ounces **Simple Syrup** (page 12)

One 2-liter bottle **chilled ginger ale**

1 **lemon**, sliced

1 **lime**, sliced

1. Fill a punch bowl three-quarters full with cracked ice. Add the bourbon, brandy, lemon juice, and simple syrup. Stir well.

2. With a nod to the many great party streets, add the ginger ale. Stir briefly, add the lemon and lime slices, and stir again. Serve in punch glasses.

"He was very confident when he had his two or three glasses of sherry at luncheon, and he was **often delightfully confident** with his cigar and brandy-and-water at night."

ANTHONY TROLLOPE, *The Prime Minister*

Speak No Evil

I would rarely put down any drink name, and never put down a monkey—unless it was a giant monkey trying to get his monkey hands on my glass of Speak No Evil, in which case every maxim about monkeys is off the table, because I tend to get antsy when paws are reaching for my punch. (Not that I'm not a sharer, because I am, but hey, monkey, ask first.) But when **whooping it up at a wingding** where everyone has to simulate one of the *sanbiki no saru*, or three wise monkeys, my suggestion is that you avoid being Iwazaru (speak no evil) because you have to cover your mouth, which seriously inhibits your ability to imbibe the drink named after that monkey. While Mizaru (see no evil) is tough, and Kikazaru (hear no evil) means you'll have dancing issues, in this case pick one of these latter two—at least you won't get parched. **Serves 10**

Ice cubes

10 ounces **dark rum**

7½ ounces **Apfelkorn**

7½ ounces **purple grape juice**

5 ounces **Cointreau**

5 ounces **Simple Syrup** (page 12)

3 ounces **freshly squeezed lemon juice**

One 25.4-ounce bottle **sparkling apple cider**

One 2-liter bottle **chilled ginger ale**

1 **lemon**, sliced

1 **tart apple**, cored and sliced

1. Fill a punch bowl halfway full with ice cubes. Add the rum, Apfelkorn, grape juice, Cointreau, simple syrup, and lemon juice. Stir well (but not, I repeat, not with a monkey's paw—not only is it cruel, but you're also tempting some serious demonic forces).

2. Add the sparkling cider, then the ginger ale, in both cases being calm about it, to ensure neither makes a break for it. Stir again, with a spoon or ladle only.

3. Add the lemon and apple slices, stir slightly, and let sit for 3 minutes (one for each symbolic monkey). Serve in punch glasses or cute monkey mugs.

⊙ *A Note: Apfelkorn is a German liqueur made with apples combined with a wheat-based spirit. It's a touch sweet, with bright apple overtones.*

Steinway Punch

After a few peg legs of this **powerful pepper-upper**, you might start singing an old-ish (but still first-class) Tom Waits song: "The piano has been drinking, not me." And after a couple more glasses, you might start conversing with phantom members of the Steinway family, who've been making pined-for pianos since 1853. If, though, after a few more, the ghost of Jacques Straub (author of the 1914 book *Drinks*, where I first gandered at this drink) begins to heckle you for making this in a punch bowl as opposed to single drinks, well, first, I'd put the glass down. Second, I'd offer to make him one. Third, blame me, since I altered the formula—I can say this, because I know that after that second suggestion the ghostly Mr. Straub will forgive us. **Serves 8**

Block of ice, or **ice cubes**

One 750-milliliter bottle **rye**

8 ounces **orange curaçao**

8 ounces **freshly squeezed lemon juice**

8 ounces **Simple Syrup** (page 12)

One 2-liter bottle **chilled club soda**

1. Place the block of ice within a punch bowl, or fill the bowl three-quarters full with ice cubes. Add the rye, curaçao, lemon juice, and simple syrup. Stir with a long spoon (one that's shaped slightly like a conductor's baton).

2. Pour the club soda carefully into the bowl. Stir again. Serve in punch glasses.

⬆ *A Note: The lack of garnish making you feel slightly out of tune? Add a lemon slice to each punch glass and bring your song back to center.*

Five to Toss Back While Listening to Tom Waits

The phrase "unbelievably intriguing inventive genius" gets thrown around too often. Tom Waits, though? He deserves the title, along with any other back-road, late-night, feather-bed-flung-from-the-window sobriquet that can be bestowed on a singer/musician/songwriter/actor of his bourbon-soaked tale-telling stature. The next evening you find yourself spinning a seedily beautiful Waits song, sip one of these, which seem like they could sail around Waits's world.

1. **Stockholm Tar** (page 223)
2. **Dutch Charlie's** (page 199)
3. **Scofflaw Cocktail** (page 218)
4. **Fish House Punch** (page 28)
5. **Steinway Punch** (above)

The Very Old Fashioned

Don't tell Andrew (drinking comrade, creative cocktailian, and bar theorist, as well as creator of this pitcher favorite and the general favorite the Sweet Louise, page 88), but when I'm in the kitchen making a batch of this eye-opener, whistling a jaunty song such as Truck Stop Love's "How I Spent My Summer Vacation," smiling from ear to ear as I anticipate the Ballard Progressive Association's arrival, scratching the Sookie dog behind the ears, and being pretty amazed at how wonderful a day can be, once in a while, childish with joy, I call out loudly to myself and the dog, "VOF!" Sometimes "VOF, VOF!" Not sure why, but that cracks me into silly pieces. When you're in this situation (and I sure hope you are at some point), try it and see if you don't start laughing.

Serves 12 to 15

1 approximately 4-inch piece **fresh ginger**, peeled and chopped (about 4 ounces)

12 ounces **Simple Syrup** (page 12)

Two 750-millimeter bottles **bourbon**

16 ounces **freshly squeezed orange juice**

½ ounce **Angostura bitters**

Ice cubes

1. Combine the ginger and the simple syrup in a sturdy large pitcher. Using a muddler or wooden spoon, muddle these new friends (don't get wacky about it, but be firm).

2. Add the bourbon, orange juice, and bitters. Stir well.

3. Fill as many punch cups (or highball glasses, or other glasses that make you grin) as there are guests three-quarters full with ice cubes. Pour the VOF (ha!) equally amongst the cups.

Xalapa Punch

Another curiosity of the cocktail and booze firmament (though not as curious as why more people haven't become utterly hooked on Sazeracs, page 45, or why there are still some people in the world who don't have a bottle of Strega in the house), the Xalapa isn't a Mexican coalescence in the least, and for that matter doesn't even have flowers as a garnish (which is curious because Xalapa is the city of flowers, as well as capital of the Mexican state Veracruz). How about this: Let's **you and I decide right now** to garnish this with flowers. The edible kind, naturally, and not just some random blossoms from the backyard or some sprayed blooms from the florist (no one needs a stomach-pumping party). That way, the name begins to match up with the town and we both have a good story. **Serves 12 to 15**

1 **lemon**

32 ounces **freshly brewed hot black tea**

16 ounces **Simple Syrup** (page 12)

24 ounces **dark rum**

24 ounces **applejack**

One 750-milliliter bottle **claret**

Ice cubes

15 **lemon wheels**

Edible flowers, such as mini carnations, violets, or **lilacs** (optional)

1. Peel the lemon, and chop the peel into 1- to 1½-inch pieces. Add the lemon peel to a large pot.

2. Pour the hot tea over the lemon peel pieces. Let stand for 10 to 15 minutes.

3. Add the simple syrup to the lemon-tea combo. Stir well. Add the rum, applejack, and claret. Stir again, and let sit for 15 minutes. Check to make sure it's completely cooled. If not, let it sit longer.

4. Fill a punch bowl three-quarters full with ice cubes. Carefully pour the mixture from the pot over the ice in the punch bowl. Add the lemon wheels and stir.

5. Directly before serving, sprinkle the flowers over the punch. Serve in punch glasses, making sure each gets some flowers and a full explanation of why there are flowers in the drink.

⬆ *A Note: Not feeling the flowers, or worried about historical accuracy in drink-naming? They can wilt by the roadside then, though you'll be droopy about it.*

⬆ *A Second Note: No actual applejack in the house? Sub in regular apple brandy. Or, if you're feeling fancy, Calvados, the apple brandy made in lower Normandy in France.*

Hot Stuff

Hot, hot, hot, hot stuff. Hot, hot, hot, hot stuff. Yeah, sing it loud and proud, you champion of the hot mixes and heated amalgamations, the steaming saucepans, bowls, goblets, and mugs brimming with combinations that are bound to take the edge off a cold evening, melt the ice in your hair, and give Old Man Winter the what for. Quit standing out there in the cold—come on in where it's cheery, and thaw out.

The cold chill doesn't stand a chance with this chapter's hits, from classic dark spirit warmers such as the Tom & Jerry and the lesser-known Black Stripe to the globetrotting favorite of young and old alike, Irish Coffee. These un-frigid drinks are specifically designed to be served anytime from that evening in late fall when you're getting ready to get on, or get off, a hay ride (the hayrack driver waiting until the "getting off" part, of course) all the way through to those mornings in mid-March when there's still over an ounce of a chance that the sidewalks will be slippery with a sheen of frozen H_2O.

You'll also find near-to-boiling beverages that make mighty fine accompaniments to winter wingdings. If it's an upscale kind of affair, with everyone wearing their finest finery, then serve up a Sophisticated. Want to make it a bit more mellow? Take the party to the streets with a Hot Brick. Morning or brunch affair, with a touch of achiness in the air? Remember, you can beat the cold and flu season with the help of a Chamomile Fairy—or at least enjoy it more. All of these succulently warm numbers have the heart to turn a snowman from frosty into fun, and they remain the reason that old Saint Nick really comes in through the chimney—poor milk and cookies don't stand a chance.

Becoming the Host/Hostess with the Most/Mostest

Want to cement your rep in the fiesta-throwing firmament? Follow the following easy-peasy steps like fairy-tale bread crumbs (before they were snapped up) and you'll raise your drinks, and your revelry repute, to a more transcendent level.

1

That old ice that's been living in the freezer next to a fish caught in 1998? Don't throw it into your drink. Get some sparkling, odor-free ice, right quick.

2

Use fresh fruit and fresh fruit juice every time. Every time, I say.

3

Try out a soda siphon instead of club soda for better bubbles. Or, at least, use a bottle that hasn't been petering out in the fridge door.

4

Check with guests before assuming they'll be okay with the mango juice in an Ognam (page 82), because those mango allergies are rough (as are other ingredient allergies).

5

Never forget: Drinking with chums and cronies is a joyous occasion, even when you're hosting. Have fun.

Ambrosia

At first glance, it may seem that something called Ambrosia (sounds a little sexy, right?) should be in the Dim the Lights, Chill the Cocktails chapter (page 137) with the other flirty ones. And, indeed, ambrosia *was* the food of the flirtatious gods, brought to them by doves, and sounds so delish rolling off the tongue. But (he says, ponderously), the word itself means "not mortal," and love is such a mortal obsession. And this Ambrosia is a hot, caffeinated drink, something that **brings life back into a cold body** that has been shoveling snow a little too long, and makes one feel alive again, like a champion against the elements. A godlike feeling, I think, and one that puts Ambrosia alongside the other warmers in this chapter.

3 ounces **hot coffee**

2 ounces **brandy**

1 ounce **Galliano**

1. Add the coffee, brandy, and Galliano to a coffee cup or mug.

2. Drink carefully—you can still get burned.

⬆ *A Note:* Under the impression that this one is lacking a little something? (It is the drink of the gods, after all.) Then I suggest you top it with a swirl or two of whipped cream.

⬆ *A Second Note:* Just because this isn't in the couple-y chapter doesn't mean you can't be sharing this with your baby cuddled up under the covers on a cold day.

Aunt Betsy's Favorite

I feel a dash sad, because I never had an Aunt Betsy to serve this to, unlike the writers of *House & Garden's Drink Guide* (Pocket Books, 1975), from which I adapted this hot wine relative. I did once have a rather nice, aunt-like boss named Betsy, who was known (in the best way) to **enjoy a fine drink** when the workday was done and wasn't opposed to encouraging her underlings to have one, too. That's the kind of boss (or aunt) you want, friends. **Serves 6**

24 ounces **red wine** (I suggest a dry Cabernet Sauvignon)

16 ounces **tawny port**

8 ounces **brandy**

4 ounces **Simple Syrup** (page 12)

1 **orange peel**

3 **whole cloves**

1 **stick cinnamon**

1. Add all of the ingredients to a medium-size saucepan. Cook on medium heat, stirring regularly, for 10 minutes. You want it to get good and hot, but not start boiling, or even simmering. Reduce the heat midway through the cooking time if needed.

2. Once the 10 minutes have passed and the room smells wonderful, ladle the mix into heavy mugs. Avoid serving the orange peel, cloves, and cinnamon stick if your pals are worried about clunking up their smiles.

Black Stripe

Ladieeeeees and gentlemen, in this corner, the cold-weather forgetter, the wild north wind un-doer, the arctic-party personified, the December morning defeater, the master of molasses, the Blaaaaaack Stripe. With that kind of introduction, aren't you glad that the Black Stripe's on your side when the temperature dips? I sure am.

2½ ounces **dark rum**

1 **teaspoon molasses**

4 ounces **water**

Lemon twist for garnish

1. Add the rum and molasses to a mug or sturdy coffee cup. Stir slightly to combine.

2. In a small saucepan, heat the water to boiling, then quickly pour it into the mug.

3. Twist the lemon over the drink, and then drop it in. Stir once, happily on the winning side.

"His bag was already on the customs bench and he opened it for a uniformed inspector who made but a cursory examination until he found the leather-covered flask. **He unscrewed it, sniffed rum, grinned**. 'Medicine,' he said. 'Medicine.' Andy grinned back at him and opened the briefcase."

GEORGE HARMON COXE, *Murder in Havana*, 1943

Brandy Skin

Once and for all, soiree attendees, when I start talking about serving up a Brandy Skin, I'm talking about neither a disgusting medical procedure nor a blue movie one might find at a video store. It's a simple and wonderful warmer, one that's been around, sure, but only because one of the first bar heroes, Tom Bullock, wrote it up in *The Ideal Bartender* (reprinted in *173 Pre-Prohibition Cocktails*, Howling at the Moon Press, 2001) for us to share. So stop being squeamish.

3 ounces **water**

1½ ounces **brandy**

½ ounce **Simple Syrup** (page 12)

Lemon twist for garnish

1. In a small saucepan (or the microwave, if you're stoveless), heat the water to just about boiling.

2. Pour the water carefully into an old-fashioned glass, then add the brandy and simple syrup. Stir to get everything cozy. Garnish with the lemon twist.

A Matter of Tastes

Taste is a defining and—this is key—individualistic thing; it's what makes us who we are. (Well, that and our choice in hats. And a few other things, such as how well we can wear a feather boa.) Sure, you're saying, all this is pretty obvious. But, given that these recipes call for you to be presenting drinks tricked out to the ¼ ounce in some cases, I think it's good to go over this salient taste point, because, friends, your taste is obviously not going to be quite the same as mine. Which means I'm not going to cry if you, when seeing me at the bar, say you altered a recipe in this book slightly because you thought it was too lemony.

The recipes are tested for my (albeit educated) taste, and I would always suggest (when reading any recipe book, by the way) following them to a T when starting out, because, well, I think they're tasty. But you shouldn't feel trapped into drinking or eating something you don't like, when you're just ¼ ounce of lemon juice away from sipping a drink that'll change your life, make memories for you and yours, and cement itself into your mind as the drink to change all drinks.

Remember, people have different tastes—but this is never a reason not to sit and swill with them. Now, if they won't wear a boa, that's a wholly different issue.

Café Brûlot

There is no doubt that New Orleans is one of the finest places to get an out-of-this-world meal accompanied by classic drinks. Is it any surprise, then, that the after-dinner coffee in that city is something exceptional, out-of-the ordinary, and triumphant? Of course not—and if you doubt it, first, you're silly. Second, check out the Café Brûlot and see how wrong you were. This incendiary mixture was supposedly created at Antoine's restaurant by Jules Alciatore, the son of the restaurant's founder, sometime in the 1890s. Today, many restaurants in the city boast a good Café Brûlot, and if you're exceptionally lucky, you'll have a meal in a fine home where your host or hostess will construct a celebratory Café Brûlot. Take heart from these folks, and try making your own next time you're holding a dinner party. **Serves 5 flame-loving folks**

- 5 ounces **Cognac**
- 4 **orange twists**
- 4 **lemon twists**
- 4½ teaspoons **granulated sugar**
- 3 **cinnamon sticks**
- ½ teaspoon **ground cloves**
- 4 ounces **hot coffee**

A Note: *The legend goes that this drink was especially popular during Prohibition, as the coffee aroma would cover up the liquor aroma. That's not only a fun fact to bring up; it also means this one's ideal for a Prohibition party.*

1. Add the Cognac, orange and lemon twists, 3 teaspoons of the sugar, the cinnamon sticks, and cloves to a silver bowl or attractive saucepan or other sturdy and heatproof serving bowl (a silver bowl is traditional, but isn't a necessity, though it sure gleams prettily).

2. Scoop a bit of the Cognac up in a large ladle and very carefully add the remaining 1½ teaspoons sugar to the ladle. Then, using a long match or other safe lighting device, light the contents of the ladle on fire.

3. Okay, here's the tricky part: Pour the flaming contents of the ladle back into the silver bowl or larger vessel, while not letting the flames go out. Then, smoothly scoop up and pour back in one ladleful of the bowl's contents to mix, again making sure the flame doesn't go out. You want to keep repeating this step until everything is mixed and the whole mixture is gently flaming.

4. Continuing to make sure the flame continues, add the coffee, as slowly as necessary, and mix it in.

5. Now, ladle the mix around, but don't worry about putting the flame out—actually, you want to put it out now, but be careful about it. Ladle into five espresso cups or small coffee cups, with a nod southward (unless you're south of New Orleans—then nod northward).

Chamomile Fairy

Gather round, my wee ones, and let me spin you a yarn of the Chamomile Fairy, a yarn that winds its windy way back through me hearing it at my grandfather's knee, as he heard it at his grandfather's, and on back throughout time itself. It's a story of strong Irish drink combined with the healing power of tea—yes, a yarn that can wake up the weary and warm up the weak, one that you yourself can pass on to a friend who's tired and wilty (much like putting a chamomile plant next to a droopy plant **tends to perk it up**). While this isn't always going to make you feel better, it sure won't make you feel ill, unless you tell the yarn too many times in a short period. Like many yarns, it has a sprinkling of lemon and sugar to balance it out, and a heap of good cheer in the ending. And speaking of endings, that's the whole yarn itself, and now you know it.

2 ounces **Irish whiskey**

½ ounce **freshly squeezed lemon juice**

½ ounce **Simple Syrup** (page 12)

4 ounces **freshly brewed chamomile tea**

Lemon slice for garnish

1. Add the Irish whiskey, lemon juice, and simple syrup to a mug or other insulated glass. Stir once.

2. Pour in the tea. Stir well, while spinning a yard-long yarn if possible. Garnish with the lemon slice and a twinkle in your eye.

⬆ *A Note: It's said in some shady spots (by elves, I think) that if you plant a whole lawn of chamomile, you could throw an egg into the air and it wouldn't break on landing. This in no way means you should try to toss an egg into this drink.*

The Eagle

This comes with a sing-along for brisk late-October evenings, when you are still able to go a cappella without getting a mouthful of snow: "I want to drink up the Eagle, against the chill, drink up the Eagle, for that double dark spirit thrill. I want to drink up the Eagle, all night long, drink that toasty Eagle until the break of dawn." Now, anyone who pretended they didn't know the tune, hang your head in shame. And give a silent apology to Steve Miller.

1 ounce **bourbon**

1 ounce **rye**

½ ounce **Simple Syrup** (page 12)

3 ounces **water**

Lemon twist for garnish

1. Add the bourbon, rye, and simple syrup to a coffee cup or mug. Stir briefly.

2. In a small saucepan or in the microwave, heat the water just to boiling. Pour it into the mug, and stir again.

3. Squeeze the lemon twist over the cup or mug, and then let it fly down in to meet the other ingredients. Exquisite, isn't it?

Hot Brick

Much like sauntering down a hot brick road in summertime—which can be, if you're not careful, a jumpy affair—drinking the Hot Brick demands care when consumed on an afternoon when the temperature is rapidly shifting in the opposite direction (meaning, arctic *brrr*-ness and general frosty stylings) for one good reason and one great one. First, you're dealing with heated items. Second, your lips are probably chapped already, and the last thing you want is to burn them on top of the chapped-ness, because, even though it's bitterly cold, you still may want to do some cold-weather kissing. Think of these reasons, take care of those lips, and make everyone happy.

2 ounces **bourbon**

1 ounce **Simple Syrup** (page 12)

½ teaspoon **butter**

¼ teaspoon **ground cinnamon**

3½ ounces **water**

1. Heat a sturdy goblet by running it under warm water, then drying it quickly. Add the bourbon, simple syrup, butter, and cinnamon.

2. Being wary and watchful, heat the water to almost boiling in a small saucepan or in the microwave. Pour the water into the goblet, and stir well. Don't (even if tempted) lick the stirring apparatus—you want to save those lips, remember.

Poetic Party Lines

Impress your friends, allure your neighbors at the bar, and realize how the poetry of a good drink is even better when accompanied by one of the lines from the following poems.

1. "I give a cocktail in the bathroom, everyone gets wet / it's very beachy; and I clear my head staring at the sign / LOI DU 29 JUILLET 1881 . . ." –Frank O'Hara, "Beer for Breakfast," *The Collected Poems* (University of California Press, 1995)

2. "But since you've asked for a poem, / my ex, my sweet and troubled one, I'll give you this / attempt, complete with starry night and bourbon shots . . ." –Albert Goldbarth, "Complete with Starry Night and Bourbon Shots," *The Kitchen Sink* (Graywolf Press, 2007)

3. "I am looking out over / the bay at sundown and getting / lushed with a fifty-nine- / year-old heavily rouged cocktail / lounge singer; this total stranger." –Denis Johnson, "Night," *Incognito Lounge* (Harper Perennial, 1982)

4. "I have taken in the religion / of pork chop and gin, tasted / red meat and confection, / nectarine and absinthe." –Amy Fleury, "Commotions of the Flesh," *Beautiful Trouble* (Southern Illinois University Press, 2004)

5. "O'Neal ran the Saturn Bar. His heart called last call / a few months after the flood, and in my fever / he raises his shirt, a pale guyaberra, to show the scar / at a party, and he serves a blue drink / in a flower vase, and one for himself." –Ed Skoog, "Memory Loss," *Mister Skylight* (Copper Canyon, 2009)

Hot Spiced Scotch

If any hot dog at your ski chalet complains about you mixing up Scotch into a hot drink, let it be said: This particular combination traces its lineage back at least to *Applegreen's Bar Book*, which, for the edition in my hands right now (the 1909 edition, published by the Hotel Monthly Press, though an earlier edition came out in 1899), sold for a dollar—a nice bit of change even if you're a darb. All of this equaling the fact that this Hot Spiced Scotch has been served much, much longer than the puffy-panted complainer has been alive. If that doesn't sell him on it, then kick the whiner back out into the snow and find some better friends.

½ ounce **Simple Syrup** (page 12)

½ teaspoon **ground allspice**

3 to 4 **whole cloves**

2 ounces **Scotch**

3½ ounces **water**

½ teaspoon **butter**

¼ teaspoon **freshly grated nutmeg** for garnish

Lemon twist for garnish

1. Heat a sturdy goblet by running it under warm water, then drying it quickly.

2. Add the simple syrup, allspice, and cloves to a cocktail shaker. Using a muddler or wooden spoon, muddle well.

3. Add the Scotch to the shaker. Swirl the contents together, and then strain into the warm goblet.

4. Heat the water in a small saucepan or in the microwave. Pour the hot water into the goblet. Add the butter and stir a couple of times (not once for every year between now and 1909, though).

5. Top the drink with the nutmeg and the lemon twist.

Hot Whiskey Sling

Sure, too many Hot Whiskey Slings added to that supposedly leisurely stroll on streets in January under those sweet stars, with a layer of black ice almost unseen on every surface—compounded by a few minutes of inspired-at-the-time tag-playing—that can equal a second, unseen sling. Your arm in a sling, that is, after the fractures have been set by the local M.D. Keep it safe: Stay indoors once the third Sling has been slurped, and save the money from the doctor's bill for more drinks. Tomorrow, friends, is a new day.

2 ounces **whiskey**

½ ounce **freshly squeezed lemon juice**

½ ounce **Simple Syrup** (page 12)

Dash of **Angostura bitters**

1½ ounces **water**

1. Add the whiskey, lemon juice, simple syrup, and bitters to a thick-walled old-fashioned glass, mug, or other vessel that can handle the heat.

2. Heat the water almost to boiling in the microwave or a small saucepan.

3. Pour the water into the glass (or wherever those other ingredients are hiding). Stir once.

A VARIATION: You can make a Hot Sling with dark rum, or even Scotch or brandy, and enjoy it immensely (as long as you're not breaking bones).

"Tip the whiskey round,
I wish to be a-blinking,
My feet sha-n-t leave this ground
While **I'm fit for drinking**."

O'BRIAN, "Tip the Whiskey Round,"
The Universal Songster: Or, Museum of Mirth, 1834

Irish Coffee

A staple of bar and restaurant menus worldwide in locales where the average outfit is at least a sweater, if not a thick fishing jacket or parka (also a staple at bars and restaurants that insist on keeping the air conditioner at torturously low temperatures—c'mon!), the Irish Coffee has myriad variations, with the best being **an unfussy grouping**, as friendly to each other as the locals at your neighborhood pub. (If, perhaps, garnished with a little more whipped cream. Not that I'm saying your neighborhood pub doesn't have locals covered in whipped cream. I'm just guessing it doesn't.) One hint: This works best with a coffee that has good body to it, like Colombian Supremo.

1½ ounces **Irish whiskey**

½ ounce **Simple Syrup** (page 12)

6 ounces **hot coffee**

Whipped cream (optional)

1. Add the whiskey and simple syrup to a mug. See how well they get along?

2. Add the coffee to the mug, with care. Stir once, and top with whipped cream (unless you're watching your figure).

A VARIATION: If this is too sweet (say, in the morning, when you don't want to frou-frou up your coffee with sugar), drop out the simple syrup until your mood lightens.

⬆ *A Note: I recently read that Irish Coffee's roots go back to an Irish port town called Foynes, which garnered a lot of incoming air and sea traffic in the 1930s and '40s. This drink was developed at the port terminal restaurant to help warm up incoming travelers. Now, that's a fine story, and shows once again the healing power of the dark spirits.*

Sophisticated

A refined drink for refined evenings when you've come in from a winter black-tie-and-white-gown event, where the dancing was slight and distanced and the food mild and undemanding, the conversation revolved around urbane and delicately mundane matters, and the farewells were said early and without much exuberance. After such an evening, you, unsurprisingly, want to start it up, kick it back, put on a loud funk record, and **shake that nonsense off**. The Sophisticated lets you accomplish those goals while still maintaining your chic.

2½ ounces **Cognac**

1½ ounces **Chambord**

1. Run a snifter or goblet carefully under warm water. Dry quickly.

2. In a small saucepan, heat the Cognac and Chambord, stirring often. You want to raise the temperature to medium, but never let the mixture come to even a simmer.

3. Once it's heated through, pour the mix into the snifter. Don't spill once the dancing starts, as it's still warm.

Movie Night Snacks and Drinks

If you're having some friends over for a night of cinematic wonderment, but you can't seem to find the right snacks or drinks to match up with the celluloid marvels that are bound to ensue, then go to the source for the snacks (the source being the movie theater itself). And look below for specific drinks to go *with* the snacks.

1. Snack: Popcorn. Drink: Corn Popper (page 100)
2. Snack: Junior Mints. Drink: Stinger (page 48)
3. Snack: Red Vines. Drink: Crimson Slippers (page 195)
4. Snack: Butterfinger Bites. Drink: Lover's Moon (page 161)
5. Snack: Nachos. Drink: Xalapa Punch (page 271)

Tom & Jerry

A drink once almost synonymous with the Professor, Jerry Thomas, a star (perhaps *the* star) bartender from the late 1800s, the Tom & Jerry is a delightful way to while away the late December hours—if a bit of a production. But **isn't pageantry itself a holiday staple**? I think so, which is why having a drink that lives up to the spectacle (and a warmer-upper at that) isn't a shabby idea. And yet, as modern-day cocktail professor David Wondrich details in his wondrous book *Imbibe!* (Perigee, 2007), which is brimming with Jerry Thomas information and enough drink lore to fill up any number of evening readings, provided your liquor cabinet is well stocked, this drink wasn't invented by Jerry Thomas after all, even though he told the story of inventing it many times (even going so far as to claim he named it after his two pet white mice). It turns out the Tom & Jerry was made in New England before ol' Thomas was even born. But many bartenders are inventive folks, and we wouldn't want it any other way, or bars would be much less enjoyable places to while away the hours within. And, as Mr. Wondrich says about Mr. Thomas not inventing it, "No matter; if he didn't invent the drink, he certainly did more than any other man to promote it." Which means you should give up a toast to him with your first Tom & Jerry.

1 **egg**, separated

¾ ounce **dark rum**

1 teaspoon **granulated sugar**

¼ teaspoon **ground allspice**

¾ ounce **brandy**

2½ ounces **milk**

Freshly grated nutmeg for garnish

1. In a small bowl, mix up the yolk of the egg with the rum, sugar, and allspice.

2. Using a hand mixer or a fork and your strong arm, whip the egg white until it gets stiff. Fold it and the brandy into the bowl with the rum mixture.

3. Using hot water, heat an actual Tom & Jerry mug or other sturdy mug and dry it quickly. Then add the mixture in the bowl to it.

4. In a small saucepan, heat the milk until it just becomes introduced to a boil, then stop. Pour it into the mug, stir briefly, then sprinkle a little nutmeg over the top.

✖ *A Warning: As this contains raw egg, do not serve to the elderly or those with compromised immune systems.*

Winter's Twilight

The curtains rise on a noirish film with this same sobriquet. The opening shot tracks a man (maybe Dick Powell) stumbling across a field covered in snow, carrying a black satchel that looks heavy with cash and heartbreak, and wearing a dented hat pulled down deep over his head, but no coat, and his pant leg is torn in the back. As the camera pans down that torn pant leg and trails behind him, spots of blood dot the white snow . . . but wait, what's in the distance? An ordinary farmhouse with a window lit by a single candle, and as he approaches the door, it's opened from the inside by a blond looker (maybe Virginia Mayo), and as he walks in the door, he opens that satchel, which doesn't contain cash, but the ingredients and tools needed to make this very drink.

4 ounces **POM Wonderful pomegranate juice**

2 ounces **Cognac**

½ ounce **Chambord**

Lemon slice for garnish

1. Add the pomegranate juice to a small saucepan and, over medium heat, let the juice come to a simmer, but not a boil. Add the Cognac and Chambord, and lower the heat to medium-low. Heat, stirring once or twice, for 2 minutes, never letting it come to a boil.

2. Pour the mix into a glass or mug that can handle the heat. Garnish with the lemon slice.

↑ *A Note: All dark nights aside, I first found this cozy combo in Mary Lou and Robert J. Heiss's book* Hot Drinks *(Ten Speed Press, 2007), which you should invest in if you ever like to make a drink during the colder mornings, afternoons, or evenings.*

WOW

I have to say it: Wow, I mean, wow, this drink is . . . wow. I'm almost speechless (which would be the first time since Trudy and Art's boy, a.k.a. me, learned to talk). But not so much that I can't dwell for a moment on this **affectionate heater's moniker**. Is it just a reference to the ingredients? Or could it mean "Warmth Over Winter"? Or, to be more literary, "Wild Oscar Wilde" in an homage to the writer and raconteur? You decide for me; I don't want to waste any WOW time talking about it.

2 ounces **whiskey**

1½ ounces **freshly squeezed orange juice**

1 ounce **Simple Syrup** (page 12)

2½ ounces **water**

Orange twist for garnish

1. Add the whiskey, orange juice, and simple syrup to a large mug. Stir wonderingly.

2. Heat the water in a tiny saucepan or the microwave (but be cautious about it), almost to boiling.

3. Pour the water into the mug, and stir briefly. Twist the orange twist over the top and drop it in. Wow, indeed.

A VIRGIN VARIATION: Take the whiskey out of the equation; up the orange juice by 1 ounce, the simple syrup by ½ ounce, and the water by ½ ounce; and add ¼ teaspoon ground cloves to the mug in step 1. But you can only call it a WO.

"Peat whiskey hot,
Tempered with well-boiled water!
These **make the long night shorter**."

ROBERT HINCKLEY MESSINGER, "A Winter Wish,"
Yale Book of American Verse, 1912

Measurement Equivalents

Please note that all conversions are approximate.

Liquid Conversions

U.S.	Imperial	Metric
1 tsp		5 ml
1 tbs	½ fl oz	15 ml
2 tbs	1 fl oz	30 ml
3 tbs	1½ fl oz	45 ml
¼ cup	2 fl oz	60 ml
⅓ cup	2½ fl oz	75 ml
⅓ cup + 1 tbs	3 fl oz	90 ml
⅓ cup + 2 tbs	3½ fl oz	100 ml
½ cup	4 fl oz	120 ml
⅔ cup	5 fl oz	150 ml
¾ cup	6 fl oz	180 ml
¾ cup + 2 tbs	7 fl oz	200 ml
1 cup	8 fl oz	240 ml
1 cup + 2 tbs	9 fl oz	275 ml
1¼ cups	10 fl oz	300 ml
1⅓ cups	11 fl oz	325 ml
1½ cups	12 fl oz	350 ml
1⅔ cups	13 fl oz	375 ml
1¾ cups	14 fl oz	400 ml
1¾ cups + 2 tbs	15 fl oz	450 ml
2 cups (1 pint)	16 fl oz	475 ml
2½ cups	20 fl oz	600 ml
3 cups	24 fl oz	720 ml
4 cups (1 quart)	32 fl oz	945 ml
		(1,000 ml is 1 liter)

Weight Conversions

U.S./U.K.	Metric
½ oz	14 g
1 oz	28 g
1½ oz	43 g
2 oz	57 g
2½ oz	71 g
3 oz	85 g
3½ oz	100 g
4 oz	113 g
5 oz	142 g
6 oz	170 g
7 oz	200 g
8 oz	227 g
9 oz	255 g
10 oz	284 g
11 oz	312 g
12 oz	340 g
13 oz	368 g
14 oz	400 g
15 oz	425 g
1 lb	454 g

Oven Temperature Conversions

°F	Gas Mark	°C
250	½	120
275	1	140
300	2	150
325	3	165
350	4	180
375	5	190
400	6	200
425	7	220
450	8	230
475	9	240
500	10	260
550	Broil	290

Index
of Drinks by Primary Liquor

Note: *Italicized* page references indicate photographs.

Amaretto
WeatherUp, 91

Apple brandy
Corpse Reviver, 192
Kitchen Sink, 208

Applejack
Corpse Reviver, 192

Armagnac
Fair Skies, 104

Bourbon
Artist's Special, 185
Buck Owens, 59
Class of the Race, *98*, 99
Debutante's Dream, 152
Demon of Destiny, 198
Derby Fizz, 103
Derby Widow, 63
The Eagle, 282
Gaslight Tiger, 202
Horsefeather, 29
Horse's Neck, 253
Hot Brick, 282
Hunter, 204
Irreverent Reverend, 72
Karlita, 74
King Cole, 206
Lazy Hazy, 116
Left Hand, 76, *77*
Lover's Moon, *160*, 161
Millennium Cocktail, 80
Mint Julep, 36–37
Old Fashioned, 38
Pony Punch, 261
Presbyterian, 124
Quickie, 165
Sazerac, *44*, 45
Sookie Cocktail, 221
Southstreet, 266
Summer Dream, 168, *169*
The Very Old Fashioned, 269
Whiskey Sour, 51
Whizz Bang, 232

Brandy. *See also* Cognac
Ambrosia, 275
Between the Sheets, 141
Black Feather, 58
Blood and Sand, 239
Blue Train, 96
Bosom Caresser, 146
Brace Up, 147
Brandy Skin, 279
Corpse Reviver, 192
Côte d'Azur Cooler, 101
Dalliance, 151
Debutante's Dream, 152
Drowsy Chaperone, 66
Fair Skies, 104
Fu Manchu, 67
Ginger Smash, 203
The Golden Panther, 250
Hoop La, 156
Hot Shot, *70*, 71
Hot Toddy, 31
The Human Factor, 72
Kitchen Sink, 208
Little Sister, 255
Ognam, 82, *83*
Saratoga, 126
Sidecar, 46
Sleepy Head, 127
Snow Ball, *128*, 129
Soother, 167
Stinger, 48, *49*
Stomach Reviver Cocktail, 225
Sweet Louise, 88
Thumper, 228
Ti Penso Sempre, 174, *175*
Tip Top, 131
Warlock, 230
Washington's Wish, *134*, 135
Williwaw, 233
Zoom, 181

Canadian Whisky
O Happy Day, 121
Whisper, 179

Champagne or **sparkling wine**
Bombay Punch, 240, *241*
Cardinal, 244
Crimean Cup à la Marmora, 247
Honolulu Punch, 252
Power to the People, 262, *263*
Rocky Mountain Punch, 265

Cherry brandy
Blood and Sand, 239

Cognac
Ambiance, 139
Bimbo Punch, 238
Black Pearl, 142
Blushing Bride, *144*, 145
Café Brûlot, 280
Champs Élysées, 245
Chicago, 97
Dirty Monkey, 199
Golden Lady, 108
Green Room Cocktail, 203
Hour Glass, 110
King's Peg, 112
Lalla Rookh, *114*, 115
Ponce de León, 122, *123*
Roffignac, 125
The Settler, 127
Sidecar, 46
Sophisticated, 288
Stinger, 48, *49*
Sweet Dream, 171
Vieux Carré Cocktail, 50
Winter's Twilight, 290, *291*
Yokohama Romance, 180–181

Cointreau
Between the Sheets, 141

Coole Swan liqueur
Dirty Monkey, 199

Corn Whiskey
Corn Popper, 100

Cynar
The Search for Delicious, 85

Gin
The Golden Panther, 250
Karlita, 74
Kitchen Sink, 208

Irish Whiskey
Brainstorm, 190, *191*
Cameron's Kick, 192
Chamomile Fairy, 281
The Curtis Hotel, 62
Irish Coffee, 287
Irish Rickey, 111
Leprechaun, 210
Mike Collins, 34, *35*
Serpent's Tooth, 219

Rum
ASAP, 56, *57*
Bayou, 186
Beach Bubble, 94, *95*
Bedroom Eyes, 140
Between the Sheets, 141
Black Stripe, 278
Blossom, 142
Bring the House Down, 242
Caesar's Bowl, 243
Caribbean Bloom, 148, *149*
Crimson Slippers, *194*, 195
Dark and Stormy, 26, *27*
Dark Mountain, 197
Dark Water, 102
Dirty Monkey, 199
Fish House Punch, 28
Football Punch, 250, *251*
Fu Manchu, 67
Haitian Witch, 69
Honey Bee, 154, *155*
KP Cocktail, 75
Lady Godiva, 158
Lalla Rookh, *114*, 115
Limbo, *212*, 213
Lion Tamer, 79
Mai Tai, 32
The Native, 258
The Natural, 162
New Orleans Buck, 120

Northside Special, 121
Nourmahal, 259
Nuit de Noces, 163
The Occidental, 81
Paradiso, 164
Parisian Blonde, 164
Planter's Punch, 39
Polynesian Donkey, 84
Quarter Deck, 214
Rumba, 166
Rum Cobbler, 216, *217*
Rum Rascal, 125
Shanghai Cocktail, 219
Short Timer, 86
Sir Henry Morgan, 220
Soother, 167
Speak No Evil, 267
Stockholm Tar, *222*, 223
Three Wishes, 173
Tom & Jerry, 289
Tropical, 176
Vick's Zither, 132
Zombie, 52–53

Rye
Black Hood, 187
Creole Cocktail, 193
Day-Off Punch, 248
Dr. Blinker, 64, *65*
Dutch Charlie's, 199
The Eagle, 282
Enchanted Field, *200*, 201
Golf Links Highball, 109
Iollas's Itch, 204, *205*
Kitchen Sink, 208
The Late Caress, 159
Leatherneck, 209
Manhattan, 33
Old Fashioned, 38
Oriental, 214
Rattlesnake Cocktail, 215
Sazerac, *44*, 45
Scofflaw Cocktail, 218
Spring in Your Step, 130
Steinway Punch, 268
Temptation Cocktail, 172
Tombstone, 89
Up in Mabel's Room, *178*, 179
Vieux Carré Cocktail, 50
Ward Eight, 229
Zazarac, *234*, 235

Scotch
Blood and Sand, 239
Bobby Burns, 189
Cameron's Kick, 192
The Curtis Hotel, 62
Foppa, *106*, 107
Highland Fling, 153
Hot Spiced Scotch, *284*, 285
Leviathan 477, 211
Mamie Taylor, 116
Morning Glory Fizz, 118
Morning Star, 119
Rob Roy, 40, *41*
Rusty Nail, 43
Tartan Swizzle, *226*, 227
Touchless Automatic, 90
Wildflower, 180

Sherry
Coronado Heights Flip, *60*, 61

Tia Maria liqueur
Black Pearl, 142

Vanilla liqueur
Lalla Rookh, *114*, 115

Vermouth
Blood and Sand, 239
Vieux Carré Cocktail, 50

Whiskey. *See also* Bourbon;
   Irish Whiskey; Rye; Scotch
Corn Popper, 100
Crow, 196
Derby Widow, 63
El Dorado, 249
The Golden Panther, 250
Hot Whiskey Punch, 254
Hot Whiskey Sling, 286
Manhattan, 33
O Happy Day, 121
Whisper, 179
WOW, 292

Wine. *See also* Champagne
   or sparkling wine
Aunt Betsy's Favorite, 276,
   277
Mercurio Punch, *256*, 257
Quintet, 264
Xalapa Punch, *270*, 271

General Index

Notes: *Italicized* page references indicate photographs.
Liquor entries include recipes where liquor is secondary ingredient.
See page 295 for Index of Drinks by Primary Liquor.

A

Absinthe
    buying, 110
    Demon of Destiny, 198
    Hour Glass, 110
    Morning Glory Fizz, 118
    Sazerac, *44*, 45
    substitute for, 198
    Zazarac, *234*, 235
Aerial M, 139
Amaretto
    Foppa, *106*, 107
    Three Wishes, 173
    WeatherUp, 91
Ambiance, 139
Ambrosia, 275
Amer Picon
    about, 193
    Creole Cocktail, 193
And a Bottle of Rum
    (Curtis), 4, 47
Angostura bitters
    about, 224
    Black Feather, 58
    Brace Up, 147
    Champs Élysées, 245
    Chicago, 97
    Dutch Charlie's, 199
    Ginger Smash, 203
    Horsefeather, 29
    Horse's Neck, 253
    Hot Whiskey Sling,
        286
    Leprechaun, 210
    Manhattan, 33
    Millennium Cocktail, 80
    Nourmahal, 259
    Old Fashioned, 38
    Planter's Punch, 39
    Rob Roy, 40, *41*
    Saratoga, 126
    Serpent's Tooth, 219
    Sir Henry Morgan, 220
    Tartan Swizzle, *226*, 227
    Tombstone, 89

The Very Old Fashioned,
    269
Vieux Carré Cocktail, 50
Williwaw, 233
Zazarac, *234*, 235
Anisette
    about, 147
    Brace Up, 147
    Hunter, 204
    Shanghai Cocktail, 219
    Zazarac, *234*, 235
Aperol
    Ognam, 82, *83*
    Ti Penso Sempre, 174, *175*
Apfelkorn
    about, 71
    Hot Shot, *70*, 71
    Speak No Evil, 267
    Washington's Wish, *134*,
        135
Apple brandy
    Calvados, about, 10
    Corpse Reviver, 192
    Kitchen Sink, 208
    Xalapa Punch, *270*, 271
Apple cider or juice
    Football Punch, 250, *251*
    Hot Shot, *70*, 71
    The Occidental, 81
    Speak No Evil, 267
Applegreen's Bar Book
    (Applegreen), 285
Applejack
    about, 30
    Corpse Reviver, 192
    Xalapa Punch, *270*, 271
Apricot brandy
    Caesar's Bowl, 243
    Vick's Zither, 132
Apricot liqueur
    Bedroom Eyes, 140
    Bombay Punch, 240, *241*
    Iollas's Itch, 204, *205*
    Lady Godiva, 158
    Zombie, 52–53

Apricots
    Power to the People, 262,
        263
Ardent Spirits (website),
    80
Armagnac
    about, 9
    Fair Skies, 104
Artist's Special, 185
The Art of Mixing Drinks,
    247
ASAP, 56, *57*
Aunt Betsy's Favorite, 276,
    277
Auntie Mae's Parlor, 29, 109

B

Baker, Charles H., 180
Baker, Tim, 71
Bar, home. *See also* Bar tools
    bar tools for, 16–20
    base dark spirits for, 4–10
    drink measurements, 16
    five essentials for, 102
    garnishes for, 14–16
    glassware, 20–22
    ice for, 13–14
    mixers for, 11–13
    preparing great cocktails,
        170, 209, 274, 279
    spirited sidekicks for,
        10–11
Bars and restaurants
    Auntie Mae's Parlor, 29,
        109
    Chubs Pub, 109
    in college towns, 109
    conversation starters, 37,
        184, 283
    Crofton on Wells, 97
    Death + Company, 72, 86
    Eighth Street Taproom,
        61

Bars and restaurants *(cont.)*
  El Rancho, 109
  Ernie K-Doe Mother-in-
    Law Lounge, 67
  Franklin Café, 67
  Hazelwood, 67
  Hibachi Hut, 75
  Little Branch, 76
  Locke-Ober, 229
  Manhattan Club, 33
  The Matchbox, 67
  Milk and Honey, 76
  Monteleone Hotel, 50
  movies with bar scenes,
    138
  PDT, 67
  Pendennis Club, 38
  Rodan, 69, 97
  Schuylkill Fishing
    Company, 28
  Taproom, 29
  Tigertail, 63
  Tiki Lounge, 67
  Town Talk Diner, 71
  Trader Vic's, 32
  22 Doors, 224
  Violet Hour, 85
  WeatherUp, 91
  Zanzibar, 109
Bartender's Choice
  ASAP, 56, *57*
  Black Feather, 58
  Buck Owens, 59
  Coronado Heights Flip,
    60, 61
  The Curtis Hotel, 62
  Derby Widow, 63
  Dr. Blinker, 64, *65*
  Drowsy Chaperone, 66
  Fu Manchu, 67
  Haitian Witch, 69
  Hot Shot, *70*, 71
  The Human Factor, 72
  Irreverent Reverend, 72
  Karlita, 74
  KP Cocktail, 75
  Left Hand, 76, *77*
  Lion Tamer, 79
  Millennium Cocktail, 80
  The Occidental, 81
  Ognam, 82, *83*
  Polynesian Donkey, 84
  The Search for Delicious,
    85
  Short Timer, 86
  Sweet Louise, 88

Tombstone, 89
Touchless Automatic, 90
WeatherUp, 91
*The Bar-Tender's Guide or
  How to Mix Drinks*
  (Thomas), 177
The Bartender's Guide
  (Duffy), 206, 264
Bar tools
  bar napkins, 20
  blender, 19
  Boston shaker, 17
  bottle opener, 20
  bottle stoppers, 20
  coasters, 20
  cobbler shaker, 17
  corkscrew, 20
  foil cutter, 20
  ice bucket and scoop,
    19–20
  jigger, 17–19
  juice squeezers, 18
  knife, 18–19
  muddler, 18
  pitcher, 19
  serving trays, 20
  spice grater, 20
  stirring spoon, 20
  straws, 20
  swizzle and stir sticks,
    20
  toothpicks, 20
  towel, 20
Bayou, 186
Beach, Donn, 32, 52
Beach Bubble, 94, *95*
Beachbum Berry's Grog Blog
  (website), 197
Bedroom Eyes, 140
Beebe, Lucius, 177, 250
Benedictine
  about, 188
  Ambiance, 139
  Black Hood, 187
  Bobby Burns, 189
  Brainstorm, 190, *191*
  Class of the Race, *98*, 99
  Creole Cocktail, 193
  Honey Bee, 154, *155*
  Mercurio Punch, *256*, 257
  Tip Top, 131
  Vieux Carré Cocktail, 50
Bergeron, Victor (Trader
  Vic), 32
Bergeron, Walter, 50
Between the Sheets, 141

Bimbo Punch, 238
Bittermens Sweet Chocolate
  Bitters
  Left Hand, 76, *77*
Bittermens (website), 76
Bitters. *See also* Angostura
  bitters; Orange bitters;
  Peychaud's bitters
  about, 13, 224
  Left Hand, 76, *77*
The Bitter Truth (website),
  86
Black Feather, 58
Black Hood, 187
Black Pearl, 142
Black Stripe, 278
Blender, 19
Blood and Sand, 239
Blossom, 142
Blue curaçao
  The Native, 258
Blue Train, 96
Blushing Bride, *144*, 145
Bobby Burns, 189
Bohrer, Andrew, 88, 224
Bombay Punch, 240, *241*
Books
  And a Bottle of Rum
    (Curtis), 4, 47
  Applegreen's Bar Book
    (Applegreen), 285
  The Art of Mixing Drinks,
    247
  *The Bar-Tender's Guide
    or How to Mix Drinks*
    (Thomas), 177
  The Bartender's Guide
    (Duffy), 206, 264
  *Cocktail Guide and Ladies'
    Companion* (Gaige),
    163, 177
  *Cocktail: Classici &
    Esotici*, 107
  Cocteles (Peysson), 204
  The Craft of the Cocktail
    (DeGroff), 47
  Drinks (Straub), 177, 199,
    268
  *The Essential Bartender's
    Guide* (Hess), 47, 58
  *The Fine Art of Mixing
    Drinks* (Embury), 51, 211
  *The Gentleman's
    Companion* (Baker), 180
  *A Guide to Pink
    Elephants*, 153

Here's How: A Round-the-World Bar Guide, 220
Hot Drinks (Heiss), 290
House & Garden's Drink Guide, 276
The Ideal Bartender (Bullock), 279
Imbibe! (Wondrich), 47, 89, 206, 289
International Cocktail Specialties from Madison Avenue to Malaya (Mayabb), 101
The Joy of Mixology (Regan), 47, 80
Mixologist (Miller), 47
The Museum of the American Cocktail's Pocket Recipe Guide (Hess), 64
The New Diner's Club Drink Book (Simmons), 164
The Official Mixer's Manual (Duffy), 141, 206
The Old Waldorf-Astoria Bar Book (Crockett), 177
173 Pre-Prohibition Cocktails (Bullock), 279
Party Potpourri, 243
quotes from classic cocktail books, 177
Ronrico's Official Mixtro's Guide, 132
The Savoy Cocktail Book (Craddock), 100, 156, 214
The Stork Club Bar Book (Beebe), 177, 250
Straight Up or On the Rocks (Grimes), 46
Vintage Spirits and Forgotten Cocktails (Haigh), 64
What Every Young Man Should Know, 202
Bosom Caresser, 146
Boston shaker, 17
Bottle opener, 19
Bottle stoppers, 20
Bourbon. *See* Index by Primary Liquor
about, 6, 37
Brace Up, 147
Brainstorm, 190, *191*

Brandy. *See also* Chartreuse; Cognac; Index by Primary Liquor
about, 8–10
Aunt Betsy's Favorite, 276, *277*
Cardinal, 244
El Dorado, 249
Honolulu Punch, 252
Hot Whiskey Punch, 254
Mercurio Punch, *256,* 257
The Natural, 162
obscure facts about, 37, 184
Polynesian Donkey, 84
Power to the People, 262, *263*
Quintet, 264
Southstreet, 266
Tom & Jerry, 289
Brandy Skin, 279
Bring the House Down, 242
Bubbly Refreshers
Beach Bubble, 94, *95*
Blue Train, 96
Chicago, 97
Class of the Race, *98,* 99
Corn Popper, 100
Côte d'Azur Cooler, 101
Dark Water, 102
Derby Fizz, 103
Fair Skies, 104
Foppa, *106,* 107
Golden Lady, 108
Golf Links Highball, 109
Hour Glass, 110
Irish Rickey, 111
King's Peg, 112
Lalla Rookh, *114,* 115
Lazy Hazy, 116
Mamie Taylor, 116
Morning Glory Fizz, 118
Morning Star, 119
New Orleans Buck, 120
Northside Special, 121
O Happy Day, 121
Ponce de León, 122, *123*
Presbyterian, 124
Roffignac, 125
Rum Rascal, 125
Saratoga, 126
The Settler, 127
Sleepy Head, 127
Snow Ball, *128,* 129
Spring in Your Step, 130
Tip Top, 131

Vick's Zither, 132
Washington's Wish, *134,* 135
Buck Owens, 59
Bullock, Tom, 279
Butler, Mark, 81

C

Cachaça
Polynesian Donkey, 84
Caesar's Bowl, 243
Café Brûlot, 280
Calvados, about, 10
Cameron's Kick, 192
Campari
about, 168
Crimson Slippers, *194,* 195
Left Hand, 76, *77*
Summer Dream, 168, *169*
Canadian Whisky
about, 7
O Happy Day, 121
Whisper, 179
Cardinal, 244
Caribbean Bloom, 148, *149*
Cask Strength (website), 88, 197
Chambord
Sophisticated, 288
Winter's Twilight, 290, *291*
Chamomile Fairy, 281
Champagne and sparkling wine. *See also* Index by Primary Liquor
about, 113
Black Pearl, 142
Blue Train, 96
Bombay Punch, 240, *241*
Chicago, 97
Class of the Race, *98,* 99
Fair Skies, 104
Golden Lady, 108
King's Peg, 112
Ponce de León, 122, *123*
Prosecco, about, 262
Tip Top, 131
Washington's Wish, *134,* 135
Champagne flute, 21
Champs Élysées, 245
Chartreuse
about, 246
Champs Élysées, 245

Chartreuse *(cont.)*
 Irreverent Reverend, 72
 Sweet Louise, 88
Cherries, maraschino, about,
  143
Cherry brandy. *See also*
   Cherry Heering
 Blood and Sand, 239
 Hunter, 204
 Kirschwasser, about, 10
 Williwaw, 233
 Yokohama Romance,
  180–181
Cherry Heering
 about, 68
 Haitian Witch, 69
 Hot Shot, *70*, 71
 O Happy Day, 121
Chicago, 97
Chubs Pub, 109
Citrónge
 about, 130
 Spring in Your Step, 130
Citrus fruit. *See also specific*
   fruits
 buying, 11–12
 juicers for, 18
 juicing, 12
 twists, creating, 15
 wedges, creating, 15
 wheels, creating, 15
Clarke, Paul, 86
Class of the Race, *98*, 99
Coasters, 20
Cobbler shaker, 17
Cocktail Chronicles (website),
  86, 197
Cocktail glasses, 20–21
Cocktail Guide and Ladies'
   Companion (Gaige),
  163, 177
Cocktail napkins, 20
Cocktails
 accented drink ideas, 101
 for anniversaries, 146
 beach house drinks,
  248
 to drown out boss's voice,
  255
 for anniversaries, 146
 finely named drinks, 167
 following recipe
   instructions, 279
 fresh mixers for, 209
 global-themed, 210
 hellacious hits, 187

information and websites,
  133, 197
innovative ingredients
   for, 91
for listening to Tom
   Waits, 268
matrimonial mixes, 140
for monster movies, 233
movie night, 288
named after animals, 74
pairing with music, 96
party packages, 73
planning, for successful
   parties, 170, 274
potions to pacify, 81
scary movie sippers, 53
seducing sippers, 165
tailgating triumphs, 228
Cocktail: Classici & Esotici,
  107
Coconut milk
 Limbo, *212*, 213
Cocteles (Peysson), 204
Coffee
 Ambrosia, 275
 Café Brûlot, 280
 Irish Coffee, 287
Cognac. *See also* Index by
   Primary Liquor
 about, 9, 184
 Crimean Cup à la
   Marmora, 247
 Fish House Punch, 28
 WeatherUp, 91
Cointreau
 Between the Sheets, 141
 Black Feather, 58
 Bombay Punch, 240, *241*
 Drowsy Chaperone, 66
 Golden Lady, 108
 Hoop La, 156
 Hour Glass, 110
 Ponce de León, 122, *123*
 Sidecar, 46
 Speak No Evil, 267
Collins glass, 21
Coole Swan liqueur
 about, 199
 Dirty Monkey, 199
Cordial glasses, 22
Corkscrew, 19
Corn Popper, 100
Corn Whiskey
 about, 6
 Corn Popper, 100
Coronado Heights Flip, *60*, 61

Corpse Reviver, 192
Côte d'Azur Cooler, 101
Craddock, Harry, 100, 156,
  214
The Craft of the Cocktail
   (DeGroff), 47
Cream-based cocktails
 Lover's Moon, *160*, 161
 Morning Star, 119
 Paradiso, 164
 Parisian Blonde, 164
 Sweet Dream, 171
 Zoom, 181
Cream of coconut
 Bring the House Down,
  242
Cream soda
 Lion Tamer, 79
Crème de cacao
 Bedroom Eyes, 140
Crème de cassis
 The Settler, 127
Crème de menthe
 Stinger, 48, *49*
Crème de pêche
 Drowsy Chaperone, 66
Creole Cocktail, 193
Crimean Cup à la Marmora,
  247
Crimson Slippers, *194*, 195
Crockett, Albert Stevens, 177
Crofton on Wells, 97
Crow, 196
Curaçao. *See also* Orange
   curaçao
 The Native, 258
Curtis, Wayne, 4, 47
The Curtis Hotel, 62
Cynar
 about, 87
 The Search for Delicious,
  85

D

Dalliance, 151
Dark and Stormy, 26, *27*
Dark Classics
 Dark and Stormy, 26, *27*
 Fish House Punch, 28
 Horsefeather, 29
 Hot Toddy, 31
 Mai Tai, 32
 Manhattan, 33
 Mike Collins, 34, *35*

Mint Julep, 36–37
Old Fashioned, 38
Planter's Punch, 39
Rob Roy, 40, *41*
Rusty Nail, 43
Sazerac, *44*, 45
Sidecar, 46
Stinger, 48, *49*
Vieux Carré Cocktail, 50
Whiskey Sour, 51
Zombie, 52–53
Dark Drinks That Go Bump in
    the Night
  Artist's Special, 185
  Bayou, 186
  Black Hood, 187
  Bobby Burns, 189
  Brainstorm, 190, *191*
  Cameron's Kick, 192
  Corpse Reviver, 192
  Creole Cocktail, 193
  Crimson Slippers, *194*, 195
  Crow, 196
  Dark Mountain, 197
  Demon of Destiny, 198
  Dirty Monkey, 199
  Dutch Charlie's, 199
  Enchanted Field, *200*, 201
  Gaslight Tiger, 202
  Ginger Smash, 203
  Green Room Cocktail, 203
  Hunter, 204
  Iollas's Itch, 204, *205*
  King Cole, 206
  Kitchen Sink, 208
  Leatherneck, 209
  Leprechaun, 210
  Leviathan 477, 211
  Limbo, *212*, 213
  Oriental, 214
  Quarter Deck, 214
  Rattlesnake Cocktail, 215
  Rum Cobbler, 216, *217*
  Scofflaw Cocktail, 218
  Serpent's Tooth, 219
  Shanghai Cocktail, 219
  Sir Henry Morgan, 220
  Sookie Cocktail, 221
  Stockholm Tar, *222*, 223
  Stomach Reviver Cocktail,
    225
  Tartan Swizzle, *226*, 227
  Thumper, 228
  Ward Eight, 229
  Warlock, 230
  Whizz Bang, 232

Williwaw, 233
Zazarac, *234*, 235
Dark Mountain, 197
Dark Water, 102
Day-Off Punch, 248
Death + Company, 72, 86
Debutante's Dream, 152
DeGroff, Dale, 47
Demon of Destiny, 198
Denny, Jeff, 29
Derby Fizz, 103
Derby Widow, 63
Dim the Lights, Chill the
    Cocktails
  Ambiance, 139
  Bedroom Eyes, 140
  Between the Sheets, 141
  Black Pearl, 142
  Blossom, 142
  Blushing Bride, *144*, 145
  Bosom Caresser, 146
  Brace Up, 147
  Caribbean Bloom, 148, *149*
  Dalliance, 151
  Debutante's Dream, 152
  Highland Fling, 153
  Honey Bee, 154, *155*
  Hoop La, 156
  Lady Godiva, 158
  The Late Caress, 159
  Lover's Moon, *160*, 161
  The Natural, 162
  Nuit de Noces, 163
  Paradiso, 164
  Parisian Blonde, 164
  Quickie, 165
  Rumba, 166
  Soother, 167
  Summer Dream, 168, *169*
  Sweet Dream, 171
  Temptation Cocktail, 172
  Three Wishes, 173
  Ti Penso Sempre, 174, *175*
  Tropical, 176
  Up in Mabel's Room, *178*,
    179
  Whisper, 179
  Wildflower, 180
  Yokohama Romance,
    180–181
  Zoom, 181
Dirty Monkey, 199
Dr. Blinker, 64, *65*
Drambuie
  Rusty Nail, 43
DrinkBoy (website), 38, 58

Drinks (Straub), 177, 199, 268
Drowsy Chaperone, 66
Dubonnet
  about, 172
  Dutch Charlie's, 199
  Gaslight Tiger, 202
  Temptation Cocktail, 172
Duffy, Patrick Gavin, 141,
    206, 264
Dutch Charlie's, 199

E

The Eagle, 282
Eighth Street Taproom, 61
Egg-based cocktails
  Bosom Caresser, 146
  Corn Popper, 100
  Coronado Heights Flip,
    60, 61
  Derby Fizz, 103
  Kitchen Sink, 208
  Morning Glory Fizz, 118
  Morning Star, 119
  Snow Ball, *128*, 129
  Tom & Jerry, 289
Ekus, Lisa, 153
Elderflower liqueur. *See*
    St-Germain elderflower
    liqueur
El Dorado, 249
El Rancho, 109
Embury, David A., 51, 211
Enchanted Field, *200*, 201
Ernie K. Doe Mother-in-Law
    Lounge, 67
*The Essential Bartender's
    Guide* (Hess), 47, 58
Estopinal, Kirk, 85

F

Fair Skies, 104
Falernum
  about, 56
  ASAP, 56, *57*
Fernet-Branca
  about, 207
  King Cole, 206
  Stomach Reviver Cocktail,
    225
*The Fine Art of Mixing
    Drinks* (Embury), 51, 211
Fish House Punch, 28

Foil cutter, 19
Football Punch, 250, *251*
Foppa, *106*, 107
Frangelico
 about, 159
 The Late Caress, 159
Franklin Café, 67
Fruit. *See also* Citrus fruit
 fresh, buying, 11–12
Fuller, Natalie, 82
Fu Manchu, 67

G

Gaige, Crosby, 163, 177
Galliano
 Ambrosia, 275
Garnishes, 14–16
Gaslight Tiger, 202
*The Gentleman's
 Companion* (Baker), 180
Giffard Ginger of the Indies
 liqueur
 about, 86
 Short Timer, 86
Gin. *See also* Index by
 Primary Liquor
 Rumba, 166
Ginger
 fresh, adding to drinks, 91
 Ginger Smash, 203
 KP Cocktail, 75
 The Very Old Fashioned,
 269
Ginger ale
 ASAP, 56, *57*
 Beach Bubble, 94, *95*
 Day-Off Punch, 248
 Foppa, *106*, 107
 Fu Manchu, 67
 Horsefeather, 29
 Horse's Neck, 253
 Mamie Taylor, 116
 New Orleans Buck, 120
 The Occidental, 81
 O Happy Day, 121
 Polynesian Donkey, 84
 Presbyterian, 124
 Rum Rascal, 125
 Snow Ball, *128*, 129
 Southstreet, 266
 Speak No Evil, 267
Ginger beer
 Dark and Stormy, 26, *27*

KP Cocktail, 75
Ginger Smash, 203
Glasser, Janet and Avery, 76
Glassware
 Champagne flute, 21
 cocktail glasses, 20–21
 Collins glass, 21
 cordial glasses, 22
 highball glasses, 21
 Martini glass, 20
 mugs, 21
 old-fashioned glasses, 21
 punch bowl, 21–22
 wine glasses, 21
Golden Lady, 108
The Golden Panther, 250
Golf Links Highball, 109
Grand Marnier
 about, 78
 Black Hood, 187
GranGala
 about, 105
 Fair Skies, 104
 Lion Tamer, 79
Grapefruit juice
 Dr. Blinker, 64, *65*
 Karlita, 74
 Ponce de León, 122, *123*
 Up in Mabel's Room, *178*,
 179
 Wildflower, 180
Grape juice
 Mercurio Punch, *256*, 257
 Speak No Evil, 267
Green Room Cocktail, 203
Grenadine
 Artist's Special, 185
 Bayou, 186
 Bosom Caresser, 146
 Corn Popper, 100
 Crow, 196
 Lady Godiva, 158
 Little Sister, 255
 The Natural, 162
 Rumba, 166
 Scofflaw Cocktail, 218
 Shanghai Cocktail, 219
 Tropical, 176
 Ward Eight, 229
 Washington's Wish, *134*,
 135
 Whizz Bang, 232
 Wildflower, 180
Grimes, William, 46
Groseille syrup, preparing, 185

A Guide to Pink Elephants,
 153

H

Haigh, Ted, 64
Haitian Witch, 69
Harrelson, Gabe, 91
Harris, Brian, 90
Hazelwood, 67
Heering cherry liqueur. *See*
 Cherry Heering
Heiss, Mary Lou and Robert
 J., 290
*Here's How: A Round-the-
 World Bar Guide*, 220
Hess, Robert, 38, 47, 58,
 64, 224
Hibachi Hut, 75
Hibiscus flowers
 adding to drinks, 91
 buying, 148
 Caribbean Bloom, 148, *149*
Highball glasses, 21
Highland Fling, 153
Holt, Jeremy, 62, 84, 224, 227
Honey
 Honey Bee, 154, *155*
 Zoom, 181
Honey Bee, 154, *155*
Honolulu Punch, 252
Hoop La, 156
Horsefeather, 29
Horse's Neck, 253
Hot Brick, 282
Hot Drinks (Heiss), 290
Hot Shot, *70*, 71
Hot Spiced Scotch, *284*, 285
Hot Stuff
 Ambrosia, 275
 Aunt Betsy's Favorite,
 276, *277*
 Black Stripe, 278
 Brandy Skin, 279
 Café Brûlot, 280
 Chamomile Fairy, 281
 The Eagle, 282
 Hot Brick, 282
 Hot Spiced Scotch, *284*,
 285
 Hot Whiskey Sling, 286
 Irish Coffee, 287
 Sophisticated, 288
 Tom & Jerry, 289

Winter's Twilight, 290,
   291
WOW, 292
Hot Toddy, 31
Hot Whiskey Punch, 254
Hot Whiskey Sling, 286
Hour Glass, 110
*House & Garden's Drink
   Guide*, 276
Hpnotiq
   Polynesian Donkey, 84
The Human Factor, 72
Hunter, 204
Husky Boy (website), 84

I

Ice, 13–14
Ice bucket and scoop, 19–20
The Ideal Bartender
   (Bullock), 279
Imbibe! (Wondrich), 47, 89,
   206, 289
*International Cocktail
   Specialties from
   Madison Avenue to
   Malaya* (Mayabb), 101
InternetWines (website), 110
Iollas's Itch, 204, *205*
Irish Coffee, 287
Irish Rickey, 111
Irish Whiskey. *See* Index by
   Primary Liquor
   about, 7
Irreverent Reverend, 72

J

Jeffrey Morgenthaler
   (website), 197
Jigger, 17–18
The Joy of Mixology (Regan),
   47, 80
Juicers, 18

K

Kahlúa
   Coronado Heights Flip,
      60, 61
   Sweet Dream, 171
Karlita, 74

King Cole, 206
King's Peg, 112
Kirschwasser, about, 10
Kitchen Sink, 208
Knives, 18
Kosevich, Nick, 71
KP Cocktail, 75
Kümmel
   about, 225
   Serpent's Tooth, 219
   Stomach Reviver Cocktail,
      225
Kyle, Keith, 59

L

Lady Godiva, 158
Lalla Rookh, *114*, 115
The Late Caress, 159
Lazy Hazy, 116
Leatherneck, 209
Left Hand, 76, *77*
Leggs, Mitchell, 90
Lemongrass simple syrup,
   59
Lemons / lemon juice
   Bimbo Punch, 238
   Crow, 196
   Day-Off Punch, 248
   El Dorado, 249
   Fish House Punch, 28
   Hot Whiskey Punch,
      254
   Hot Whiskey Sling, 286
   Leprechaun, 210
   Leviathan 477, 211
   Little Sister, 255
   Quintet, 264
   Rocky Mountain Punch,
      265
   The Search for Delicious,
      85
   Southstreet, 266
   Steinway Punch, 268
   Whiskey Sour, 51
Leprechaun, 210
Leviathan 477, 211
Lillet
   about, 157
   Hoop La, 156
   The Human Factor, 72
Limbo, *212*, 213
Limes / lime juice
   Blossom, 142

Blushing Bride, *144*, 145
Caribbean Bloom, 148, *149*
Irish Rickey, 111
Nourmahal, 259
Nuit de Noces, 163
Tartan Swizzle, *226*, 227
Tropical, 176
Ward Eight, 229
Yokohama Romance,
   180–181
Zombie, 52–53
Limoncello
   about, 230
   Warlock, 230
Lion Tamer, 79
Little Branch, 76
Little Sister, 255
Locke-Ober, 229
Loft lavender liqueur
   about, 72
   The Human Factor, 72
Lover's Moon, *160*, 161
LUPEC (Ladies United for
   the Preservation of
   Endangered Cocktails),
   197

M

Macadamia nut liqueur
   about, 221
   Lover's Moon, *160*, 161
   Sookie Cocktail, 221
Mai Tai, 32
Mamie Taylor, 116
Mamunes, Anthony, 132
Mango juice
   adding to drinks, 91
   Beach Bubble, 94, *95*
   Ognam, 82, *83*
Manhattan, 33
Manhattan Club, 33
Maple syrup
   Nuit de Noces, 163
Maraschino cherries, about,
   143
Maraschino liqueur
   about, 150
   Bombay Punch, 240,
      241
   Crimean Cup à la
      Marmora, 247
   Dalliance, 151
   Pony Punch, 261

Maraschino liqueur *(cont.)*
　Rocky Mountain Punch,
　　265
　Saratoga, 126
Martini glass, 20
The Matchbox, 67
Mayabb, James, 101
Mead
　about, 214
　Quarter Deck, 214
Meister, Joel, 69
Mercurio Punch, *256, 257*
Mike Collins, 34, *35*
Milk and Honey, 76
Millennium Cocktail, 80
Mint
　Ginger Smash, 203
　Iollas's Itch, 204, *205*
　KP Cocktail, 75
　Mint Julep, 36–37
　Sleepy Head, 127
Mint Julep, 36–37
Mixers. *See also specific*
　types
　buying, 11–13, 209
　lemongrass simple syrup,
　　preparing, 59
　modified sour mix,
　　preparing, 69
　rich simple syrup,
　　preparing, 89
　Simple Syrup, 12
Mixologist (Miller), 47
Molasses
　Black Stripe, 278
Monteleone Hotel, 50
Morgenthaler, Jeffrey,
　197
Morning Glory Fizz, 118
Morning Star, 119
Muddler, 18
Museum of the American
　Cocktail, 133
The Museum of the
　American Cocktail's
　Pocket Recipe Guide
　(Hess), 64

The Native, 258
The Natural, 162
New Orleans Buck, 120
The New Diner's Club Drink
　Book (Simmons), 164

Northside Special, 121
Nourmahal, 259
Nuit de Noces, 163

The Occidental, 81
The Official Mixer's Manual
　(Duffy), 141, 206
Ognam, 82, *83*
O Happy Day, 121
Old Fashioned, 38
Old Fashioned, The Very, 269
Old-fashioned glasses, 21
The Old Waldorf-Astoria Bar
　Book (Crockett), 177
173 Pre-Prohibition Cocktails
　(Bullock), 279
Orange bitters
　Highland Fling, 153
　The Human Factor, 72
　Regan's Orange Bitters
　　No. 6, about, 224
　Scofflaw Cocktail, 218
　The Search for Delicious,
　　85
　Whizz Bang, 232
　Zazarac, *234,* 235
Orange curaçao
　Bosom Caresser, 146
　Chicago, 97
　Green Room Cocktail, 203
　Leatherneck, 209
　Little Sister, 255
　Mai Tai, 32
　Oriental, 214
　Parisian Blonde, 164
　Rum Rascal, 125
　Soother, 167
　Steinway Punch, 268
　Temptation Cocktail, 172
Oranges / orange juice
　Bayou, 186
　Blood and Sand, 239
　Bombay Punch, 240, *241*
　Bring the House Down,
　　242
　Dark Mountain, 197
　Debutante's Dream, 152
　Enchanted Field, *200,* 201
　Golden Lady, 108
　The Golden Panther, 250
　Hunter, 204
　King Cole, 206
　The Late Caress, 159

Lazy Hazy, 116
Leviathan 477, 211
Little Sister, 255
The Native, 258
New Orleans Buck, 120
Northside Special, 121
Paradiso, 164
Planter's Punch, 39
Power to the People, 262,
　263
Quintet, 264
Sleepy Head, 127
Summer Dream, 168, *169*
The Very Old Fashioned,
　269
WOW, 292
Orgeat syrup
　about, 32
　Cameron's Kick, 192
　Crimean Cup à la
　　Marmora, 247
　Mai Tai, 32
　The Natural, 162
Oriental, 214

Papaya
　Limbo, *212,* 213
Paradiso, 164
Parisian Blonde, 164
Parties
　Citrus Fantastic party
　　package, 73
　Hayrack Roundup party
　　package, 73
　Painters on Parade party
　　package, 73
　pairing drinks with music,
　　96
　planning, 2–3, 170, 274
　Speakeasy Evening party
　　package, 73
　Summer Camp Revisited
　　party package, 73
　Summer Solstice Soiree
　　party package, 73
Party Potpourri, 243
PDT, 67
Peach brandy
　Fish House Punch, 28
Peaches
　Power to the People, 262,
　　263
　Summer Dream, 168, *169*

Peach schnapps
  Millennium Cocktail, 80
Pendennis Club, 38
Pernod
  Gaslight Tiger, 202
  Morning Glory Fizz, 118
  Rattlesnake Cocktail, 215
  Temptation Cocktail, 172
  Whizz Bang, 232
Petraske, Sasha, 91
Peychaud's bitters
  about, 224
  Class of the Race, *98*, 99
  Crimson Slippers, *194*,
    195
  The Curtis Hotel, 62
  The Human Factor, 72
  Rattlesnake Cocktail,
    215
  Sazerac, *44*, 45
  Stomach Reviver Cocktail,
    225
  Vieux Carré Cocktail, 50
  Warlock, 230
Peysson, R.S., 204
Pineapple / pineapple juice
  ASAP, 56, *57*
  Beach Bubble, 94, *95*
  Blossom, 142
  Blue Train, 96
  Caesar's Bowl, 243
  Cardinal, 244
  Côte d'Azur Cooler, 101
  Dalliance, 151
  Golf Links Highball, 109
  Honolulu Punch, 252
  King Cole, 206
  Planter's Punch, 39
  Polynesian Donkey, 84
  Pony Punch, 261
  Rum Rascal, 125
  Saratoga, 126
  Tropical, 176
  Zombie, 52–53
Pingleton, Ken, 75, 90
Pitchers, 19
Planter's Punch, 39
Plums
  Sweet Louise, 88
Polynesian Donkey, 84
Pomegranate juice
  Polynesian Donkey, 84
  Winter's Twilight, 290,
    291
Ponce de León, 122, *123*
Pony Punch, 261

Port
  Aunt Betsy's Favorite,
    276, *277*
  Morning Star, 119
Power to the People, 262,
    263
Presbyterian, 124
Punch
  Bimbo, 238
  Blood and Sand, 239
  Bombay, 240, *241*
  Bring the House Down,
    242
  Caesar's Bowl, 243
  Cardinal, 244
  Champs Élysées, 245
  Crimean Cup à la
    Marmora, 247
  Day-Off, 248
  El Dorado, 249
  Fish House, 28
  Football, 250, *251*
  The Golden Panther, 250
  Honolulu, 252
  Horse's Neck, 253
  Hot Whiskey, 254
  Little Sister, 255
  Mercurio, *256*, 257
  The Native, 258
  Nourmahal, 259
  Planter's, 39
  Pony, 261
  Power to the People, 262,
    263
  Quintet, 264
  Rocky Mountain, 265
  Southstreet, 266
  Speak No Evil, 267
  Steinway, 268
  The Very Old Fashioned,
    269
  Xalapa, *270*, 271
Punch bowl, 21

Q

Quarter Deck, 214
Quickie, 165
Quintet, 264

R

Raspberries
  Blushing Bride, *144*, 145

Raspberry syrup
  adding to drinks, 91
  Dr. Blinker, 64, *65*
  Roffignac, 125
Rattlesnake Cocktail, 215
Regan, Gary, 47, 80
Regan, Mardee, 80
Regan's Orange Bitters No. 6
  about, 224
  The Search for Delicious,
    85
Rhum Clément Créole
    Shrubb
  about, 117
  Lazy Hazy, 116
  Short Timer, 86
  Three Wishes, 173
Rob Roy, 40, *41*
Rocky Mountain Punch, 265
Rodan, 69, 97
Roffignac, 125
*Ronrico's Official Mixtro's
    Guide*, 132
Ross, Sam, 76
Rum. *See also* Index by
    Primary Liquor
  about, 4–6, 37, 184
  Caesar's Bowl, 243
  Cardinal, 244
  Crimean Cup à la
    Marmora, 247
  El Dorado, 249
  Honolulu Punch, 252
  Ponce de León, 122, *123*
  Pony Punch, 261
  Quickie, 165
  Quintet, 264
  Rocky Mountain Punch,
    265
  Xalapa Punch, *270*, 271
  Zazarac, *234*, 235
Rumba, 166
Rum Cobbler, 216, *217*
Rum Rascal, 125
Rusty Nail, 43
Rye. *See* Index by Primary
    Liquor
  about, 6

S

Saratoga, 126
The Savoy Cocktail Book
    (Craddock), 100, 156,
    214

Sazerac, *44*, 45
Schuylkill Fishing Company,
     28
Scofflaw Cocktail, 218
Scotch. *See* Index by Primary
     Liquor
     about, 7–8
The Search for Delicious, 85
Serpent's Tooth, 219
The Settler, 127
7UP or Sprite
     Bring the House Down,
        242
     Ginger Smash, 203
Shakers, 16–17
Shanghai Cocktail, 219
Sherry
     Artist's Special, 185
     Coronado Heights Flip,
        60, 61
Short Timer, 86
Sidecar, 46
Sidener, Jeremy, 29, 61, 203
Simmons, Matty, 164
Simple Syrup, 12
     lemongrass, 59
     rich, 89
Sir Henry Morgan, 220
Skoog, Ed, 66
Sleepy Head, 127
Snacks
     antipasto, 260
     chocolate-covered
        strawberries, 260
     hummus, 260
     pizza puffs, 260
Snow Ball, *128*, 129
Sookie Cocktail, 221
Soother, 167
Sophisticated, 288
Sour mix, preparing, 69
Southstreet, 266
Speak No Evil, 267
Spice grater, 19
Spring in Your Step, 130
St. Elizabeth Allspice Dram
     about, 90
     Touchless Automatic, 90
Steinway Punch, 268
St-Germain elderflower
     liqueur
     about, 63
     Derby Widow, 63
Stinger, 48, *49*
Stirring spoon, 19
Stockholm Tar, *222*, 223

Stomach Reviver Cocktail,
     225
The Stork Club Bar Book
     (Beebe), 177, 250
Straight Up or On the Rocks
     (Grimes), 46
Straub, Jacques, 177, 199, 268
Strega
     about, 231
     Enchanted Field, *200*, 201
     Warlock, 230
Summer Dream, 168, *169*
Swangard, Andrea, 79
Sweet Dream, 171
Sweet Louise, 88
Swizzle and stir sticks, 20
Syrup, Simple, 12
     lemongrass, preparing, 59
     rich, preparing, 89

T

Tales of the Cocktail
     (website), 133
Taproom, 29
Tartan Swizzle, *226*, 227
Tea
     Chamomile Fairy, 281
     Pony Punch, 261
     Xalapa Punch, *270*, 271
Temptation Cocktail, 172
Thomas, Jerry, 177, 289
Three Wishes, 173
Thumper, 228
Tia Maria
     Black Pearl, 142
     Dark Mountain, 197
Tigertail, 63
Tiki Lounge, 67
Ti Penso Sempre, 174, *175*
Tip Top, 131
Tombstone, 89
Tom & Jerry, 289
Toothpicks, 20
Touchless Automatic, 90
Towel, for home bar, 20
Town Talk Diner, 71
Trader Vic's, 32
Trays, for serving, 20
Triple sec
     Crimson Slippers, *194*, 195
     Quickie, 165
Tropical, 176
Tuaca
     about, 56

ASAP, 56, *57*
Thumper, 228
22 Doors, 224

U

Up in Mabel's Room, *178*, 179

V

Vanilla liqueur
     Lalla Rookh, *114*, 115
Vermouth
     about, 42
     Black Feather, 58
     Blood and Sand, 239
     Bobby Burns, 189
     Brainstorm, 190, *191*
     Cardinal, 244
     Carpano Antica, about, 76
     Corpse Reviver, 192
     Creole Cocktail, 193
     The Curtis Hotel, 62
     Day-Off Punch, 248
     Demon of Destiny, 198
     Dutch Charlie's, 199
     Football Punch, 250, *251*
     Foppa, *106*, 107
     The Golden Panther, 250
     Golf Links Highball, 109
     Green Room Cocktail, 203
     Highland Fling, 153
     Iollas's Itch, 204, *205*
     Lady Godiva, 158
     Left Hand, 76, *77*
     Manhattan, 33
     The Native, 258
     Oriental, 214
     Punt e Mes, about, 85
     Rob Roy, 40, *41*
     Scofflaw Cocktail, 218
     The Search for Delicious,
        85
     Serpent's Tooth, 219
     Short Timer, 86
     Sir Henry Morgan, 220
     Thumper, 228
     Vieux Carré Cocktail, 50
     Whisper, 179
     Whizz Bang, 232
The Very Old Fashioned,
     269
Vick's Zither, 132
Vieux Carré Cocktail, 50

Vintage Spirits and Forgotten Cocktails (Haigh), 64
Violet Hour, 85
Vodka
  Blushing Bride, *144*, 145
  Buck Owens, 59
  Dark Mountain, 197
  Dark Water, 102

W

Ward, Phil, 86
Ward Eight, 229
Warlock, 230
Washington's Wish, *134*, 135
WeatherUp, 91
Weatherups, Kathryn, 91

What Every Young Man Should Know, 202
Whiskey. *See also* Index by Primary Liquor
  American, about, 6–7
  bourbon, about, 6
  Irish, about, 7
  obscure fact about, 37
  rye, about, 6
  Scotch, about, 7–8
Whiskey Sour, 51
Whisper, 179
Whizz Bang, 232
Wildflower, 180
Williwaw, 233
Wine. *See also* Champagne and sparkling wine; Index by Primary Liquor
  Cardinal, 244
  claret, about, 244

Wine, fortified. *See* Dubonnet; Port; Sherry; Vermouth
Wine glasses, 21
Winter's Twilight, 290, *291*
Wondrich, David, 47, 89, 206, 289
WOW, 292

XYZ

Xalapa Punch, *270*, 271
Yokohama Romance, 180–181
Zanzibar, 109
Zazarac, *234*, 235
Zombie, 52–53
Zoom, 181